CURRENT RESEARCH AND
TECHNOLOGICAL DEVELOPMENTS
ON THE DEAD SEA SCROLLS

STUDIES ON THE TEXTS OF THE DESERT OF JUDAH

EDITED BY

F. GARCÍA MARTÍNEZ
A. S. VAN DER WOUDE

VOLUME XX

CURRENT RESEARCH AND TECHNOLOGICAL DEVELOPMENTS ON THE DEAD SEA SCROLLS

*Conference on the Texts from the Judean Desert,
Jerusalem, 30 April 1995*

EDITED BY

DONALD W. PARRY

AND

STEPHEN D. RICKS

E.J. BRILL
LEIDEN · NEW YORK · KÖLN
1996

The paper in this book meets the guidelines for permanence and durability of the Committee on Production Guidelines for Book Longevity of the Council on Library Resources.

Library of Congress Cataloging-in-Publication Data

Conference on the texts from the Judean Desert (1995 : Jerusalem)
    Current research and technological developments on the dead Sea
scrolls : Conference on the texts from the Judean Desert, Jerusalem,
30 April, 1995 / edited by Donald W. Parry and Stephen D. Ricks.
       p. cm. — (Studies on the texts of the desert of Judah ; v.
20)
    Includes index.
    ISBN 9004106626 (cloth : alk. paper)
    1. Dead Sea scrolls—Congresses. I. Parry, Donald W. II. Ricks,
Stephen David.   III. Title.   IV. Series.
BM487.C575   1996
296.1'55—dc20   96–26931
                                              CIP

Die Deutsche Bibliothek - CIP-Einheitsaufnahme

**Current research and technological developments on the dead
sea scrolls** / Conference on the Texts from the Judean Desert,
Jerusalem, 30 April 1995. Ed. by Donald W. Parry and Stephen
D. Ricks. – Leiden ; New York ; Köln : Brill, 1996
   (Studies on the texts of the desert of Judah ; Vol. 20)
   ISBN 90–04–10662–2
NE: Parry, Donald W. [Hrsg.]; Conference on the Texts from the Judean
Desert <1995, Yerûšālayim>; GT

ISSN 0169-9962
ISBN 90 04 10662 6

CONTENTS

Contents

Abbreviations

DJD	*Discoveries in the Judean Desert*
DSD	*Dead Sea Discoveries*
DSST	Florentino García Martínez, *The Dead Sea Scrolls Translated—The Qumrân Texts in English,* trans. Wilfred G. E. Watson (Leiden: Brill, 1994)
HUCA	*Hebrew Union College Annual*
JBL	*Journal of Biblical Literature*
JJS	*Journal of Jewish Studies*
NTS	*New Testament Studies*
RB	*Revue biblique*
RQ	*Revue de Qumran*
ZAW	*Zeitschrift für die alttestamentliche Wissenschaft*

Introduction

On April 30, 1995, scholars from Israel, Europe, and the United States met at Brigham Young University's Jerusalem Center for Near Eastern Studies to present the results of their research at a conference cosponsored by the Foundation for Ancient Research and Mormon Studies (FARMS) and Brigham Young University. This volume includes both papers that were presented at this conference and one by invitation.

The major focus of this volume reflects further insights on the discoveries from Cave 4 that have only recently been made available to the public. The first two papers, contributed by Frank Moore Cross and Florentino García Martínez, examine the identity of the messiahs in *4Q246* and *4Q521*. Cross reaffirms his view that only a priestly messiah and a messiah of Israel are mentioned in the Dead Sea texts, while García Martínez sees these documents as providing us a view of the figure of the heavenly and prophetic messiahs. Emanuel Tov provides a thorough and painstaking analysis of scribal markings in the Dead Sea texts. Eugene Ulrich examines the various biblical manuscripts of Cave 4 and concludes that the history of the text was preceded by variant literary editions. Torleif Elgvin sees *Sapiential Work A* (preserved in several fragmentary copies) as a "bridge between the apocalyptic Enoch literature" and the Qumran community.

Three papers were contributed by younger scholars, all of them from Brigham Young University. David R. Seely has been collaborating with Professor Moshe Weinfeld of the Hebrew University on the *Barki Nafshi* texts (*4Q434-439*). Seely examines textual and physical evidence of the texts and concludes that the first five sets of fragments represent different copies of the same text or the same collection of texts and reviews evidence that the texts are of sectarian origin. Dana M. Pike, who has studied nearly 1,000 fragments, identifies several of these as coming from the book of Numbers. Although in Pike's view Numbers is the least represented of the first five books of the Old Testament at Qumran, the fragments of Numbers nevertheless provide important information concerning the life of the community. Donald W. Parry, who is collaborating with Professor Cross on the *4QSam^a* and *4QSam^b* texts of Samuel, comes to a number of striking conclusions about the way in which the Tetragrammaton is used—or not used—in the Samuel fragments.

The final papers focus on the contributions of technology to an understanding of the Scrolls. Scott Woodward and his colleagues at the Hebrew University analyze and consider the interesting implications of DNA testing on the Scrolls parchment materials, which represent the majority of the Dead Sea Scrolls. The last contribution, by Donald W. Parry and Steven W. Booras, outlines the capabilities of the database on CD-ROM currently being developed by Brigham Young University and FARMS.

The papers in this volume—reflecting the maturity and sober judgment of senior scholars, the energy and intensity of younger scholars, and the fruitful applications of technology—hold out the rich promise of the future in Dead Sea Scrolls studies.

We wish to acknowledge the assistance of many individuals who have contributed to the success of this conference and the completion of this volume: S. Kent Brown, Alison V. P. Coutts, Brent Hall, Noel B. Reynolds, Shirley S. Ricks, Eric Smith, and members of the staff of FARMS.

We also appreciate the support and encouragement of Florentino García Martínez, series editor of Studies on the Texts of the Desert of Judah, and Hans van der Meij, editor, E. J. Brill.

Stephen D. Ricks
Provo, Utah
January 2, 1996

Notes on the Doctrine of the Two Messiahs at Qumran and the Extracanonical Daniel Apocalypse (4Q246)

FRANK MOORE CROSS

Harvard University

Since the publication of Jean Starcky's programmatic paper arguing for a series of four stages in the messianism of the Qumran community, a near consensus has developed holding that different messianic doctrines—perhaps even four—exist in its literature.[1] A parade example has been the *Damascus Docu-*

---

[1]   Jean Starcky, "Les quatre étapes du messianisme à Qumran," *RB* 70 (1963): 481–505. The literature on messianism at Qumran is rich. An important early work that still retains value is Adam S. van der Woude, *Die messianischen Vorstellungen der Gemeinde von Qumran* (Assen: Van Gorcum, 1957). An extensive bibliography on the subject of Qumran messianism may be found in Joseph A. Fitzmyer, *The Dead Sea Scrolls: Major Publications and Tools for Study,* ed. W. Lee Humphreys, rev. ed. (Atlanta: Scholars Press, 1990). To his items may be added a number of important recent studies: Émile Puech, "Fragment d'une apocalypse en araméen (4Q246 + pseudo-Dan[d]) et le 'royaume de Dieu,' " *RB* 99 (1992): 98–131 and the literature cited; John J. Collins, "Teacher and Messiah? The One Who Will Teach Righteousness at the End of Days," in *The Community of the Renewed Covenant: The Notre Dame Symposium on the Dead Sea Scrolls*, ed. Eugene Ulrich and James C. VanderKam (Notre Dame, Ind.: University of Notre Dame Press, 1994), 195–210; two other essays in this symposium are important both for their content and bibliography: James C. VanderKam, "Messianism in the Scrolls," 211–34; and Émile Puech,

ment, in which different messianic doctrines have been detected in the two sections of the work. I wish to argue that this is not so. Rather, I believe, a consistent doctrine of only two messiahs—one of Aaron and one of Israel—is evident throughout the sectarian Qumran literature.[2]

The doctrine of two messiahs has its roots in the restoration establishment of a diarchy. Joshua the high priest and the "scion," namely Zerubbabel, are the two "anointed ones," *běnê hay-yišhar,* who "shall take office standing by the side of the Lord of the whole earth."[3] The elaboration of a doctrine of two ages took place in later apocalypticism, in which a typology of the events and offices of old Israel was projected into the new age. David, the ideal king of the old days, is taken as the archetype of the ideal king of the New Age. Zadok, priest of David and high priest in Solomon's temple, scion of Aaron, is the archetype of the new Zadok, the messiah of Aaron. The two figures, priestly and royal, persist in later Jewish doctrines of eschatological offices down to Christian times.[4] At Qumran, in the *Damascus Document,* the *Rule,* the *War Scroll,* the *Testimonia (4Q175),* and in the *Testaments of the Twelve Patriarchs* as

---

"Messianism, Resurrection, and Eschatology at Qumran and in the New Testament," 235–56.

[2] This near consensus appears to be breaking down somewhat at present. See Devorah Dimant, "Qumran Sectarian Literature," in *Jewish Writings of the Second Temple Period,* ed. Michael Stone (Assen: Van Gorcum, 1984), 538–42; Frank Moore Cross, "Some Notes on a Generation of Qumran Studies," in *The Madrid Qumran Congress: Proceedings of the International Congress on the Dead Sea Scrolls, Madrid, 18–21 March 1991,* ed. Julio Trebolle Barrera and Luis Vegas Montaner (Leiden: Brill, 1992), 1–21. Most recently see the discussion by VanderKam and Puech in the studies cited in n. 1.

[3] Zechariah 4:14; cf. Zechariah 3:8–9; 6:12–13.

[4] See, for example, *Jubilees* 31:16–20 and the coinage of the Second Jewish Revolt, which preserves the institution of diarchy, bearing the names and titles of Simon (bar Koseba), prince of Israel, and Eleazar, the Priest.

well,[5] is found the doctrine of the two messiahs, with the *Balaam Oracle* concerning the Star and the Scepter—the two eschatological figures—a favorite proof text.

Confusion has been introduced by a reading in *CD* XIV, 19: [*mšy*]*ḥ ʾhrwn wyśrʾl.*[6] It is to be read "the messiah of Aaron and the one of Israel." This constitutes no problem in Hebrew grammar as L. Ginzberg recognized long ago in his *Eine unbekannte jüdische Sekte.*[7] This expression cannot mean anything but the (priestly) messiah of Aaron and the (secular) messiah of Israel.[8] The expression *Aaron and Israel* regularly refers to the priestly and the secular division of the community. A single priestly messiah would be called simply "the messiah of Aaron." Further confusion has also been created by the following phrase: *ykpr ʿwnm* [ ]. The verb is singular, but must be taken as a passive, *yĕkuppar.* Compare the passive constructions with this verb, the *nitpaʿel* in Deuteronomy 21:8 and in 1 Samuel 6:3 (*4QSamᵃ* and *OG*), or the more familiar *puʿal* as in Isaiah 22:14 and 27:9. Were *ʿwnm* the object of the verb *ykpr* here, and *mšyḥ* the subject, the word *ʿwnm* would have been preceded by the particle *ʾet.* So the case is clear: the putative single messiah is a phantom of bad philology.

It is true that the royal messiah is usually meant when otherwise unspecified. Even in *1QSa* II, 11–13 (*1Q28a*)—the rule for the celebration of the eschatological banquet—the messiah of

---

5   See especially *Testament of Levi* 18:1–14; cf. *Testament of Reuben* 6:8–12; *Testament of Simeon* 7:1–3; *Testament of Judah* 21:1–5.

6   See especially *CD* XX, 1, which reads *mšyḥ mʾhrwn wmyśrʾl*—even more obviously referring to two messiahs; cf. *CD* XII, 23; and *1QS* IX, 11.

7   Louis Ginzberg, *Eine unbekannte jüdische Sekte*, a 1922 work translated and updated as *An Unknown Jewish Sect* (New York: Ktav, 1976); see below in *4Q246* the expression *mlk ʾtwr wmṣrym* (I, 6), which means "the king of Assyria and the one of Egypt." The reference is obviously to the Ptolemies and the Seleucids. In *4Q246* II, 2, the use of plurals, "their rule," and *ymlkwn*, "they shall rule" make clear that two kings are meant.

8   Thus it has the same meaning as משיחי אהרון וישראל in *1QS* IX, 11.

Israel is juxtaposed to "the Priest," the *latter* taking precedence. Further, texts exist that mention only the royal messiah; but to argue that these texts represent circles in which the traditional doctrine of the diarchy had been replaced by a merging of the two figures into one—as happened in Christianity, and to some degree in later Judaism after the fall of the temple (indeed after the Second Jewish Revolt against Rome) when the rule of the high priest was permanently broken—is a precarious argument from silence. It has long been argued—against Josephus's plain testimony—that the Essenes of Qumran had no doctrine of resurrection. But a recently published text makes reference to a proof text promising resurrection: "As it is written, he shall heal the slain, and the dead he shall resurrect (literally, 'make alive')."[9] I know of no reason not to reckon this text as sectarian.

The reverse case may be illustrated by reference to the Daniel literature. Here scholarly consensus has held that while the book of Daniel testifies explicitly to a doctrine of the resurrection of the righteous, the author (or editor) possessed no doctrine of the messiah(s). In fact, in a famous document belonging to the wider Daniel literature from Qumran Cave 4, *4Q246* or *pseudo-Daniel^d* (so-called because it is not a part of the canon), dramatic reference to the expected messiah is made using familiar sobriquets to identify him, including "Son of God" and "Son of the Most High." The *editio princeps* of *4Q246* (= *4QpsDan^d*) is by Émile Puech, to whom J. T. Milik assigned the text.[10] Puech

---

[9]   For a preliminary edition of this text, *4Q521*, see Robert M. Eisenman and Michael O. Wise, *The Dead Sea Scrolls Uncovered* (Shaftesbury, Dorset: Element, 1992), 19–23, and pl. 1.

[10]   Puech, "Fragment d'une apocalypse en araméen"; see also the reconstructions of Joseph Fitzmyer in his latest studies of the text, "4Q246: The 'Son of God' Document from Qumran," *Biblica* 74 (1993):153–74; and "The Aramaic 'Son of God' Text from Qumran Cave 4," in *Methods of Investigation of the Dead Sea Scrolls and the Khirbet Qumran Site: Present Realities and Future Prospects*, ed. Michael O. Wise et al. (New York: New York Academy of Sciences, 1994), 163–78; Florentino García Martínez, *The Dead Sea Scrolls Translated: The Qumran Texts in English*, trans.

has produced an exemplary edition. He argues strongly for a messianic interpretation of these titles.

I have held a messianic interpretation of the "Son of God" text since J. T. Milik read a paper on the text at Harvard University in 1972. Indeed I sent to him my reconstruction of the text of *4Q246* recorded below shortly after his American visit, arguing strongly against his interpretation of the epithets as belonging to a Seleucid king (Alexander Balas).[11]   The text reads as follows:

I

1 [ ]   ע]לוהי שרת נפל קדם כרסיא

2 [ואמר לה חיי מ]לכא [ל]עלמא אתה רגז ושנוך

3 [זיוך ואפשר מלכ]א חזוך וכלא אתה עד עולם

4 [חזיתא][12] די ישפלון ר]ברבין עקה תתא על ארעא

5 [להוה קרב בעממיא] ונחשירון רב במדינתא

6 [ולקצת יומיא יאבדון] מלך אתור [ומ]צרין

7 [ויקום בר אנש מלך] רב להוה על ארעא

Wilfred G. E. Watson (Leiden: Brill, 1994), 138; Eisenman and Wise, *The Dead Sea Scrolls Uncovered*, 68–71.

[11]   See John J. Collins, "A Pre-Christian 'Son of God' among the Dead Sea Scrolls," *Bible Review* 9 (1993): 34–38 and 57, esp. n. 4; John J. Collins, *Daniel: A Commentary on the Book of Daniel*, ed. Frank Moore Cross (Minneapolis: Fortress, 1993), 77–79. Collins shares my view that the text is messianic; he also argues eloquently, if briefly, for the closeness of the text to canonical Daniel. J. T. Milik has described his views in "Les modèles araméens du livre d'Esther dans la grotte 4 de Qumrân," *RQ* 15 (1992): 383–84. David Flusser has also opted for an interpretation of the "Son of God" as an Antichrist figure: "The Hubris of the Antichrist in a Fragment from Qumran," *Immanuel* 10 (1980): 31–37. Florentino García Martínez holds yet another view, which, while seeing the figure as an eschatological savior, does not identify him with the royal messiah: "The Eschatological Figure of 4Q246," in *Qumran and Apocalyptic: Studies on the Aramaic Tests from Qumran* (Leiden: Brill, 1992), 162–79.

[12]   On the orthography, see *4Q246* II, 2, and Daniel 2:41.

8 [כלה וכל אנש לה י]עבדון וכלא ישמשון

9 [לה קדיש אלהא ר]בא יתקרא ובשמה יתכנה

II

1 ברה די אל יתאמר ובר עלין יקרונה כזיקיא

2 די חזיתא[13] כן מלכותהן תהוה שנ[ין] ימלכון על

3 ארעא וכלא ידשון עם לעם ומדינה למד[ינ]ה

4 vacat עד יקום עם אל וכלא ינוח מן חרב vacat

5 מלכותה מלכות עלם וכל ארחתה בקשוט ידי[ן]

6 ארעא בקשוט וכלא יעבד לשלם חרב מן ארעא יסף

7 וכל מדינתא לה יסגדון אל רבא באילה

8 הוא יעבד לה קרב עממין ינתן בידה וכלהן

9 ירמה קדמוהי שלטנה שלטן עלם וכל תהומי

I

(1) [   ] on him settled;
He fell before the throne,
(2) [and said to him, "Live O k]ing forever!
You are disturbed and your (3) [appearance] changed
[And I shall interpret O kin]g your dream
And all that comes to pass unto perpetuity;
(4) [You saw in your vision that the] might[y shall be humbled];
Affliction shall come on earth.
(5) [There shall be war with the nations,]
And great carnage among the countries.
(6) [And at the end of days] the king of Assyria and of Egypt
[shall perish].
(7) [And there shall arise a son of man]
He shall be a great [king] over the [whole] earth (8)
[And all of mankind] shall serve [him],

And all shall minister (9) [to him.]
[The Holy One of the g]reat [God] he shall be called,
And by his name he shall be surnamed.

II

(1) Son of God he shall be called,
And Son of the Most High he shall be surnamed.

Like comets (2) that you saw (in your vision), thus will be their kingdom.
For some years they will reign over (3) the earth;
And they will trample on all.
One nation shall trample on another nation,
And one province (will trample on) another province.
(4)[vacat] Until the people of God arise
And all rest from the sword. [vacat]
(5) His kingdom shall be an eternal kingdom,
And all his ways truth.
He shall judge (6) the earth with truth,
And all will make peace (with him).
The sword shall cease from the earth,
(7) And all the countries shall worship him.
The great God shall be his patron.
(8) He will make war for him;
People he will give in his hand
And all of them (9) he shall cast before him.
His rule shall be an eternal rule.

Notes to the Text

Line 1.

Joseph Fitzmyer, following Puech for the most part, reconstructs וכדי דחלה רבה ע[לוהי as "[When great fear] settled on them." For both readings, compare Daniel 10:7. Fitzmyer's reading is plausible and fits the space.

Line 2.

Puech reconstructs line 2 to read: {ל} מ[לכא](?)ל דניאל ואמר]
<בג>עלמא אתה רגז ושניך. I prefer to read this differently, avoiding
the double emendation: ואמר] לה חיי מ[לכא לעלמא אתה רגז ושנוך.
For the cliché חיי מלכא לעלמא, see חיי מלכא לעלמין in Daniel
2:4; 3:9; and 5:10, in which the king is being addressed.
Fitzmyer reconstructs the passage as אדין] אמר למלכא חיי מ[לכא.
His reading is an improvement on that of Puech, but is decidedly too long for the space. One need only pen the letters proposed for the lacuna in the script of this scribe to see that his
reconstruction is impossible.

Lines 2/3.

At the end of line 2, and the beginning of line 3, Puech reads
אתה רגז ושניך [בדחלה, which he translates "*tu t'irrites et tes
années se déroulent* (3) *dans la crainte!*" I believe the material
reading is wrong. I read אתה רגז ושנוך [זיוך] as "You are disturbed and your (3) [appearance] changed." The reading ושנוך זיוך
I regard as certain. The lower part of the *waw* may be slightly
marred, but the form is identical with the *waw* in חזוך found later
in line 3. ושנוך זיוך is precisely the impersonal use with suffix as
subject found in Daniel 5:6 with the same terms: זיוהי שנוהי.
Fitzmyer recognized that *zyw* should be read here, and *šnyk*
somehow derived from *šny*, but his solution produced a grammatical anomaly, as he himself recognizes. Puech and Milik's
reading of *šnyk* as "your years" throws line 3 off and, in my
view, is impossible.

Line 3.

Puech's reconstruction בדחלה הן אש [רא or בדחלה הן אק [רא
is too short for the space. Moreover, neither *qrʾ* nor *šrʾ* is a natu-
ral way to introduce the interpretation of a dream. I would
expect, rather, *pšr*. Fitzmyer's reconstruction fits the space, but
leaves the dream interpretation without an introduction. In my
reconstruction, the speaker (Daniel) promises to interpret the
king's dream using the language of Daniel 5. Both Puech and

Fitzmyer have misunderstood the expression וכלא אתה עד עלמא, "and all that comes to pass unto perpetuity." The seer is to relate all that will happen in the future. This use of אתה, here a participle, is well known both in Hebrew and Aramaic. Note its use in line 4.

Line 4.

The seer then relates the future events seen in the dream. Both Puech and Fitzmyer have failed to recognize that the bicolon ends at the end of line 3. This throws off their reconstructions of the beginning of line 4. Puech's poetry breaks down. I believe that it is easiest to have the seer explain what the king saw. For the use of הזית[א] די to introduce the content of a vision of the future, see, for example, Daniel 2:45 and 4:17.

Line 5.

My reconstruction is very close to those of Puech and Fitzmyer.

Line 6–7.

The expression לקצת יומיא appears in Daniel 4:31. The line should signal the end of the war and carnage, and the perishing or defeat of the Seleucids and Ptolemies (i.e., the king of Assyria and of Egypt). Puech has no reference to the demise of the great powers in his reconstruction (nor has Milik). Fitzmyer's reconstruction of the beginning of line 6 is much too short. He too proposes no reference to the defeat of the powers. In line 7, he reconstructs ברם אף ברך רב להוה על ארעא, translating "[. . . but your son]shall also be great upon the earth." Whose son? Evidently the son of the king addressed. In an apocalypse written in the name of Daniel—as Milik correctly labeled this fragment, a conclusion I believe is clear from shared linguistic and literary traits—the king in question presumably would be either Nebuchadnezzar, Darius, Belshazzar, or Cyrus, the kings addressed in the Daniel literature. But to give the son of one of these kings the eschatological titles to follow in the next lines of the text, is surely far-fetched, if not impossible. Fitzmyer ultimately rejects a messianic interpretation, to be sure, and opts for a historical Jewish king.

The reconstruction of these lines is, of course, speculative. But I believe certain elements must have been included in the development of the apocalypse: the war among the nations (line 5), the defeat of the great powers, Assyria and Egypt—that is, the Seleucids and Ptolemies (line 6)—and the rise of the eschatological king, the Davidic messiah (line 7). Certainly lines I, 8–9, and II, 1 describe the king of the end time. [14]

Line 7.

In this line, I believe we must read מלך] רב לחה על ארעא כלה].[15] The epithet *mélek rāb* is found in Psalm 48:3 (cf. Daniel 2:10):

הר ציון ירכתי צפון
קרית מלך רב

I believe that in the apocalypse the term was taken to refer to the son of David, the future king, as in "city of the great king" understood as equivalent to "city of David." In Luke 1:32 we read οὗτος ἔσται μέγας καὶ υἱὸς ὑψίστου κληθήσεται καὶ δώσει αὐτῷ κύριος ὁ θεὸς τὸν θρόνον Δαυὶδ τοῦ πατρὸς αὐτοῦ, "He will be great, and will be called the son of the Most High, and the Lord God will give to him the throne of David his father." I am interested here in the epithet *great* (μέγας = רב), the basis of my reconstruction.

Lines 8–9.

I believe these lines must be reconstructed in a bicolon with *yʿbdwn* and *yšmšwn* in parallelism. The latter verb, *yšmšwn*, is

---

[14] In *4Q246* II, 5, the expression מלכותה מלכות עלם echoes Daniel 7:27 and recalls Luke 1:33.

[15] *klh*, literally "all of it," is an idiomatic usage found in Imperial Aramaic. See, for example, *ʾAḥiqar* [2:]12, [4:]55 (*ʾtwr klh*, "the whole of Assyria").

used in Daniel 7:10, "Thousands upon thousands served him [the Ancient of Days]; myriads upon myriads attended him."

[וכל אנש לה י]עבדון

וכלא ישמשון [לה]

[And all of mankind] shall serve [him]

And all shall minister (9) [to him.]

We could just as well reconstruct [וכל עממיא לה י]עבדון וכלא [ישמשון [לה]. Both *kl ʾnš* and *kl ʿmmyʾ* are expressions found in the book of Daniel.

I, line 9–II, line 1.

I reconstruct the quatrain as follows (note the parallelism of *ytqrʾ*, *ytknh*, *ytʾmr*, and *yqrwnh*):

[קדיש אלהא ר]בא יתקרא

ובשמה יתכנה

ברה די אל יתאמר

ובר עליון יקרונה

[The holy one of the of the g]reat [God] he shall be called,

And by His name he shall be surnamed.

(II, 1) Son of God he shall be called,

And Son of the Most High he shall be surnamed.

In lines I, 7–9 and II, 1 we have a sequence of messianic epithets. We have discussed *[mlk] rb* above and compared the passage in Luke 1:32. In line 9, I have reconstructed *[qdyš ʾlhʾ r]bʾ*, "the Holy One of the Great God." The basis of this reconstruction is twofold. In Luke 1:35b we read τὸ γεννώμενον ἅγιον κληθήσεται υἱος θεοῦ, "the child to be born will be called the holy one, Son of God." The term *qdyš* is applied to the elect of Israel in Daniel 7. Here the manlike figure, *kbr ʾnš*, who is given eternal kingship, is interpreted in Daniel 7:18–28 to be corporate Israel, or at least the holy ones of Israel, *qdyšy ʿlywnym*. However, I believe it can be argued convincingly that the manlike figure in Daniel 7 was originally the future king, the "holy one of the great God," namely the Son of God. In other words, the editor or author of Daniel democratized the messianic figure. In origin, of course, the vision of the Ancient of Days goes back to the Canaanite myth of the young god (Baᶜl-Haddu) riding his cloud chariot up to the throne on the mount of the council of the gods, there receiving kingship from the head of the pantheon, ʾEl.

I have reconstructed the titles [Son of Man], Great [King], [Holy One of the g]reat [God], which fit nicely into the lacunae, and which go well with the titles that are fully preserved on the leather: "Son of God" and "Son of the Most High." The epithets found in Luke 1:32–35 (in which the messianic interpretation is patent)—"Great," "Holy One," "Son of the Most High," and "Son of God"—are so striking as to suggest, if not require, that the author of the hymn quoted in Luke is dependent on a Danielic text very much like the one in *4Q246*. I would argue this even if some of my reconstructed titles prove not to be correct.[16]

It should be noted that in the Aramaic epithets, the names of god—ʾEl and ᶜElyon—are given their Hebrew forms—not their Aramaic forms. This makes it most implausible that they be applied to any but an Israelite king. If these were pagan titles or, rather, titles claimed by a foreign king, we should expect *ʾlhʾ* and *ᶜlyʾ*, the ordinary Aramaic words for "god" and "most high." There would no reason for the evil king, or, *a fortiori*, for a pious Jew to substitute the specifically Jewish names of god in the epithets of a hated enemy.

I will confine myself to a few, brief remarks on the remainder of column II of the text. The section that starts at the end of line 1 begins a new section of the interpretation of the dream of the king (mentioned in column I, lines 3–4). The pattern A_1B_1: A_2B_2 features a reversion to the sequence of the dream. First (A_1), the evil kingdoms and their wars are described (I, 4–6); then (B_1) comes the appearance of the great king, the Son of God who shall establish universal rule (I, 7–II, 1). Then the

---

[16] For example, an alternate reconstruction of the lacuna in line 9 might be *ᶜbd ʾlhʾ hyʾ*, an epithet applied to Daniel in 6:21.

sequence is repeated (A_2). The kings will rule briefly for some years, like flashes in the pan, like the falling of comets (II, 1b–3); then (B_2) the people of God arise, peace is restored, and their king establishes a just, peaceful, and eternal kingdom (II, 4–9).

Note that in II, 2, the usage is plural: "Thus shall be their kingdom; . . . they will reign over the earth." The reference is to the two kings of column I, the king of Assyria and the king of Egypt. The antecedent of the third singular pronouns in II, 5–9 is not explicit. It is clear from line 7 that the pronouns do not refer to the deity. Conceivably they could refer to the "people of God," but the structure of the poetry described above requires that the pronouns refer to the future king, the messiah whose kingdom is eternal and who judges justly the nations.

One final text may be cited: the *Apocryphon of Levi* (*4Q540* and *4Q541*).[17] If Puech's interpretations and reconstructions are roughly sound, these writings discuss a salvific figure who is evidently the messiah priest. At the same time the royal messiah goes without mention—which by no means can be construed to mean that the author of the *Testament of Levi* possessed no doctrine of the royal messiah, son of David.

In dealing with the traditional materials of apocalyptic and related genres occupied with things at the end of the world, it is dangerous to assume that a writer's or a sect's complete doctrine is recorded in a single work—or in a single layer of a complex work. Arguments from silence, always precarious, are particularly dangerous in dealing with such literature.

---

[17]   The *editio princeps* is by Émile Puech, "Fragments d'un apocryphe de Lévi et le personnage eschatologique: 4QTestLevi^c-d(?) et 4QAJa," in *The Madrid Qumran Congress* 2:449–501.

Two Messianic Figures in the Qumran Texts

FLORENTINO GARCÍA MARTÍNEZ

University of Groningen

In the twenty-five years following the discoveries and first publications of the texts from Qumran, few topics were so widely discussed as the messianic expectations of the Qumran Community.[1] This interest is easy to understand. In most of the other Jewish writings of the Second Temple period, the figure of the Messiah either is not featured or plays a very secondary role. By contrast, the new texts express not only the hope of an eschatological salvation but also introduce into this hope the figure (or figures) of a messiah, to use technical terminology. Thus they promised to clarify the origins of the messianic hope that occupies such a central position in Christianity. However, the expectations of the first years of research were not fulfilled, and the subsequent reaction was not long in coming. Interest in Qumran messianism plunged to a low level in the agenda of

---

[1] From the basic work by Adam S. van der Woude, *Die messianischen Vorstellungen der Gemeinde von Qumran* (Assen: Van Gorcum, 1957). A bibliography of the most important works from these twenty-five years is found in Joseph A. Fitzmyer, *The Dead Sea Scrolls: Major Publications and Tools for Study*, ed. Wayne A. Meeks (Missoula, MT: Scholars Press, 1975), 114–18. An updated bibliography will be published in 1996: Florentino García Martínez and Donald W. Parry, eds., *A Bibliography of the Finds in the Desert of Judah, 1970–1994* (Leiden: Brill, forthcoming).

Qumran studies, and the topic remained dormant for a long time.[2]

The situation has changed dramatically in recent years. In 1992, Émile Puech published several texts that brought new light to Qumran messianism.[3] As a result, scholars started to study Qumran messianism again, and a flood of new publications appeared.[4] I wrote a long overview collecting the evidence

---

[2]   It is significant that the 1990 edition of Fitzmyer's bibliography, *The Dead Sea Scrolls: Major Publications and Tools for Study*, ed. W. Lee Humphreys, rev. ed. (Atlanta: Scholars Press, 1990), 164–67, adds only six titles to the list published in 1975.

[3]   They are the *editio princeps* of three Aramaic texts completed by Émile Puech—"Fragment d'une apocalypse en araméen (4Q246 = pseudo-Dan^d) et le 'Royaume de Dieu,'" *RB* 99 (1992): 98–131; "Une apocalypse messianique (*4Q521*)," *RQ* 15 (1992): 475–522; and "Fragments d'un apocryphe de Lévi et le personnage eschatologique—*4QTestLevi^{c-d}* et *4QAJa*," in *The Madrid Qumran Congress*, ed. Julio Trebolle Barrera and L. Vegas Montaner (Leiden: Brill, 1992), 449–501 and plates 16–22, and of a Hebrew fragment published by Geza Vermes, "The Oxford Forum for Qumran Research: Seminar on the Rule of War from Cave 4 (*4Q285*)," *JJS* 43 (1992): 85–94.

[4]   Among the studies published recently see Martin G. Abegg, "Messianic Hope and *4Q285:* A Reassessment," *JBL* 113 (1994): 81–91; Otto Betz, "Spricht ein Qumran-Text vom gekreuzigten Messias?" in Otto Betz and Rainer Riesner, *Jesus, Qumran, und der Vatikan* (Giessen: Brunner Verlag, 1993), 103–20 (published in English as "Does the Qumran Text Speak of a Crucified Messiah" in *Jesus, Qumran, and the Vatican: Clarifications*, trans. John Bowden [London, SCM, 1994], 83–97); Markus Blockmuehl, "A 'Slain Messiah' in *4Q Serek Milhamah (4Q285)*?" *Tyndale Bulletin* 43 (1992): 155–69; George J. Brooke, "The Messiah of Aaron in the *Damascus Document*," *RQ* 15 (1991): 215–30; George J. Brooke, "*4QTestament of Levi^d*(?) and the Messianic Servant High Priest," in *From Jesus to John: Essays on Jesus and New Testament Christology in Honour of Marinus de Jonge*, ed. Martinus C. de Boer (Sheffield: JSOT, 1993), 83–100; Andrew Chester, "Jewish Messianic Expectations and Mediatorial Figures and Pauline Christology," in *Paulus und das antike Judentum*, ed. Martin Hengel and Ulrich Heckel (Tübingen: Mohr, 1992), 17–89; John J. Collins, "A Pre-Christian 'Son of God' among the Dead Sea Scrolls," *Bible Review* 9/3 (June 1993): 34–38 57; John J. Collins, "The Works of the Messiah," *Dead Sea Discoveries* 1/1 (1994): 98–112; John J. Collins,

"Messiahs in Context: Method in the Study of Messianism in the Dead Sea Scrolls," in *Methods of Investigation of the Dead Sea Scrolls and the Khirbet Qumran Site: Present Realities and Future Prospects,* ed. Michael O. Wise et al. (New York: New York Academy of Sciences, 1994), 213–29; Craig A. Evans, "The Recently Published Dead Sea Scrolls and the Historical Jesus," in *Studying the Historical Jesus: Evaluations of the State of Current Research,* ed. Bruce Chilton and Craig A. Evans (Leiden: Brill, 1994), 547–65; Joseph A. Fitzmyer, "*4Q246:* The 'Son of God' Document from Qumran," *Biblica* 74 (1993): 153–74; Florentino García Martínez, "Nuevos textos mesiánicos de Qumrán y el Mesías del Nuevo Testamento," *Communio* 26 (1993): 3–31; Florentino García Martínez, "Los Mesías de Qumrán: Problemas de un traductor," *Sefarad* 53 (1993): 345–60; Michael A. Knibb, "The Teacher of Righteousness—A Messianic Title?" in *A Tribute to Geza Vermes: Essays on Jewish and Christian Literature and History,* ed. Philip R. Davies and Richard T. White (Sheffield: JSOT, 1990), 51–65; Michael A. Knibb, "The Interpretation of *Damascus Document* VII,9b–VIII,2a and XIX,5b–14," *RQ* 15 (1991): 243–51; Corrado Martone, "Un testo qumranico che narra la morte del Messia? A proposito del recente dibattito su *4Q285,*" *Rivista Biblica* 42 (1994): 329–36; Gerbern S. Oegema, *Der Gesalbte und sein Volk: Untersuchungen zum Konzeptualisierungsprozeß der messianischen Erwartungen von den Makkabäern bis Bar Koziba* (Göttingen: Vandenhoeck und Ruprecht, 1994), 86–99, 108–15; Kenneth E. Pomykala, *The Davidic Dynasty Tradition in Early Judaism: Its History and Significance for Messianism,* ed. William Adler (Atlanta: Scholars Press, 1995), 171–216; Paolo Sacchi, "Ésquisse du développement du messianisme juif à la lumière du texte qumranien *11QMelch,*" *ZAW* 100 supplement (1988): 202–14; Lawrence H. Schiffman, "Messianic Figures and Ideas in the Qumran Scrolls," in *The Messiah: Developments in Earliest Judaism and Christianity,* ed. James H. Charlesworth (Minneapolis: Fortress, 1992), 116–29; Lawrence H. Schiffman, *Law, Custom, and Messianism in the Dead Sea Sect* (Jerusalem: Merkaz Zalman Shazar le Toldot Yisraʾel, 1993), 286–311 (in Hebrew); Lawrence H. Schiffman, *Reclaiming the Dead Sea Scrolls: The History of Judaism, the Background of Christianity, the Lost Library of Qumran* (Philadelphia: Jewish Publication Society, 1994), 315–50; Frederick M. Schweitzer, "The Teacher of Righteousness," in *Mogilany 1989: Papers on the Dead Sea Scrolls,* ed. Zdzislaw J. Kapera (Cracow: Enigma Press, 1991), 2:53–97; Shemaryahu Talmon, "Waiting for the Messiah—The Conceptual Universe of the Qumran Covenanters," in *The World of Qumran from Within—Collected Studies,* ed. Shemaryahu Talmon (Jerusalem: Magnes, 1989), 273–300 (this article originally appeared as "Waiting for of the use of of the term *messiah* from all the scrolls at Qumran for the *Jahrbuch für biblische Theologie.*[5] Two lengthy contributions dealing with messianism in the scrolls appeared in the compilation of presentations given at the Notre Dame Symposium on the Dead Sea Scrolls of 1993,[6] and in 1995 a book-length study on the topic by John J. Collins was published.[7] Thus it is not lack of recent treatment that has motivated the choice of my topic, nor, to be honest, the incomparable cadre assembled at this meeting—in a setting across from the closed Golden Gate, to which so many messianic legends are attached. The reason for my choice is that some elements of the messianism of the Scroll remain unclear and problematic to me, and I hope that discussing them here might help to elucidate them. If a solution is not available, at least your comments will help me see the problems more clearly.

---

the Messiah: The Spiritual Universe of the Qumran Covenanters," in *Judaisms and Their Messiahs at the Turn of the Christian Era,* ed. Jacob Neusner, William S. Green, and Ernest S. Frerichs [Cambridge: Cambridge University Press, 1987], 111–37); Shemaryahu Talmon, "The Concept of Masiah and Messianism in Early Judaism," in *The Messiah,* ed. Charlesworth, 79–115; Clemens Thoma, "Entwürfe für messianischen Gestalten in frühjüdischer Zeit," in *Messiah and Christos: Studies in the Jewish Origins of Christianity,* ed. Ithamar Gruenwald, Shaul Shaked, and Gedalyahu G. Stroumsa (Tübingen: Mohr, 1992), 15–29; James C. VanderKam, "Jubilees and the Priestly Messiah of Qumran," *RQ* 13 (1988): 353–65; and Michael O. Wise and James D. Tabor, "The Messiah at Qumran," *Biblical Archaeology Review* 18/6 (November/December 1992): 60–61, 65.

[5]   Florentino García Martínez, "Messianische Erwartungen in den Qumranschriften," *Jahrbuch für biblische Theologie* 8 (1993): 171–208.

[6]   James C. VanderKam, "Messianism in the Scrolls," in *The Community of the Renewed Covenant: The Notre Dame Symposium on the Dead Sea Scrolls,* ed. Eugene Ulrich and James VanderKam (Notre Dame: University of Notre Dame Press, 1994), 211–34; Émile Puech, "Messianism, Resurrection, and Eschatology at Qumran and in the New Testament," in ibid., 235–56.

[7]   John J. Collins, *The Scepter and the Star: The Messiahs of the Dead Sea Scrolls and Other Ancient Literature* (New York: Doubleday, 1995).

I would like to bring two points to your attention: (1) the heavenly messiah and (2) the messianic character of the expected prophet.

The Heavenly Messiah

Most scholars agree that the people of Qumran expected more than one eschatological figure whose coming would herald the era of salvation; they used the technical term *anointed ones* or *messiahs* to refer to these figures. The key text is *1QS* IX, 9–11:[8]

> [9] They should not depart from any counsel of the law in order to walk [10] in complete stubbornness of their heart, but instead shall be ruled by the first directives which the men of the Community began to be taught [11] until the prophet comes, and the messiahs of Aaron and Israel. *Blank.*

The text is clear and expresses firmly the hope, within the Qumran community, of the future coming of two anointed ones—the messiah of Aaron and the messiah of Israel—two figures who correspond to the priestly messiah and the royal messiah. A third figure, the Prophet, will occupy our attention later on in this discussion.

---

[8]   Text and plates in *The Dead Sea Scrolls of St. Mark's Monastery,* ed. Millar Burrows, vol. 2 (New Haven: American Schools of Oriental Research, 1951). Color photographs by John C. Trever in *Scrolls from Qumran Cave 1,* ed. Frank Moore Cross, David Noel Freedman, and James A. Sanders (Jerusalem: Albright Institute of Archaelogical Research and Shrine of the Book, 1972); translation in Florentino García Martínez, *The Dead Sea Scrolls Translated—The Qumran Texts in English*, trans. Wilfred G. E. Watson (Leiden: Brill, 1994), 13–14 (hereafter cited as *DSST*).

The Messiah Figure in the Bible

General consensus seems to indicate that the Dead Sea Scrolls can refer to these eschatological agents of salvation without using the term *messiah*. In fact texts vary in their use of the technical term when talking about the *same* eschatological figure. After all, the Old Testament texts, which later on will be used to express the hope of an eschatological savior, do not use the word *messiah*, and in none of the thirty-nine instances in which the Hebrew Bible uses the word *messiah* does this word have the precise technical meaning of the title used later to denote one of the figures who would bring eschatological salvation. Texts such as the blessings of Jacob (Genesis 49:10), Balaam's oracle (Numbers 24:7), Nathan's prophecy (2 Samuel 7), and the royal psalms (such as Psalms 2 and 110) would be developed by Isaiah, Jeremiah, and Ezekiel in the direction of hope in a future royal messiah, heir to the throne of David. The promises of the restoration of the priesthood in texts such as Jeremiah 33:14–26 (missing from the Septuagint) and the oracle of the high priest Joshua included in Zechariah 3 were to act as a starting point for later hope in a priestly messiah. Similarly, the double investiture of the "sons of oil"—Zerubbabel and Joshua (Zechariah 6:9–14)—would be the starting point of the hope in a double messiah, reflecting a particular division of power already present since Moses and Aaron. In the same way, the presence of the triple office—king, priest, prophet—combined with the announcement of the future coming of a Prophet like Moses in Deuteronomy 18:15–18 and with the hope in the return of Elijah found in Malachi 4:5–6, would act as the starting point for the development of a hope in the coming of another agent of eschatological salvation. Similarly, the presentation of the mysterious figure of the Servant of YHWH in chapters 40–55 of Isaiah, as an alternative to traditional messianism in the perspective of the restoration, would result in the development of a hope in a suffering messiah. Also, the announcement in Malachi 3:1 that God was to send his angel as a messenger to prepare his coming would permit the development of hope in an eschatological mediator of nonterrestrial origin.

Thus we do not need to limit our search to texts which expressly use the term *messiah*; we can expect to find messianic figures designated by other titles as well. Expectation is fulfilled precisely with the first of the figures discussed here, designated as a heavenly messiah.

Messiah Figure as Both Human and Heavenly

It is perfectly understandable that the hope in a superhuman agent of eschatological salvation could have developed in the Judaism of the period. But to consider this agent of eschatological salvation as a messiah could appear to be not only an unacceptable broadening of the concept of messiah, but also an expansion which robs the concept of its deepest characteristic—its human dimension. It is difficult to imagine the possibility of a superhuman person being considered as anointed; angels, it appears, did not receive an anointing.[9] The human character of all other messiahs is strongly stressed in the Davidic succession of the messiah-king and in the cultic perspective in which the messiah-priest performs his atonement.[10]

And yet it seems difficult to avoid using the adjective *messianic* to characterize this figure, since the functions attributed to him are messianic in nature. This seems to require a semantic widening of the term *messiah* to enable us to apply it to figures which are presented not only as human but also as superhuman.

Other Jewish writings not from Qumran, the *Parables of Enoch* and *4 Esdras*, describe a superhuman agent of eschatological salvation, using the technical term *messiah* as one of the names for the saving figure. This suggests that the widening of the semantic field of *messiah* had already taken place in the Judaism of the period. We cannot, therefore, exclude *a priori*

---

[9]   Although some angels did appear ministering as priests in the heavenly temple in the *Songs of the Sabbath Sacrifice*.

[10]   Within the sacrificial cult of the Jerusalem temple.

from our consideration the Qumran texts—which may refer to such figures without using the technical term—under pain of ignoring one of the possible developments of messianic hope reflected in the preserved manuscripts. In the *Parables of Enoch* 48:10 and 52:4 the term *messiah* is occasionally used together with the more common titles of *Chosen One* and above all *Son of Man* to denote an existing, transcendental figure of celestial origin.[11] In the vision of *4 Esdras* 13, a person "like a man" (called *messiah* in 7:28 and 12:32 and more often *son/servant of God*) is clearly presented as a preexisting, transcendental person of celestial origin.[12] The figures in these texts are called *messiah*, in spite of their superhuman nature and their description using images traditionally associated with divinity. Accordingly, as Collins correctly observes, "the understanding of 'messiah' is thereby qualified."[13] These parallels in compositions whose Jewish origin does not seem to be in question justify the use of the term *heavenly messiah* to designate an eschatological savior figure found in two of the Qumran texts, in which the word *messiah* itself is not used.

---

[11]   See recently James C. VanderKam, "Righteous One, Messiah, Chosen One, and Son of Man in 1 Enoch 3–71," in *The Messiah,* ed. Charlesworth, 169–91, with references to previous studies.

[12]   Michael E. Stone, "The Question of the Messiah in 4 Ezra," in Michael E. Stone, *Selected Studies in Pseudepigrapha and Apocrypha*, ed. Albert M. Denis and Marinus de Jonge (Leiden: Brill, 1991), 317–32 (the article appeared earlier in *Judaisms and Their Messiahs,* ed. Neusner, Green, and Frerichs, 209–24); and Michael E. Stone, "Excursus on the Redeemer Figure," in Michael E. Stone, *Fourth Ezra: A Commentary on the Book of Fourth Ezra,* ed. Frank Moore Cross (Minneapolis: Fortress, 1990), 207–13.

[13]   In an excellent article in which he stresses how both figures represent a particular messianic interpretation of Daniel 7, John J. Collins, "The Son of Man in First-Century Judaism," *NTS* 38 (1992): 466 n. 78, suggests that *4Q246* could contain a similar messianic interpretation of the Daniel figure, an intuition that seems absolutely correct and matches my own understanding of the text.

The Heavenly Messiah in a Midrash from Cave 11

The first of the Qumran texts *(11QMelch)* referred to is a midrash of eschatological content, which was preliminarily published by A. S. van der Woude as part of the Dutch lot of Cave 11.[14] The protagonist of this text is a heavenly person, an *elohim*, called Melchizedek, who, at the end of times, will execute justice and be the instrument of salvation. The central part of the fragment (col. II 6–19) can be translated as follows:[15]

[6] He (Melchizedek) will proclaim liberty for them, to free them from [the debt] of all their iniquities. And this will [happen] [7] in the first week of the jubilee which follows the ni[ne] jubilees. And the day [of atonem]ent is the end of the tenth jubilee [8] in which atonement will be made for all the sons of [God] and for the men of the lot of Melchizedek. [And on the heights] he will decla[re in their] favor according to their lots: for [9] it is the time of the "year of grace" for Melchizedek, to exa[lt in the tri]al the holy ones of God through the rule of judgment, as is written [10] about him in the songs of David, who said: "Elohim will stand up in the assem[bly of God,] in the midst of the gods he judges." And about him he said: "Above it [11] return to the heights, God will judge the

---

[14] It will be included in a volume of the series *Discoveries in the Judaean Desert*, which we are preparing with the generous support of Alan Ashton.

[15] See the manuscript published by Adam S. van der Woude, "Melchisedek als himmlische Erlösergestalt in den neugefundenen eschatologischen Midraschim aus Qumran Höhle XI," *Oudtestamentische Studiën* 14 (1963): 354–73; it was placed in the context of other Qumran writings by Jozef T. Milik, "Milkî-sedeq et Milkî-rešaᶜ dans les anciens écrits juifs et chrétiens," *JJS* 23 (1972): 95–144, and has been extensively studied, for example, in Paul J. Kobelski, *Melchizedek and Melchireša* (Washington: Catholic Biblical Association of America, 1981). My translation (García Martínez, *DSST*, 139–40) incorporates most of the readings and reconstructions proposed by Émile Puech, "Notes sur le manuscrit de 11QMelkîsédeq," *RQ* 12 (1987): 483–513.

peoples." As for what he sa[id: "How long will yo]u judge unjustly and show partiality to the wicked? Selah." *12* Its interpretation concerns Belial and the spirits of his lot, who were rebels [all of them] turning aside from the commandments of God [to commit evil.] *13* But, Melchizedek will carry out the vengeance of God's judges [on this day, and they shall be freed from the hands] of Belial and from the hands of all the sp[irits of his lot.] *14* To his aid (shall come) all "the gods of [justice": he] is the one [who will prevail on this day over] all the sons of God, and he will pre[side over] this [assembly.] *15* This is the day of [peace about which God] spoke [of old through the words of Isa]iah the prophet, who said: "How beautiful *16* upon the mountains are the feet of the mess[enger who announces peace, of the messenger of good who announces salvation,] saying to Zion: "Your God [reigns."] *17* Its interpretation: The mountains are the pro[phets . . .] *18* And the messenger is [the anoi]nted of the spirit about whom Dan[iel] spoke [. . . and the messenger of] *19* good who announces salv[ation is the one about whom it is written that . . .

In spite of the uncertainty of the reconstructions, the content seems clear. Here we need only to note the details concerning the messianic figures to whom the text refers. The weave of the text is formed by Leviticus 25:8–13 concerning the jubilee year, Deuteronomy 15 concerning the year of release, and Isaiah 52, which proclaims the liberation of the prisoners. The author also develops his ideas from interpretions of other texts from Isaiah, the Psalms, and Daniel, which he uses to refers to Melchizedek, the protagonist.

Melchizedek's intervention is set specifically in the first week of the tenth jubilee, the final jubilee of human history in the text's chronological system, equivalent to the last of the seventy weeks of other systems. The remission of debts in the biblical text is interpreted as referring to the final liberation that will occur during the Day of the Expiation. The agent of this liberation is Melchizedek, presented as the eschatological judge found in Psalm 7:8–9 and Psalm 82:1–2. This liberation will be preceded by a battle between Melchizedek and Belial and his spirits, and Melchizedek's victory will usher in an era of salvation described in Isaiah 52:7 and 61:2–3. In a typical *pesher* way the four key words of the biblical text are interpreted: the *mountains* are the prophets, the *messenger* is the anointed of the spirit, *Sion* is the faithful to the covenant, and *elohim* is Melchizedek himself.

The midrash text presents Melchizedek as the chief of the heavenly armies—the leader of the sons of God who destroys the armies of Belial—and identifies this figure, in terms of practical functions, with the "Prince of Light" (a figure we find in *1QS* III, 30, *CD* V, 8 and *1QM* XIII, 10) and with the angel Michael (a figure appearing in *1QM* XVII, 6–7). But Melchizedek, although being presented as a heavenly being, is not described simply as an angel (he is called *elohim* but not *malak*), and his earthly origins seem to serve as a backdrop for his exalted heavenly position. This fact suggests that this heavenly being is the same earthly Melchizedek of the Bible, the mysterious king of Genesis 14:17–20 and the eternal priest of Psalm 110:4. Although he is clearly a heavenly being and is called *elohim*, the text speaks of "the lot of Melchizedek" or "the year of grace of Melchizedek," using Melchizedek's name in expressions that in the Bible are typically related to God himself.

Because the three basic functions the text ascribes to this heavenly being are messianic, we can designate this heavenly being as a heavenly messiah. These three functions are (1) to be an avenging judge (with reference to Psalms 82:1–2 and 7:1), (2) to be a heavenly priest who carries out atonement for his inheritance on the Day of Atonement, and (3) to be the ultimate savior of "the men of his lot," destroying the kingdom of Belial in the eschatological battle and restoring eternal peace.

The Heavenly Messiah in *4Q246*

The same sort of heavenly messiah seems to be the protagonist of an Aramaic composition partially preserved in *4Q246*.[16]
From this manuscript, copied in the first half of the first century,
a complete column of nine lines and approximately half of the
preceding column have reached us. The text can be translated as
follows:[17]

4Q246 col. I

1 [. . .] settled upon him and he fell before the throne
2 [. . .] eternal king. You are angry and your years
3 [. . .] they will see you, and all shall come for ever.

---

[16] The text was presented by Jozef T. Milik in a lecture given at
Harvard University in 1972 and was made known by Joseph A. Fitzmyer in
his study "The Contribution of Qumran Aramaic to the Study of the New
Testament," *NTS* 20 (1973–74): 382–407, and reprinted with an important
supplement in Joseph A. Fitzmyer, *A Wandering Aramean: Collected Aramaic Essays* (Missoula, MT: Scholars Press, 1979), 85–107. It has since
then been extensively studied; see David Flusser, "The Hubris of the Anti-
christ in a Fragment from Qumran," *Immanuel* 10 (1980): 31–37; also in
David Flusser, *Judaism and the Origins of Christianity* (Jerusalem: Magnes,
1988), 207–13; Florentino García Martínez, "*4Q246:* ¿Tipo del Anticristo o
Libertador escatológico?" in *El misterio de la Palabra: Homenaje a
L. Alonso Schöckel,* ed. Vicente Collado and Eduardo Zurro (Madrid:
Ediciones Cristiandad, 1983), 229–44 (published in English as "The
Eschatological Figure of *4Q246*," in Florentino García Martínez, *Qumran
and Apocalyptic* [Leiden: Brill, 1992], 162–79); and Georg Kuhn, "Röm
1.3 f und der davidische Messias als Gotessohn in den Qumrantexten," in
Lese-Zeichen für Annelies Findeiß zum 65. Geburtstag am 15. März 1984,
ed. Christoph Burchard and Gerd Thiessen (Heidelberg: Burchard and
Thiessen, 1984), 103–13. The recent complete publication by Puech
("Fragment d'une apocalypse") of the last five lines of column II now
allows a fuller analysis. See Fitzmyer, "*4Q246:* The 'Son of God'
Document"; John J. Collins, "The *Son of God* Text from Qumran," in
From Jesus to John, ed. de Boer, 65–83; and Émile Puech, "Notes sur le
fragment d'apocalypse *4Q246*—'Le fils de dieu,' " *RB* 101 (1994): 533–58.

[17] García Martínez, *DSST,* 138.

4 [. . .] great, oppression will come upon the earth
5 [. . .] and great slaughter in the city *6* [. . .] king of
Assyria and of Egypt *7* [. . .] and he will be great over
the earth *8* [. . .] they will do, and all will serve *9* [. . .]
great will he be called and he will be designated by his
name.

Col. II

1 He will be called son of God, and they will call him
son of the Most High. Like the sparks *2* of a vision, so
will their kingdom be; they will rule several years over *3*
the earth and crush everything; a people will crush
another people, and a city another city. *4* *Blank* Until he
rises up the people of God (or the people of God arise)
and makes everyone rest from the sword. *5* His kingdom
will be an eternal kingdom, and all his paths in truth and
uprigh[tness] *6* The earth (will be) in truth and all will
make peace. The sword will cease in the earth *7* and all
the cities will pay him homage. He is a great God among
the gods (?) (or: The great God will be his strength). *8*
He will make war with him; he will place the peoples in
his hand and cast away everyone before him. *9* His
kingdom will be an eternal kingdom, and all the abysses.

Although the first column is fragmentary, the broad meaning of
the passage can be understood and has been accepted since
1974. The protagonist of the story falls down before the throne
of a king and reveals to him a vision of a future conflagration in
which the kings of Assur and Egypt will play a role. Then
appears a mysterious personage to whom the names *Son of God*
and *Son of the Most High* are given. Chaos will follow, but it
will be resolved and followed by eternal peace and his eternal
kingdom once the enemies are destroyed.

This mysterious person has been diversely interpreted—
Milik identified him with a historical king, Alexander Balas;

Fitzmyer applied the titles to an heir to David's throne, a royal but nonmessianic person; and Flusser saw in this person a reference to the Antichrist.[18] In 1983, after analyzing all these interpretations and pointing out why they seemed insufficient, I proposed interpreting the person to whom the text refers as an eschatological liberator of angelic (or nonhuman) nature, a figure similar in functions to those which *11QMelch* ascribes to Melchizedek or *1QM* assigns to the Prince of Light or to the archangel Michael.

Émile Puech, the editor of the whole text, thinks the preserved text does not allow definitive resolution between a "historicizing" interpretation like Milik's and a messianic interpretation, toward which his preferences seem inclined. Puech seems to exclude my interpretation of the text for two reasons: (1) because it is not certain that *4Q246* is a composition originating in Qumran, and because, in his opinion, "les figures 'célestes' qui sont les médiateurs de salut dans le judaïsme ancien, Hénoc, Elie, Melkîsédek ou le Fils de l'Homme, n'ont pas, à proprement parler, reçu le titre de 'messie.' "[19] However, as indicated, the preceding statement is not completely accurate. Also, the parallels with ideas contained in other Qumran writings, although they may not be determinative in assigning a sectarian origin to the composition, do at least make the text compatible with the outlook of the Qumran group.

I maintain, therefore, that my interpretation of the first fragmentary column and of the first four lines of column II still best explains the elements preserved. But I do recognize, however, that the adjective *angelic* could be misleading. My description of

---

[18] All these interpretations are discussed in García Martínez, "*4Q246:* ¿Tipo del Anticristo?" ("The Eschatological Figure of *4Q246*"); Puech, "Fragment d'une apocalypse"; and Collins, "The *Son of God* Text from Qumran."

[19] Puech, "Fragment d'une apocalypse," 102 n. 14, 124–25: "The 'celestial' figures who are the mediators of salvation in ancient Judaism— Enoch, Elias, and Melchizedek or the Son of Man—have not, strictly speaking, been given the title of *messiah.*"

the person in question as angelic was based on the parallel with
other superhuman figures of the Qumran texts. But, as has been
noted in the case of Melchizedek, the human components serve
as backdrop for the heavenly figure. Although the human character of the mysterious personage of *4Q246* is not particularly
emphasized, one can assume that he is understood to be, as
Melchizedek, human and heavenly at the same time. Therefore it
will be more correct to denote this superhuman figure of *4Q246*
as heavenly rather than as angelic. The new lines now available
confirm and emphasize this conclusion, since they ascribe to this
figure the features of Daniel's Son of Man.[20]

The quotations in *4Q246* from Daniel 7 are especially striking. "His sovereignty/kingdom will be an eternal sovereignty/
kingdom" (col. II 5) comes from Daniel 7:27; here the phrase is
applied to the "people of the holy ones of the Most High." "His
kingdom will be an eternal kingdom" (col. II 9) comes from
Daniel 7:14 and refers to the Son of Man. In the biblical text, the
parallelism of both expressions in the vision and in its explanation could favor the interpretation of the Son of Man as a collective figure. The author of our composition, however, seems to
attribute both expressions to the mysterious protagonist of the
narrative, whom he considers as an individual, thus anticipating
the clear interpretation as an individual we find in the *Book of
Parables.*

The preserved text does not completely exclude the possibility that the third person pronominal suffixes used, beginning
with column II 5, could refer to the people of God. In fact, biblical equivalents could be found for most of the expressions,
some of which refer to an individual person and some to a person representing the people as a whole. In spite of this ambiguity, though, the lines published recently by Puech in *Revue
biblique*[21] suggest that I modify my 1983 position, in which I

---

[20]   On the interpretation of the Son of Man in Daniel 7 as an individual with an angelic nature, see John J. Collins, *The Apocalyptic Vision of
the Book of Daniel* (Missoula, MT: Scholars Press, 1977), 144–47.

[21]   Puech, "Fragment d'une apocalypse."

attributed these pronouns to the "people of God." Puech's interpretation of that as the protagonist mentioned at the end of column I and at the beginning of column II now seems more plausible to me.

Puech notes that "qu'il relève" ("he raises them [the people
of God] up") can be read in column II 4 instead of "que se
(re)lève" ("they [the people of God] rise up themselves"), and
"(qu')il fasse tout reposer" ("he causes them to lie down")
instead of "tout reposera" ("all will lie down"). This enables line
4 to be understood as the climax of the period of crisis described
beforehand; the lofty titles given to the protagonist to be understood, since the task he has to fulfill is to bring in the situation
of eschatological peace; and the particle used to be given the
value of "term/limit."[22] This interpretation is strengthened by the
use of the phrase *he will judge* in column II 5 and by the statement of the cosmic dimension of his kingdom in column II 9.

This reading of the text is also strengthened by the way in
which the phrase, *Until he raises up the people of God*, is set
out in the manuscript. The *blank* that comes before mention of
the people of God seems intended to emphasize that this situation of eschatological peace is precisely the conclusion of the
situation described previously and is due to the activity of the
protagonist, to whom the lofty titles *Son of God* and *Son of the
Most High* are given. The *blank* that follows this expression on
the same line removes the necessity of making a whole series of
suffixes in the following lines refer to the nearest antecedent (the
people of God, the object of the preceding phrase). They can
refer to the subject of the phrases, the *son of God* and *son of the
Most High*.

Understood in this way, *4Q246* describes an eschatological
liberator, a heavenly being similar to Melchizedek of *11QMelch*
or the Son of Man of Daniel 7, called *son of God* and *son of the
Most High*. He will be the agent who will bring eschatological
salvation, judge all the earth, and conquer all the kings through

---

22   Puech, "Fragment d'une apocalypse," 116–17.

God's power and rule over the whole universe. He is thus a messiah, an almost divinized messiah, similar to Melchizedek and the heavenly Son of Man. This is precisely the element that needs to be emphasized. In Qumran the coming of an agent of eschatological salvation, together with a messiah-king and a messiah-priest, was expected to be as exalted as the preexistent Son of Man of the *Parables of Enoch* or as the messiah of *4 Esdras*.

The Messianic Prophet

The figure of the eschatological prophet remains elusive. We have seen him appear in the first text quoted, *1QS* IX, 11: "until the prophet comes, and the messiahs of Aaron and Israel . . ." It is obvious from his juxtaposition with the two messiah figures that this person is an eschatological being. It is less evident that he is a true messianic figure, since, unlike the other two, he is not termed *anointed* here. The text speaks only of the hope in his coming, detailing nothing about his functions, the biblical basis that allowed this hope to develop, or his possible identification with other titles used in the texts for these figures. The text does not allow us to determine whether this figure—a prophet—does or does not have messianic features. Its contrast to the messiah would seem rather to indicate it does not in this text.

More promising is the material found in the text already quoted from *11QMelch*. As indicated, the messenger of Isaiah 52:7 is identified there as *the anointed of the spirit*, an expression certainly identifying prophets, but used here clearly in the singular and referring thus to *a* prophet, an anointed one, or messiah, who is expected at the time of Melchizedek. Unfortunately, neither the text of Daniel nor further precision has been preserved. All we can assert about him, therefore, is that the text clearly distinguishes this prophet from the prophets of the past and seems to consider him as a precursor to the heavenly messiah. His identification as the eschatological Prophet cannot be considered completely proven, although it is certainly the most probable reading.[23] It cannot here be positively ascertained if his role was described as messianic.

The Prophet as a Messianic Figure

Other texts, however, enable us to determine that this expected prophet was at times considered a messianic figure. The first of these texts is *4QTestimonia*, a well-preserved, rectangular sheet written at the beginning of the first century.[24] It contains four quotations, without comments, separated by marks in the margin. Nevertheless, the contents and order of the quotations make clear the purpose of the writing—to collect references to the coming of the different messianic and anti-messianic figures at the end of time. The texts quoted are (1) Exodus 20:21b according to the Samaritan Pentateuch, giving a text that combines Deuteronomy 5:28–29 and Deuteronomy 18:18–19 according to the Masoretic Text; (2) Numbers 24:15–17; (3) Deuteronomy 33:8–11; and (4) a fragment of the *Psalms of Joshua*, a composition known through two copies found in Cave 4.[25] The first quotation is the base text, which forms the foundation for hope in the coming of a Prophet like Moses, the Prophet awaited at the end of time. The second text, which concerns the scepter and star of Balaam's oracle, is the foundation for hope in the messiah-king. The third text, taken from the blessing of Levi, is the foundation for hope in the messiah-

---

[23]   According to an explanation by Adam S. van der Woude in a joint article with Marinus de Jonge, "*11QMelchizedek* and the New Testament," *NTS* 12 (1966): 307.

[24]   Text and plates in John M. Allegro, *Qumran Cave 4.1* (4Q158–4Q186), *DJD* 5:57–60 and plate 21; translation in García Martínez, *DSST*, 137.

[25]   Published by Carol Newsom, "The 'Psalms of Joshua' from Qumran Cave 4," *JJS* 39 (1988): 56–73. See also Hanan Eshel, "The Historical Background of the Pesher Interpreting Joshua's Curse on the Rebuilder of Jericho," *RQ* 15 (1992): 409–20; and Timothy H. Lim, "The 'Psalms of Joshua' (*4Q379* fr. 22 col. 2): A Reconsideration of Its Text," *JJS* 44 (1993): 309–12.

priest. The fourth quotation, from the *Psalms of Joshua*, announces the coming of "an accursed man, one of Belial," an antagonist to these messianic figures, or an antimessiah.

In essence, my reasoning for the above interpretation consists of two elements:

1. *4QTestimonia* contains a collection of texts that the community interprets messianically[26]—these texts correspond, in the same order, to the three figures of *1QS* IX, 11. The three quotations parallel each other and therefore must refer to similar figures.

2. This figure of the prophet is identical to the figure denoted in the other texts as the Interpreter of the Law—the one who "teaches justice at the end of times"—and the messenger figures, which have a clear prophetic character and are considered as messianic figures. Like them, then, the Prophet must be considered a messianic figure.

We are told expressly in *11QMelch* II 18 that the last of these figures, the messenger, is "anointed by the spirit." In other words, the technical term, which in *1QS* IX, 11 is applied to the other two messianic figures, is applied to him in the singular. Accordingly, it seems justifiable to consider this Prophet, whose coming is expected at the same time as the messiah of Aaron and the messiah of Israel, as a true messianic figure.

The first item in my argument is obvious and needs no explanation, although perhaps it might be useful to note that *anointed* can be applied to all three figures referred to by the biblical texts of this collection of testimonia. The choice of Deuteronomy 18:18–19 shows that the expected Prophet is a "Prophet like Moses." At Qumran, both Moses and the prophets are called *anointed ones*, a title which seems to be based on the

---

[26] The interpretation of John Lübbe, "A Reinterpretation of *4QTestimonia*," *RQ* 12 (1986): 187–97, who sees the text as a condemnation of the apostasy of early dissenters from the sect and as essentially concerned with contemporary rather than future issues, has failed to oust the traditional interpretation, in which the text is viewed as a collection of messianic prooftexts.

parallel between anointed ones and prophets in Psalm 105:15 and in the Old Testament allusions to the anointing of prophets. The parallel with seers and the functions of announcing and teaching attributed to them in *1QM* and *CD* make it clear that the anointed ones spoken of are none other than the prophets. *1QM* XI, 7 declares: "By the hand of your anointed ones, seers of decrees, you taught us the times of the wars of your hands." And in *CD* II, 12 we read: "And he taught them by the hands of his anointed ones through his holy spirit and through seers of the truth." This allows us to interpret *CD* VI, 1 in the same way, in that those who lead Israel astray rise not only against Moses but also against "the holy anointed ones."[27] This seems to be nothing less than a description of Moses as a prophet.

It will be useful, perhaps, to quote Deuteronomy 18:18–19 as presented in *4QTestimonia*, since it clarifies that this expected prophet, like Moses, is portrayed in the biblical text as a true interpreter of the Law:

> [5] I would raise up for them a prophet from among their brothers, like you, and place my words [6] in his mouth, and he would tell them all that I command them. And it will happen that the man [7] who does not listen to my words, that the prophet will speak in my name, I [8] shall require a reckoning from him." *Blank*. (*4Q175* 5–8)[28]

The second element of this argument is more complex and implies an examination of the texts in which these figures—such

---

[27] A still-unpublished fragment of a pseudo-Mosaic composition, to be published by Devorah Dimant, can be read as "through the mouth of Moses, his anointed one"; cf. *4Q377* 2 ii 5, PAM 43.372. The manuscript is labeled "Sl 12" in the *Preliminary Concordance to the Hebrew and Aramaic Fragments from Qumran Caves II–X*, in which the phrase in question is transcribed.

[28] Translation in García Martínez, *DSST*, 137.

as the Interpreter of the Law—occur. The first such text is
4QFlorilegium:[29]

> [10] And "YHWH de[clares] to you that he will build you a
> house. I will raise up your seed after you and establish
> the throne of his kingdom [11] [for ev]er. I will be a father
> to him and he will be a son to me." This (refers to the)
> "branch of David," who will arise with the Interpreter of
> the Law who [12] [will rise up] in Zi[on in] the last days,
> as it is written: "I will raise up the hut of David which
> has fallen." This (refers to) "the hut of [13] David which
> has fallen," who will arise to save Israel. *Blank* (*4Q174*
> I, 11–12).

This text refers to the Interpreter of the Law by name, together
with the *branch of David*, a familiar expression to denote the
messiah-king, called the "Prince of the whole congregation" in
other texts. His identity with the messiah of Israel presents no
problem. Apart from their future coming, the text reveals nothing about both figures. The requirement that this coming take
place in the last days remains important since it stresses his clear
eschatological character.

The second text is *CD* VII, 18–21:[30]

> [18] *Blank* And the star is the Interpreter of the law, [19] who
> will come to Damascus, as is written [Numbers 24:13]:

---

[29]   Text and plates in Allegro, *Qumran Cave 4.1,* in *DJD* 5:53–57
and plates 19–20; translation in García Martínez, *DSST*, 136. For commentary and bibliography see George J. Brooke, *Exegesis at Qumran:*
4QFlorilegium *in Its Jewish Context* (Sheffield: JSOT, 1985).

[30]   I use the critical edition prepared by Elisha Qimron and included in
The Damascus Document Reconsidered, ed. Magen Broshi (Jerusalem: Israel
Exploration Society, Shrine of the Book, Israel Museum, 1992), which is
accompanied by photographs of excellent quality, and which contains cross-
references to the copies found in Qumran. *CD* 7:18–21 is found in part in
the copy *4QD^b (4Q267)* frag. 3 col. IV 9–10 (PAM 43.270), and possibly
in *4QD^f (4Q271)* frag. 5 (PAM 43.300), although this is very uncertain;
translation in García Martínez, *DSST*, 38.

"A star moves out of Jacob, and a scepter arises [20] out of Israel." The scepter is the prince of the whole congregation and when he rises he will destroy [21] all the sons of Seth. *Blank*.

The Prince of the whole congregation is the already familiar messianic figure. As in other texts, he is equated here with the scepter. Therefore, no doubt exists about his identification with the messiah-king, the Davidic messiah of Jewish tradition, and the messiah of Israel in other texts in which the Davidic character of such titles is muted. This text only tells us about the one who "will destroy all the sons of Seth," using the expression from Numbers 24:17, but without specifying its meaning (which in the original biblical text is not clear). Who is the Interpreter of the Law who appears here in parallel with him? Is he a figure from the past or from the future?

In *CD* VI, 7 the staff of Numbers 21:18 is identified as the Interpreter of the Law to whom the text of Isaiah 54:16 is applied. In this case, the wording and context of the text are sufficient proof that he is a person from the past. Most scholars identify him as the historical Teacher of Righteousness, also a person from the past.[31] One of the great merits of van der Woude's work is his convincing argument that the epithets *Interpreter of the Law* and *Teacher of Righteousness* are used as titles in *CD* to denote both a figure from the past as well as an eschatological figure whose coming is expected in the future. This argument enabled him to resolve the problem posed by the reference to an Interpreter of the Law in *CD* VI, 7 as a figure from the past. He was also able to solve the problem posed by the subsequent text (*CD* VI, 11), which mentions a clearly

---

[31] See the arguments put forth by van der Woude in *Die messianischen Vorstellungen,* 69–71, and in "Le Maître de Justice et les deux messies de la communauté de Qumrân," *La secte de Qumrân et les origines chrétiennes* (Bruges: Desclée de Brouwer, 1959), 123–24. This figure occurs frequently in *1QpHab* and in *CD,* in which works he is called "Teacher of Righteousness," "Unique Teacher," "he who teaches justice," or "the unique teacher" in alteration.

eschatological figure from the future, with a title identical to that of *Teacher of Righteousness*: "until there arises he who teaches justice at the end of days."

The ambiguity of *CD* VII, 18–21 arises from the use of a participle form that can have a past or future value. Some authors, convinced that only one messianic figure is spoken of in this Amos-Numbers Midrash,[32] consider the Interpreter of the Law as a figure from the past, whereas those who see in the text an allusion to two messianic figures view in this same Interpreter of the Law a future figure contemporary with the Prince of the whole congregation.[33] The strict parallelism between the two figures, the fact that both are interpreted beginning with the same biblical text (to which later tradition was to give a clear messianic value) and, above all, the details that *4Q174* brings us about this Interpreter of the Law who will come at the end of time together with the "shoot of David"—a figure whom *4Q174* explicitly identifies with the Prince of the congregation—are enough to resolve the ambiguity of the text in favor of the interpretation which sees reflected here hope in two messianic figures.

The Role of the Interpreter of the Law

A determination of the role of this Interpreter of the Law would seem to be more difficult, although two interpretations have been suggested. Starcky identified him with the expected eschatological prophet,[34] although this identification starts from a seemingly false premise—the union of the two messiahs of

---

[32] As, for example, André Caquot, "Le messianisme qumrânien," in *Qumrân: Sa piété, sa théologie, et son milieu*, ed. Matthias Delcor (Paris: Duculot, 1978), 241–42.

[33] For example, George J. Brooke, "The Amos-Numbers Midrash (*CD* 713b–81a) and Messianic Expectation," *ZAW* 92 (1980): 397–404. See most recently the detailed study of the passage by Knibb, "The Interpretation of the *Damascus Document*," 248–51.

[34] Jean Starcky, "Les quatre étapes du messianisme à Qumrân," *RB* 70 (1963): 497.

Aaron and of Israel in *CD*. The more prevalent opinion, following van der Woude,[35] identifies this Interpreter of the Law
with the messiah of Aaron, i.e., the priest-messiah who should
be identified with the eschatological figure of Elijah. Van der
Woude's reasoning is essentially as follows: The Interpreter of
the Law is a person from the future and thus distinct from the
Interpreter of the Law in *CD* VI, 7, a person from the past; the
Interpreter of the Law parallels the Prince of the whole congregation, a messianic figure identical with the messiah of Israel;
this suggests he must also be a messianic figure. The title given
him, *Interpreter of the Law*, is very general and can denote various figures, but the specification "who will come to Damascus"
(meaning Qumran) is more significant. The clause comes from 1
Kings 19:15, in which Elijah receives from God the order to go
to Damascus to anoint the king of Syria, the king of Israel, and
the prophet Elisha. In later tradition,[36] and in the Karaite material
collected by N. Wieder,[37] Elijah is portrayed as the eschatological high priest who performs the anointing of the messiah. In
rabbinic tradition, Elijah is also portrayed as one who will
resolve the halakhic problems the rabbis are unable to solve,
when he returns at the end of time as a forerunner of the messiah. This permits van der Woude to conclude that the Interpreter of the Law denotes Elijah, whose coming is expected at
the end of time. This figure is seen as a priestly messiah and
thus is indistinguishable from the messiah of Aaron of the other
Qumran texts.

---

[35] Van der Woude, *Die messianischen Vorstellungen,* 43–61.

[36] Justin, *Dialogus cum Tryphone* 49; see most recently Peter
Pilhofer, "Wer salbt den Messias? Zum Streit um die Chronologie im ersten
Jahrhundert des judisch-christlichen Dialogs," in *Begegnungen zwischen
Christentum und Judentum in Antike und Mittelalter: Festschrift für Heinz
Schreckenberg,* ed. Dietrich-Alex Koch and Hermann Lichtenberger
(Göttingen: Vandenhoeck und Ruprecht, 1993), 335–45.

[37] Naphtali Wieder, "The Doctrine of the Two Messiahs among the
Karaites," *JJS* 6 (1955): 14–23.

The problems with this reasoning are that the two texts that mention the eschatological figure of the Interpreter of the Law describe nothing of his priestly character and that the features of prophet seem more characteristic of Elijah than those of a priest. Accordingly, for very different reasons from those of Starcky, it seems to make more sense to identify this messianic figure of the eschatological Interpreter of the Law with the messianic figure of the Prophet. He is the Prophet expected at the end of times, whose identification with Elijah *redivivus* can be accepted without difficulty.

Van der Woude assembled the main arguments provided by the text, proving that the historical figure referred to as Teacher of Righteousness and Interpreter of the Law was seen as a true prophet. This allowed him to conclude that this historical figure had been perceived as a Prophet like Moses, whose coming is foretold in *1QS* IX, 11. In my view this conclusion is wrong.

A text such as *CD* XIX, 35 to XX, 1 demonstrates that the period of existence of the "unique Teacher" (or of the "Teacher of the Community") is seen as different from the future coming of the messiahs with whom the coming of the Prophet is associated. However, his arguments demonstrating the prophetic character of the person appear completely valid. Van der Woude's points indicate that the figure called Interpreter of the Law or "he who teaches justice at the end of days" must be identified with this Prophet, expected together with the messiahs of Aaron and of Israel. Precisely because the historical Teacher of Righteousness was perceived as a true prophet like Moses, it was possible to use the titles *he who teaches justice* and *Interpreter of the Law* for this figure expected at the end of time and described as a Prophet like Moses.

The fundamental difference between my interpretation and van der Woude's is that for him the Prophet is not a messianic figure, but a forerunner of the messiahs. I, however, believe that the eschatological Prophet is a messianic figure. He can only be identified with a historical person from the past if this person is considered as *redivivus*. His messianic character is not an obstacle to his character as a forerunner, as shown by the messenger of *11QMelch*—together with the heavenly messiah, whose coming is expected in the final jubilee of history. Furthermore, the manuscript presents this messenger not only as *prophet*, but also as one *anointed of the spirit*.

John J. Collins has speculated that the same messianic figure of the Prophet appears in another very important text, *4Q521*.[38] This text does indeed mention a messiah;[39] however, because a full discussion would take too long and I am not sure that this messiah should be identified with the expected eschatological Prophet,[40] I will not review his arguments here.

Although not directly related to the two topics discussed, it seems appropriate to conclude this presentation by quoting one of the most beautiful fragments of the Qumran texts in which messianic expectation appears:

> *1* [for the heav]ens and the earth will listen to his messiah, *2* [and all] that is in them will not turn away from the holy precepts. *3* Be encouraged, you who are seeking the Lord in his service! *Blank 4* Will you not, perhaps, encounter the Lord in it, all those who hope in their heart? *5* For the Lord will observe the devout, and call the just by name, *6* and upon the poor he will place his

---

[38]   Collins, "The Works of the Messiah," 98–112; and Collins, *The Scepter and the Star,* 102–35.

[39]   Published by Puech in "Fragment d'une apocalypse," and studied in greater detail in his *La croyance des esséniens en la vie future: Immortalité, résurrection, vie éternelle? Histoire d'une croyance dans le Judaïsme ancien* (Paris: Gabalda, 1993), 627–92.

[40]   The ambiguity of the fragmentary text cannot be resolved, as Jean Duhaime has indicated for frag. 2 in "Le Messie et les Saints dans un fragment apocalyptique de Qumrân *(4Q521),*" in *Ce Dieu qui vient: Mélanges offerts à Bernard Renaud* (Paris: Cerf, 1995), 265–74. I have considered the interpretation of frag. 2 as referring to the Royal or Davidic Messiah as the more likely (García Martínez, "Messianische Erwartungen," 182–85), and it cannot be ignored that other fragments of the same manuscript talk also of other messianic figures, such as the "priestly messiah" (frag. 8–9), and even of the "eschatological Prophet" (frag. 5–6).

spirit, and the faithful he will renew with his strength. [7]
For he will honor the devout upon the throne of eternal
royalty, [8] freeing prisoners, giving sight to the blind,
straightening out the twisted. [9] Ever shall I cling to those
who hope. In his mercy he will jud[ge,] [10] and from
no-one shall the fruit [of] good [deeds] be delayed, [11]
and the Lord will perform marvelous acts such as have
not existed, just as he sa[id] [12] for he will heal the badly
wounded and will make the dead live, he will proclaim
good news to the meek, [13] give lavishly [to the need]y,
lead the exiled and enrich the hungry, [14] [. . .] and all
[. . .].[41]

---

[41] *4QMessianicApocalypse (4Q521)*, in García Martínez, *DSST,* 394.

Scribal Markings in the Texts from the Judean Desert

EMANUEL TOV

Hebrew University, Jerusalem

The texts from the Judean Desert, especially from Qumran,[1] contain various scribal markings, some of which recur in several individual texts. A few of these signs may have been simply scribbles (e.g., the bottom margin of *1QIsa^a* col. XXXII [fig. 16] and the slightly curved diagonal line before the first letter of וחל[לו] below the writing surface of *4QJer^c* XXII 2 = Jeremiah 31:5); however, most signs were intentional even if their meaning is often not clear to us. Since there are hardly any differences between the scribal practices displayed in biblical and nonbiblical texts, scribal signs occur in both types of text. A few signs are also known from Aramaic secular sources preceding the time of the earliest biblical witnesses (the *paragraphos* sign [fig. 1.1] and the paleo-Hebrew *ʾaleph* [fig. 3]) as well as from Greek sources concurrent with the earliest Qumran texts (the *paragraphos* sign [fig. 1.1], cancellation dots [figs. 6.1–4], and parentheses [figs. 8.1–3]). Similar signs were probably also used in Hebrew texts preceding the earliest Qumran texts, but our information about Hebrew nonlapidary texts from the period

---

[1]   For bibliographical references relating to the published and unpublished documents the reader is referred to Emanuel Tov and Stephen J. Pfann, *Companion Volume to the Dead Sea Scrolls Microfiche Edition,* 2nd ed. (Leiden: Brill, 1995).

preceding the mid-third century B.C.E. is very fragmentary.[2]
Some of these markings have been studied by Martin within the
framework of his study of the scribal practices of the Cave 1
texts.[3] They are described here in greater detail with regard to all
the texts from the Judean Desert, with attention to their nature,
frequency, and background, but because of incomplete information available at this stage, our analysis is preliminary. It should
be stressed that although the detailed discussion may create the
impression that these scribal markings are widely used in the
Qumran texts, *their use is almost exclusively limited to the texts
written according to Qumran scribal practice* (see the discussion
below). Similarly, the majority of the texts using paleo-Hebrew
letters for the divine names are written in accordance with the
Qumran scribal practice. It should also be remarked that the
occurrence of these signs is almost exclusively confined to the
Hebrew (and not the Aramaic) texts. Exceptions are *TLevi[a] ar*
(*paragraphos*), *4QTob[a] ar* (paragraph indicator and dots representing tetragrammaton), and *4QEn[a]* (omission sign).

The proportionally largest number of signs is found in
1QIsa[a] and *1QS–1QSa–1QSb* (the latter three compositions
were written by the same scribe who also inserted some corrections in *1QIsa[a]*), *4Q502–511*, *4QpIsa[c]*, and *4QCant[b]*. Some of
the signs used in the different texts resemble each other, while
others are idiosyncratic.[4]

When signs show a certain resemblance in shape or usage,
this similarity is usually not distinctive enough to warrant a connection between individual scribes or readers of different texts.

---

[2]   Most of the nonlapidary sources are ostraca for which scribal practices different from those used for papyrus and leather may have been used.
[3]   Malachi Martin, *The Scribal Character of the Dead Sea Scrolls*, 2
vols. (Leuven: Leuven University Press, 1958).
[4]   Note further the various signs used in the Samaritan writing tradition; however, it is not known in which period they originated. The various
grammatical treatises explaining the use and meaning of these signs have
been collected by Zev Ben-Hayyim, *The Literary and Oral Tradition of
Hebrew and Aramaic amongst the Samaritans* (in Hebrew), vol. 2
(Jerusalem: Mosad Bialik, 1957), especially *Qanun Dartha fi l-Maqra*.

At the same time, certain conclusions can be made: (1) A few of the signs in *1QIsaᵃ* and *1QS* resemble each other strongly (see sections 1b and 1g), and (2) the texts using letters in the Cryptic A script are of a sectarian nature (see section 3 below).

We consider any element that is not part of the content of the running text, but is additional to it, as a scribal mark. This definition thus excludes the guide dots written at the beginning and end of sheets to guide the drawing of lines on the parchment, since these were inserted before the writing of the text. Having been written, signs could be transferred to subsequent copies of the same text and in that case could easily be misunderstood,[5] although they were not usually meant to be transferred. Most of the shapes of these signs are distinct from the letters of the script in which the text was written, although in some texts, letters in the square, paleo-Hebrew, and Cryptic A script are also used as signs. Some markings were inserted by the original scribes, but probably a greater number were inserted by later scribes and generations of readers, although usually we are not able to distinguish between these three levels. Sometimes the color of the ink or the shape of the sign shows that the sign was written after the text was completed.

Scribal markings have been identified—in varying degrees of frequency—in several texts, more in nonbiblical than in biblical manuscripts. They can be subdivided into the following categories:[6]

---

[5] For example, when the parentheses were not understood any more, they became the inverted *nunim* in the Masoretic tradition of the Bible, which only in some exegetical traditions preserved their original meaning (for a discussion, see Emanuel Tov, *Textual Criticism of the Hebrew Bible* [Minneapolis–Assen/Maastricht: Fortress–Van Gorcum, 1992], 54–55). Cancellation dots were misunderstood in the same tradition, in which they came to denote doubts regarding the letters or words thus indicated. On both issues, see section 2 below. Note also the ʾ*aleph* at the end of the line in *1QpHab*, col. II, line 5, which probably reflects a misunderstood X sign serving as a line-filler (see section 6 below).

[6] I am aware of only one attempt to classify these signs; see Maurice Baillet, "Index des mots et des signes," in *Qumrân Grotte 4. III (4Q482–*

1. signs pertaining to the division of the text into different paragraphs,

2. marks pertaining to scribal intervention, mainly for the correction of errors,

3. letters in the Cryptic A script denoting matters of special interest,

4. paleo-Hebrew letters designating matters of special interest,

5. marks drawing attention to certain matters in the text,

6. marks written at the ends of lines as line-fillers,

7. separation dots between words,

8. marks numbering content units and sheets.[7]

1. Signs Pertaining to the Division of the Text into Different Paragraphs

In addition to the indication of new sections by systems of spacing at the ends of the lines, in the middle of the line, and between lines as described above, scribes often indicated new sections with an additional type of paragraph marking. Thus the small document *4QTest* consistently indicates each paragraph with a paragraph marker. Also in *1QS* the division between paragraphs is rather consistently indicated, referring not only to "open" sections, but also to some "closed" sections (V, 13, 25; VI, 8; VIII, 5; X, 5).[8] However, in the majority of the texts in which one or more of these paragraph markers appear, the marks were inserted sporadically and very inconsistently, as far as we can judge, unless the very use of the marking has a spe-

---

4Q520), DJD, vol. 7 (Oxford: Clarendon, 1982), 339: (1) signes de division, (2) séparation des mots, (3) signes de correction, (4) autres signes.

[7] Numbers used in the documents themselves are excluded from this list.

[8] In three cases the paragraph marker occurs in *1QS* neither in conjunction with a spacing system nor with an apparent break in the context (III, 18–19; IX, 5–6, 19–20; XI, 15 [used in conjunction with two dots placed as a colon in the line itself—see fig. 17 and the analysis in section 1h below]).

cial meaning that escapes us. For example, since the paragraph markers usually appear together with one of the spacing systems, the very use of a paragraph marker in conjunction with a spacing device could indicate a greater content break than mere spacing. In *1QIsa^a* one often has the impression that the paragraph markers are arranged in pairs setting apart the section between two paragraphs (see, e.g., columns VIII, XXIII, XXIV, XXXIV, XL, XLI, XLVIII). This practice could point to the insertion of the paragraph signs by readers.

The paragraph markers, although occurring between two lines, usually mark the end of the preceding section, and not the beginning of the next one (for exceptions see further discussion in this section). These marks therefore occur sometimes at the ends of sections before blank lines (e.g., *1QS* IX, 11) and even at the end of compositions (see below).

The following markings appear in the Qumran scrolls, almost exclusively between the lines or protruding into the margin, in a few cases under the last text unit (see below), or in two instances (*4QpapPrQuot [4Q503]; 4QDecrees of Sect [4Q477]*) in the middle of the text on the line itself:

a. A horizontal line (*paragraphos*), often shaped with a downstroke to the left (fig. 1.1) or to the right (fig. 1.2) slightly curved like a fishhook, or with a more developed downstroke in a 45-degree angle, often gently rounded and with a small stroke on top of it (figs. 1.3, 1.4), is used in two biblical (*1QIsa^a* and *4QPs^h*) and many nonbiblical texts from Qumran. The straight line (occurring already in the Aramaic scribal tradition of the fifth century B.C.E.) occurs in *1QIsa^a*, *1QpHab*, *4Qpap apocrJer B?* (*4Q384*), and *4QSap Work A^d* (*4Q415*), in the latter case almost completely in the margin itself. A sign similar to fig. 1.2 is used in some manuscripts of the Samaritan Pentateuch in the middle of empty lines between sections.

The *paragraphos* usually occurs in conjunction with a system of notation of open or closed sections, almost exclusively in manuscripts displaying the Qumran orthography and morphology. The various forms of this *paragraphos* sign occur in the following nonbiblical texts: *1QH^a, 1QpHab, 1QS, 1QSa, 4QpIsa^c, 4QTest, 4Qpap apocrJer B? (4Q384), 4QBaptismal Liturgy (4Q414), 4QSap Work A^d (4Q415), 4QDecrees of Sect (4Q477), 4QHod^b, 4QM^a (4Q491), 4QpapM^f (4Q496), 4QpapRitMar (4Q502), 4QpapPrQuot (4Q503), 4QDibHam^a (4Q504), 4QPrFêtes^c (4Q509), 4QpapRitPur (4Q512),* and *4QOrd^b (4Q513).* All these texts are sectarian (with the exception of *4Qpap apocrJer B? [4Q384]*) and are written according to the Qumran scribal practice. The paragraph sign in *1QSb* col. V noted in the Burrows edition is not visible on the plate. The following biblical texts written in the Qumran scribal practice display a paragraph sign: *1QIsa^a* and *4QPs^h*. Paragraph signs also occur in the following texts not written according to the Qumran scribal practice: *4QNoncanonical Psalms A (4Q380), 4QTLevi^a ar* and beyond Qumran also in *MasSir*. The paragraph sign is also found once in a slightly different form (fig. 1.4) in *4QNoncanonical Psalms A (4Q380,* 1, 7), not displaying that scribal tradition (see below).

This *paragraphos* sign—the most frequent of all signs in the Qumran texts—is usually drawn at the right side of the column between the lines of the text, with the greater part of the sign protruding into the right margin, referring to a content division indicated by spacing either in the line above or in the line below. In *1QpHab, 1QIsa^a, 4Qpap apocrJer B? (4Q384),* and *4QBaptismal Liturgy (4Q414)* the *paragraphos* sign is written completely or almost completely in the margin itself. The different shapes of the *paragraphos* show that scribes developed their own forms, slightly differing one from another. Because it cannot usually be determined whether these *paragraphos* signs were written by the original scribes, later scribes, or readers of the text, one should not draw any conclusions on the basis of the shapes or use of this or any other sign.

Not only do the shapes of the *paragraphos* signs differ, but their usages also differ slightly in the various texts. For example, in *1QIsa^a* the *paragraphos* is written under the line in which an open or closed section occurs (e.g., col. V, 21 [Isaiah 6:1];

VIII, 9 [Isaiah 8:16]), and, in the case of an indentation, above the indented space (e.g., col. VII, 10 [Isaiah 7:21]). Likewise, most of the signs in *1QS* are written above the indented space and in a few cases under lines in which a closed section occurs (e.g., *1QS* V, 13, 25; VI, 8), but also above such lines (VIII, 5). Since the shapes of the signs differ in the two parts of *1QIsaᵃ*, it is not impossible that the scribes inserted these signs themselves. Thus in the section written by scribe A, there appear two forms of the *paragraphos*—the straight line and, more frequently, the line with a curve to the left (fig. 1.1)—without distinguishable difference in meaning between them. However, in the section written by scribe B we find the straight *paragraphos*, the *paragraphos* with a hook to either the left or the right (figs. 1.1, 1.2), and the composite *paragraphos* as described in (b) below (fig. 1.6).

Many texts use a developed *paragraphos* form shaped like a fishhook, often gently rounded, in a 45-degree angle (fig. 1.3): *1QS, 1QSa, 1QHᵃ, 4QTest, 4QBaptismal Liturgy (4Q414), 4QDecrees of Sect (4Q477), (4Q496), 4QpapRitMar (4Q502), 4QpapPrQuot (4Q503), 4QPrFêtesᶜ (4Q509), 4QpapRitPur (4Q512), 4QHodᵇ*, and the *4QTLeviᵃ ar*. The fishhook shape (not the gently rounded form) is rather similar to the διπλῆ, which functions in a similar way in the Greek scribal tradition.[9] Several new sections in *MasSir* are denoted with a marginal sign consisting of two lines in a 90-degree angle (fig. 1.5).

As part of the paragraph system in *1QSa*, the *paragraphos* is written at the very end of the text, under the last line. Likewise, the sign in *4QNoncanonical Psalms A (4Q380), 1*, line 7 (fig. 1.4) marks the end of a poem. Similar markings may have appeared also at the ends of other compositions (e.g., *4QTest*) whose ends have not been preserved. By the same token, the

---

[9]   Cf. Eric G. Turner, *Greek Manuscripts of the Ancient World*, ed. Peter J. Parsons, 2nd ed. (London: Institute of Classical Studies, 1987), 14. Viktor E. Gardthausen, *Griechische Palaeographie*, 2 vols. (Leipzig: Veit, 1911–1913), 2:411–12.

curved line in *4QPs^h* marks the beginning of a new couplet in Psalm 119.

The horizontal as well as the curved paragraph signs are evidenced already in Aramaic secular texts from the fifth century B.C.E. onward,[10] as well as in many Greek documents from Egypt contemporary with the Qumran texts.

b. The slightly curved horizontal line with a semicircle on top (fig. 1.6) is a variation of the aforementioned curved *paragraphos*, evidenced only in the second part of *1QIsa^a* (six times) and in *1QS* col. IX, 3 as part of a composite sign (fig. 11.2; see section 4b below). It is not impossible that this sign denotes a larger content division, as it occurs mostly at places which form beginnings of chapters in the MT (e.g., XXVIII, 29 = Isaiah 36:1; XXXII, 29 = Isaiah 40:1; XXXVIII, 6 = Isaiah 45:1). Like the simple *paragraphos*, it is written between the lines in *1QIsa^a*, after a closed or open section (e.g., col. XXVIII, 29 [Isaiah 36:1]; XXXII, 29 [Isaiah 40:1]), or above an indentation (e.g., XXXV, 23 [Isaiah 42:13]).[11] It is not impossible that the circle on top of the *paragraphos* is the same circular shape recorded below as appearing in *1QIsa^a* XVII, 1 and XXVIII, 18 (fig. 10.4) and explained in section 3 as a letter in the Cryptic A script.

---

[10] See Eduard Sachau, *Aramäische Papyrus und Ostraka aus einer jüdische Militär-Kolonie zu Elephantine* (Leipzig: Hinrichs, 1911). Arthur E. Cowley, ed., *Aramaic Papyri of the Fifth Century B.C.* (Oxford: Clarendon, 1923). Emil G. Kraeling, ed., *The Brooklyn Museum Aramaic Papyri* (New Haven: Yale University Press, 1953). G. R. Driver, *Aramaic Documents of the Fifth Century B.C.* (Oxford: Clarendon, 1954). Jonas C. Greenfield and Bezalel Porten, *The Bisitun Inscription of Darius the Great—Aramaic Version* (London: Corpus Inscriptionum Iranicarum, 1982). Judah B. Segal, *Aramaic Texts from North Saqqâra* (London: Egypt Exploration Society, 1983).

[11] According to Jacob L. Teicher, "Material Evidence of the Christian Origin of the Dead Sea Scrolls," *JJS* 3 (1952): 128–32, this sign indicated messianic passages, and it resembles the "sign of life" in the Egyptian scribal system indicating future eschatological events.

c. A sloping line in the margin (fig. 2.1) to the right of the text in *1QIsa^a* col. III, lines 3, 22 also indicates a new section.

d. A sign resembling a hyphen written to the right of the words in the right margin of *4QM^a (4Q491)* 1–3, lines 1, 4, 6, 14, 16, 18–19 indicates a division of the text into content units.

e. Three signs indicating a minor division of the text—two variations of the apostrophe (fig. 2.2) and a period—listed by Baillet[12] for several texts from Cave 4, possibly indicate a subdivision of some kind: *4QDibHam^a (4Q504), 4QShir^a-b (4Q510, 4Q511),* and *4QOrd^b (4Q513)*. It is therefore relevant to note that in *4QDibHam^a* 1–2, col. vii, line 4, the apostrophe follows a heading. However, for all these instances the evidence is not clear. Nor is the evidence clear for a few additional markings in *4QDibHam^a* for which detailed drawings were presented by Baillet in the text,[13] although these shapes are not visible on the plates themselves, nor on photographs PAM 43.611: 1–2, vi, 2 (on the plate this sign has the appearance of a parenthesis sign), and 1–2, vii, 4 (see fig. 2.2) and 10 (both at the beginning of new sections).

f. In several instances in *4QNum^b* (probably indicating new sections), in *4QD^e* (heading), and in *2QPs*[14] (the first two lines of Psalm 103), new content units are written with red ink. For parallels to this practice, compare the Aramaic inscription from Deir ʿAllah from the eighth century B.C.E.,[15] which uses red ink for denoting the title and new paragraphs,[16] as well as

---

[12] Baillet, "Index des mots et des signes," in *DJD* 7:339.

[13] Baillet, "Paroles des luminaires," in *DJD* 7:138–68.

[14] Maurice Baillet, Jozef T. Milik, and Roland de Vaux, *Les "Petites Grottes" de Qumrân, DJD,* vol. 3 (Oxford: Clarendon, 1962), 70.

[15] For the date, cf. Jacob Hoftijzer and Gerrit van der Kooij, eds., *The Balaam Text from Deir ʾAllah Re-Evaluated: Proceedings of the International Symposium Held at Leiden, 21–24 August 1989* (Leiden: Brill, 1991). On page 237 in that volume, Émile Puech mentions the first part of the eighth century B.C.E., and on page 257 Gerrit van der Kooij speaks about the period between 800 and 720 B.C.E.

[16] Jacob Hoftijzer and Gerrit van der Kooij, *Aramaic Texts from Deir ʾAllah* (Leiden: Brill, 1976), 184.

other sources. For parallels in Egyptian, Greek, and Roman documents, as well as references to usages mentioned in the Talmud, see the discussion of *2QPs* in *DJD* 3[17] and Jastram's work.[18]

g. *Paleo-Hebrew ʾaleph and waw.* Scribal habits documented in texts preceding the period of the Qumran manuscripts provide parallels to two practices.

Paleo-Hebrew ʾaleph. A few Aramaic texts from the fifth century B.C.E.[19] contain a scribal sign in the form of a paleo-Hebrew ʾaleph written in the middle of closed or open sections (fig. 3), indicating a new paragraph or a major subdivision. These signs occur frequently in closed sections in the non-proverbial sections of Ahiqar.[20] The shape of this paleo-Hebrew ʾaleph, especially the one in a major content break in the court record TAD 2, B8.5 from 431 B.C.E., is very similar to the sign written in the right margin of *4QpIsa^c* at the beginning of a new section after a blank line (fig. 4a). The shape and function of the sign in *4QpIsa^c* are thus similar to the scribal tradition in some Aramaic documents. Compare also the paleo-Hebrew ʾaleph in *4QSap. Work A^a* (*4Q418*, PAM 43.480, top row second fragment), without any context, apparently in the margin (fig. 4b). This use of the paleo-Hebrew ʾaleph is paralleled by occurrences of a paleo-Hebrew ʾaleph or *waw* in the margins of manuscripts.

Paleo-Hebrew waw. The use of the paleo-Hebrew *waw* in *11QpaleoLev^a* and *4QpaleoExod^m* is paralleled by some of the Arad ostraca, from the end of the First Temple period.[21] In these

---

[17] Maurice Baillet, "Psautier (Pl. xii)," in *DJD* 3:69–71.

[18] Nathan Jastram, "4QNum^b (Pls. xxxviv–xlix)," in *Qumran Cave 4. VII, Genesis to Numbers, DJD* 12:221–22.

[19] See note 10 above.

[20] Thus Ahiqar (closed sections)—cf. Cowley, *Aramaic Papyri*, 215–19, and Bezalel Porten and Ada Yardeni, ed. and trans., *Textbook of Aramaic Documents from Ancient Egypt* (Winona Lake, Ind.: Eisenbrauns, 1986), 3:25–53, and the court record in 2:B8.5 (a major content break).

[21] See Yohanan Aharoni, *Judean Desert Studies—Arad Inscriptions* (Jerusalem: Bialik Institute and the Israel Exploration Society, 1975). The similarity was first pointed out by Émile Puech, "Notes en marge de

ostraca, in which words were split between two lines when there was no space for the remainder of the word, sometimes a single *waw* was left at the end of the line when there was space for the whole word (ostraca 2, lines 3–4; 3, line 6; 11, line 4).

It is unclear what the relation is between the paleo-Hebrew *ʾaleph* of the Aramaic texts (paragraph indicator) and the paleo-Hebrew *waw* of the Arad inscriptions. The scribal traditions of some of the Qumran texts apparently reflect both traditions. The paleo-Hebrew *waw* written in these texts as part of the running text probably continues the same tradition as in the Arad inscriptions, while its occurrence in the margin reflects a tradition similar to that of the Aramaic documents. The following occurrences of these paleo-Hebrew letters are documented in the Qumran texts.

• *Part of the running text of Qumran scrolls.* The use of the paleo-Hebrew *waw* in the Arad ostraca resembles that of three texts from Qumran. In these biblical texts the *waw* is generally placed in an open section when the first word of the new section would have started with a conversive *waw*, which is now omitted, since the *waw* was written separately in the middle of the space. In *4QpaleoExod^m* this pertains both to the bulk of the scroll and the patch in col. VIII (the shape of the *waw* in the patch [fig. 5.1] and its position are almost identical to the *waw* in *4QPs^b* [fig. 5.2]). This use is paralleled by *11QpaleoLev^a* (fig. 5.3) in which the *waw* occurs only in some open sections, possibly indicating a major subdivision,[22] while the practice of

---

11QpaléoLévitique—Le fragment L, des fragments inédits et une jarre de la grotte 11," *RB* 96 (1989): 161–83, esp. 165.

[22] Thus D. N. Freedman and K. A. Mathews, *The Paleo-Hebrew Leviticus Scroll (11QpaleoLev)* (Winona Lake, Ind.: Eisenbrauns, 1985), 11. That is, in this scroll some sections merely indicate the new paragraph with an open space (frg. I,7 = Leviticus 19:1; col. 2,6 = Leviticus 23:26; frg. K,6 = Leviticus 21:10), while other ones have both an open space and a *waw* in the middle of that space (frg. J,1 = Leviticus 20:1; col. 2,2 = Leviticus 23:23; col. 3,3;8 = Leviticus 24:10, 13). It seems to us, however, that there is not enough evidence for supporting the assumption that the use of a *waw* denotes a major subdivision.

4QpaleoExod^m cannot be analyzed well since the ends of most lines are missing. Likewise, a single *waw* is written in the square script in the space between two sections in *4QNum^b* col. XXI, 28 in Numbers 27:22.

•   *In the margin of Qumran scrolls.* Variations of these paleo-Hebrew *waw*s are found in the margins of a few texts written in the square script: *4QPs^b* (fig. 5.2), *1QIsa^a* (col. VI, 22; fig. 5.4), and in *1QS* col. V, 1 (fig. 5.5). Cf. also the truncated *waw* in the paleo-Hebrew script in the bottom margin of *5QLam^a* col. II (fig. 11.3). In *1QIsa^a*, *4QpIsa^c*, and in *1QS* the sign is written in the margin between the columns, indicating the beginning of a new paragraph, while in *4QPs^b* and *5QLam^a* it was written in the bottom margin, without any context. All these letters probably reflect the paleo-Hebrew *waw*, although the shape of some of them reminds us more of an *ʾaleph* than a *waw*. The shape of this paleo-Hebrew *waw* obviously differs from the paleo-Hebrew *ʾaleph*; the former has a straight line as well as an angular line facing to the right, while in the *waw* these lines are facing to the left. However, rotations of this type are well known in the development of scripts. In any event, the function of these letters is probably close to that of the paleo-Hebrew *ʾaleph* in the fifth-century Aramaic texts.

h.   *4QtgLev* consistently uses a colon (:) as a division mark between verses. This type of marking constitutes the best evidence for a division into verses of any of the Qumran texts in Hebrew, Aramaic, or Greek. Likewise, in *1QS* XI, 15 a single colonlike indication is found written in the space between the words above and below the writing surface (fig. 17). No space was left by the scribe before the beginning of the benediction starting with ברוך אתה אלי, and this was corrected by both the paragraph sign in the margin and by the colon in the text itself. A similar use of the colon is found in the medieval manuscripts of the MT and the Samaritan Pentateuch (*qiṣṣah*) at the ends of verses.

i. *4QMess. Apoc.* 2, ii, line 4 contains a sign in the margin adjacent to a new paragraph (fig. 5.6); its shape and meaning are not clear.[23]

Several additional signs (see sections 3–4 below) occur at the beginning of new paragraphs as well; however, they probably do not indicate the beginning of a new paragraph, but rather draw attention to a feature connected with the content of that paragraph.

2. Marks Pertaining to Scribal Intervention, Mainly for the Correction of Errors

When a scribe wanted to correct or change the original text, various systems of notation were used in the text itself, in the margin, or between the lines. Of the systems listed below, practices a and c may have been carried over from Alexandrian scribal practices.[24]

a. *Cancellation dots* placed above (fig. 6.1), below (fig. 6.2), or both above and below the letters (fig. 6.3), or (in the case of added words) on both sides of the added word (fig. 6.4), were used to omit letters or words already written.

This application is evidenced in the following texts written in the Qumran practice: *1QIsa^a*, *1QH^a*, *1QS*, *1QM*, *1QpHab*, *4QSam^c*, *4QD^a*, *4QTanh (4Q176)*, *4QCatena^a (4Q177)*, *4QpsJub^{a,g}*, *4QpGen^b (4Q253)*, *4QToh A (4Q274)*, *4QRP^{b,c} (4Q364, 365)*, *4QT^a? (4Q365a)*, *4QH^a (4Q417)*, *4QOrd^{b,c} (4Q513, 4Q514)*, *4QShirShabb^f*, *11QPs^a*, and *11QT^a*. The same system is evidenced in the following texts not written in

---

[23]   For some speculations on the meaning of the sign, see Émile Puech, "Une apocalypse messianique *(4Q521)*," *RQ* 15 (1992): 482.

[24]   Cf. Turner, *Greek Manuscripts*, 16. Saul Lieberman, *Hellenism in Jewish Palestine*, 2nd ed. (New York: Jewish Theological Seminary of America, 1962), 38–43.

the Qumran practice: *4QIsa^d*, *4QJer^a*, and *4QApocrLam A (4Q179).*^25

Two little strokes written in *1QpHab* VIII, 14, above and below the *waw*, perform the same function. These dots written on a few letters have been transmitted as such (named *puncta extraordinaria*) in the Masoretic Text of the Hebrew Bible, losing their original meaning in transmission.^26

b. *Crossing out a word with a horizontal line,* sometimes combined with the addition of the corrected text above the line (for an example, see fig. 7). This practice is evidenced in the following texts written in the Qumran practice: *1QIsa^a*, *1QS*, *1QSb*, *4QDan^a*, *4QD^a (olim: 4QD^b)* frg. 5 ii, *4QRP^c (4Q365)*, *4QShirShabb^f*, *4QNarrative C (4Q462)*, *4QM^a (4Q491)*, *4QApocrLam B (4Q501)*, *4QpapPrQuot (4Q503)*, and *4QPrFêtes^c (4Q509)*. The same system is evidenced in the following texts not written in the Qumran practice: *4QCant^b* and *4QApocrLam A (4Q179)*.

c. *Parentheses.* These signs denote an omission or addition of words by enclosing the elements to be omitted or, in rare cases, to be added within two scribal signs, known from the Greek scribal tradition as *sigma* and *antisigma* (cf. figs. 8.1–3).

For indicating omissions this practice is evidenced in the following texts written in the Qumran practice: *1QM*, col. III, line 1 (fig. 8.1); *1QS*, col. VII, line 8. The same system is used in the following texts not written in accordance with the Qumran practice: *11QpaleoLev^a*, *4QJer^a*, *4QCant^b*, frg. 2 col. ii, line 12. In *11QpaleoLev^a* the notation of a *sigma* and *antisigma* written

---

25   See Eduard Y. Kutscher, *The Language and Linguistic Background of the Isaiah Scroll (1QIsa^a)* (Leiden: Brill, 1974), 531–36.

26   Tov, *Textual Criticism*, 55–57. Shemaryahu Talmon, prolegomenon to Romain Butin, *The Ten Nequdoth of the Torah, or The Meaning and Purpose of the Extraordinary Points of the Pentateuch (Massoretic Text)*, ed. Harry M. Orlinsky (New York: Ktav, 1969). Avigdor Shinan, "The Midrashic Interpretation of the Ten Dotted Passages of the Pentateuch," in *The Bible in the Light of Its Interpreters: Sarah Kamin Memorial Volume* (in Hebrew), ed. Sara Japhet (Jerusalem: Magnes, 1994), 198–214.

in the middle of Leviticus 18:27 indicates verses inserted in the wrong place (Leviticus 20:23–24). Parentheses possibly also occur in *4Q504* 1–2, col. vi, line 2.

For indicating additions note the following example: Three words added in the top margin above *4QQoh^a* II, line 1 in Qohelet 6:4, omitted by way of homoioteleuton, are enclosed between parentheses (fig. 8.2). The omission of the words was probably indicated by a mark in the text (now in the lacuna). See photographs PAM 43.092 and 40.967.[27]

In the Masoretic tradition of the Bible these signs were misunderstood and reinterpreted as inverted *nunim*.

d. *Addition sign denoting supralinearly added elements to be added in the running text.* A long vertical line with a short horizontal line at the bottom turning to the right in a 90-degree angle written in the space between words on the line (fig. 9) indicated an addition above the line in *4QpapTob^a ar* 3:13.[28]

Note also the following correction systems that do not employ any signs:

e. *Erasing*—the technique of erasing words with a sharp instrument (named גרר or גרד in rabbinic literature) is known from various texts—see for example, *1QS* cols. VII and VIII and *11QpaleoLev^a*, E 3, and col. 4, 6. The erased area was sometimes left blank and at other times letters or a word were written in or above the erased area. In other cases words were erased after they had first been denoted with cancellation dots (e.g., *1QS* VII, 20).

---

[27] For a different presentation of the evidence, see Eugene Ulrich, "Ezra and Qoheleth Manuscripts from Qumran (4QEzra, 4QQoh^a,b)," in *Priests, Prophets, and Scribes: Essays on the Formation and Heritage of Second Temple Judaism in Honour of Joseph Blenkinsopp*, ed. Eugene Ulrich et al. (Sheffield: JSOT, 1992), 139–57. According to Jozef T. Milik, *The Books of Enoch: Aramaic Fragments of Qumran Cave 4* (Oxford: Clarendon, 1976), 150, a square bracket, used in conjunction with a single round parenthesis sign in *4QEn^a* II, line 1 (PAM 41.360; see fig. 8.3) indicates either an omission or an insertion.

[28] Joseph Fitzmyer, "4QpapTobit^a ar," in *Qumran Cave 4. XIV, Parabiblical Texts, Part 2, DJD* 19:13 (frg. 6, line 8).

f. *The supralinear addition of a single letter or letters*, a word or words above an element in the text as a correcting addition—this method, accepted by *y. Meg.* 1.71c, is used frequently in *1QIsaᵃ* and in many other texts. Supralinear additions occasionally continue horizontally into the margins, but also vertically, alongside the text in *1QIsaᵃ* cols. XXX, XXXII, XXXIII, and even below the text, in reverse writing in *4QJerᵃ* col. III.

g. *Reshaping letters*—in attempting to correct a letter or letters, a scribe would sometimes reshape the form of a letter into another one; for example, in *1QIsaᵃ* VI, 25 (= Isaiah 7:11) שאל (original *ʾaleph* of אאל changed to שאל = שׁ); מעם (= שׁ) probably changed from מאל.

h. *Expunging letters or words with liquids.*

3. Letters in the Cryptic A Script Denoting Matters of Special Interest[29]

It is suggested here that individual letters in the Cryptic A script (see this section) as well as paleo-Hebrew letters (section 4) were used as scribal marks in several Qumran scrolls. The markings in Cryptic A script have not been recognized in the past, but some instances of the paleo-Hebrew letters have been noted. For both groups the known samples are listed below. It seems that both groups of scribal markings point to a sectarian background of either the writing of these texts or of the use of the manuscripts in the Qumran community.

A category of scribal markings that has not been recognized previously pertains to single letters that can now be safely identified as belonging to the Cryptic A script, represented by *4QHoroscope (4Q186)*, *4QpapCryptA Midrash Sepher Moshe (4Q249)*, *4QCryptA Words of Sage to Sons of Dawn (4Q298)*, and *4QCryptA Phases of the Moon (4Q317)*, as well as by a

---

[29]   This section is also published separately in Emanuel Tov, "Letters of the Cryptic A Script and Paleo-Hebrew Letters Used as Scribal Marks in Some Qumran Scrolls," *DSD* 2/3 (1995): 330–39.

few fragmentary texts: *4Q250, 4QCal. Document C^f (4Q324c),*
and *4Q313* (unclassified frgs.). This script is described by
Pfann as a development from the late Phoenician scripts,[30] and it
is used for a few texts of a Qumran sectarian nature written in
this script. In these texts a few individual letters of the Cryptic A
script are written between the lines and, more frequently, in the
margins of other Qumran texts. They may well refer to a sectarian code message of some kind. Although the meaning of these
notes is not known to us, it is clear that they occur irregularly,
as is evident from *4QpIsa^c*, in which only one column is copi-
ously annotated in the margin (frgs. 4–7, col. ii). The scribal
markings in this script—consisting of one, two, or three letters—are listed in this section and in fig. 10, together with their
parallels in the Cryptic A script, especially in *4Q298*, but also in
4Q317 and *4Q186*. In *1QIsa^a* these signs may refer to the sectarian reading of certain passages[31] or to matters of sectarian
interest. At the same time, one of the signs (fig. 10.4) possibly
draws attention to elements lacking in the text in comparison
with the MT.[32] In any event, since the identification of the
Cryptic A script for texts using sectarian terminology is solid,[33]
the new evidence clearly shows that at least some of the biblical Qumran texts were used by the Qumran community
or copied by the sectarian scribes. The evidence pertains to
the following sectarian writings: *4QSap Work A^c (4Q417),
4QDibHam^a (4Q504), 4QShir^b,* and *4QMyst^c,* and possibly also
to *4QpIsa^c* (see section 4d below). In *4QMyst^c* the existence of
an encoded sectarian message is not surprising (see below).

---

[30]   Stephen J. Pfann, "4Q298: The Maskil's Address to All Sons of
Dawn," *Jewish Quarterly Review* 85 (1994): 203–35. The addendum to that
article (233–35) was not available when this article was written.
[31]   A phenomenon noted by John C. Trever, "The Isaiah Scroll," in
The Dead Sea Scrolls of St. Mark's Monastery, ed. Millar Burrows (New
Haven: American Schools of Oriental Research, 1950), xvi, and Martin,
Scribal Character, 1:186–87, although neither recognized the cryptic letters.
[32]   This is an unlikely assumption since there is no real evidence for
the collation of any of the Qumran scrolls with the MT.
[33]   See Pfann, "4Q298."

This type of message also pertains to the biblical texts *1QIsaᵃ*, written according to the Qumran scribal practice, and possibly also *4QExodᵏ* and *4QCantᵇ*. The use of letters in Cryptic A should be discussed in conjunction with that of individual letters of the paleo-Hebrew script, which probably served a similar purpose in *1QIsaᵃ*, *1QS*, and *5QLamᵃ* (see section 4). The appearance of letters in the Cryptic A script obviously has important implications for our understanding of the literature of the Qumran community, in particular of the biblical texts *1QIsaᵃ*, *5QLamᵃ*, *4QCantᵇ*, and of works whose sectarian nature is not immediately obvious: *4QSap. Work Aᶜ (4Q417)*, *4QDibHamᵃ (4Q504)*, *4QShirᵇ*, and *4QMystᶜ*. All these compositions were annotated, although very rarely, with paleo-Hebrew letters and letters of the Cryptic A script. These letters were written by either the original scribes, later scribes, or readers.

A relatively large number of *zayin*s are recognizable (figs. 10.6, 10.7 [2x], 10.12, 11, 11.1, 11.2, and 12.1). It is suggested here that individual letters in the Cryptic A script and paleo-Hebrew letters were used as scribal marks in several Qumran scrolls. The former type of note has not been recognized in the past, while some of the latter have been listed. For both groups the known samples are listed below. It seems that both groups of scribal markings point to a sectarian background of either the writing of these texts or of the use of the manuscripts in the Qumran community.

Several signs occur at the beginning of new sections to which they refer as a whole: figs. 5.5, 10.2, 10.3, 10.5, 10.9, 10.10, 11.1, and 11.2. Other signs are written above single words: figs. 10.4, 10.6 (2x), 10.7 (2x).[34]

a.   Several signs occur in the margin of *1QIsaᵃ* (or rarely in the text itself as noted below) without any recognizable pattern[35]

---

[34]   On the difficulty concerning the distinction between the Cryptic script and paleo-Hebrew letters, see section 4 below.

[35]   It is difficult to know whether the paragraphs indicated by the signs are of any specific sectarian importance. Martin, *Scribal Character,* 1:184, notes that fig. 10.1, referring to Isaiah 7:20, pertains to Babylon and Egypt,

and, with one exception, not more than once. These signs are listed below. That the signs are not related to a system of paragraphing is shown by fig. 10.2, which occurs in conjunction with a *paragraphos* sign.

• *1QIsaᵃ* col. VII, between lines 7 and 8 (Isaiah 7:20).[36] This sign (fig. 10.1) represents a lengthened form of the *resh* in the Cryptic A script. This sign appears at the beginning of a paragraph.

• *1QIsaᵃ* col. VIII, 9 (Isaiah 8:16).[37] This sign (fig. 10.2) is identical to the *heth* in the Cryptic A script.

• *1QIsaᵃ* col. XI, 4 (Isaiah 11:15).[38] This sign (fig. 10.3) probably reflects the *qoph* in the Cryptic A script of *4Q298* or a *bet* = *beta* in the script of *4Q186*. This sign appears at the beginning of a paragraph in *1QIsaᵃ*.

• *1QIsaᵃ* col. XVII, 1 (Isaiah 21:16) and between cols. XXVIII, 18 and XXIX, 18.[39] This circular sign (fig. 10.4) above שלוש, possibly indicating the lack of that word in the MT, may represent a *kaph* in the Cryptic A script or an *ᶜayin* in the paleo-Hebrew script. It also occurs in XXVIII, 18, in which it probably indicates the lack of a long stretch of text in the original text of the scroll, which was subsequently added by a later hand. It occurs also (with a different function?) in the margin to the right of the text in *4QSap. Work Aᶜ (4Q417),* frg. 1, col. ii, line 23 (fig. 10.8; cf. also *4QSap. Work Aᶜ* 2, i, 11) and in *4QCantᵇ* col. I, line 7 (as a line-filler?; see fig. 12.2). The same

---

often mentioned in the Qumran writings, e.g., in *1QM*. Probably an explanation of this kind is behind some of these signs in *1QIsaᵃ*, but it is hard to press this point, as the passages that are most central for the Qumran community are not indicated in this way. Another thought that comes to mind is that some of the signs could be cross-references to the *pesharim* of Isaiah, but this assumption cannot be examined as the relevant sections of the *pesharim* have not been preserved.

[36] Trever, "The Isaiah Scroll," fig. 2.
[37] Ibid., fig. 3.
[38] Ibid., fig. 4.
[39] Ibid., fig. 5.

circular form appears in conjunction with a paragraph sign in
1QIsaᵃ (see fig. 1.6).

•   *1QIsaᵃ* col. XXI, 23 (Isaiah 27:13).[40] This sign (fig.
10.5) represents the *tsade* in the Cryptic A script. This sign
appears at the beginning of a paragraph.

•   *1QIsaᵃ* col. XXVII, 21 (Isaiah 33:19)[41] contains a *zayin*
(fig. 10.6). This sign, written above תראו, and differing from
MT תראה, may reflect the notation of a variant reading. This letter represents either a *zayin* in the Cryptic A script or a paleo-
Hebrew *zayin*.

•   *1QIsaᵃ* col. XXXIII, 1 (Isaiah 40:2),[42] occurring above
כפלים in the text. This sign (fig. 10.7) represents either the *zayin*
in the Cryptic A script or a paleo-Hebrew *zayin*. A similar sign
in col. XL, 19 (Isaiah 48:14), occurs above בבבל in the text.
Note also the similar *zayin* in the margin of *4QShirᵇ* 18, iii, 8
(fig. 10.12; see further section 4 on this scroll).

b.   In *4QSap. Work Aᶜ* *(4Q417;* PAM 42.578) the circle in
the margin before the text of frg. 1, col. ii, line 23 (fig. 10.8)
probably reflects the Cryptic A letter *kaph*. The context does not
help us understand the sign, which also occurs in *4QCantᵇ* col.
1, line 7 (as a line-filler?; see fig. 12.2).

c.   In *4QDibHamᵃ (4Q504)* 1–2, col. v, line 3[43] in the margin to the right of the text, the sign (fig. 10.9) reflects a *mem* in
the Cryptic A script, at the beginning of what is probably a new
section.

d.   The three signs in *4QMystᶜ*, frg. 3, lines 2–4, written
one above the other (fig. 10.10), are probably letters in the
Cryptic A script. The top letter is a *samekh*, followed by an
ᶜ*ayin*, while the third letter could be a *shin/sin*. The context does
not help us understand the mystery of these signs, but the exis-

---

[40]   Ibid., fig. 6.

[41]   Ibid., fig. 8.

[42]   Ibid. Trever incorrectly combines his transcription of three similar
shapes into one sign.

[43]   Not iv, 3, as recorded by Baillet, "Paroles des luminaires," in *DJD*
7:147–48.

tence of a sectarian cryptic message in this text is not surprising. *4QMyst^c* frg. 3 resembles *4QHoroscope (4Q186),* since both compositions are of a physiognomical nature and both contain encoded messages written in the Cryptic A alphabet. If our explanation is correct,[44] the three letters are not scribal signs, but are part of the composition, as in *4QHoroscope.*

e. *4QExod^k*, of which merely one fragment has been preserved, has a sign (fig. 10.11) in the upper right corner, above the center of the first word, that is very similar to the *lamed* in the Cryptic A script of *4Q317.* The place of the sign could reflect a numbering system (see section 8).

f. The function of the *zayin* in the margin of *4QShir^b* 18, iii, 8 (fig. 10.12) cannot be determined because of the fragmentary context.

g. Frg. 5 of *4QpPs^b* contains the word לאל written in unusual letters. Allegro named them "some cryptic form,"[45] while Skehan speaks of "distorted, unnatural paleohebrew lettering."[46] The letters look like Greek and Latin letters in mirror writing with Hebrew values (α = א and L = ל), and therefore resemble the Cryptic A script of *4QHoroscope*, which includes a few Greek letters.

---

[44] The text to the left of the letters has not been preserved. It is more likely that the three letters constituted the beginning of a three-line heading or note written in the middle of the text, than that they constituted a three-letter note written one above the other. The three signs are preceded by blank spaces, the spaces being preceded by the remnants of two letters written in the square script, like the remainder of the document. If our explanation is correct, the word סעש does not need to be explained; rather, the three letters form the beginnings of three words starting three lines—the first one started with a *samekh* (ס פר ?).

[45] John M. Allegro, "173. Commentary on Psalms (B)," in *Qumran Cave 4 (4Q158–4Q186), DJD* 5:53.

[46] Patrick W. Skehan, "The Divine Name at Qumran, in the Masada Scroll, and in the Septuagint," *Bulletin of the International Organization for Septuagint and Cognate Studies* 13 (1980): 27.

4. Paleo-Hebrew Letters Designating Matters of Special Interest

Several individual letters in the paleo-Hebrew script written in the margins of some compositions (*1QIsaᵃ*, *1QS*, *4QpIsaᶜ*, and *5QLamᵃ*) and at the ends of lines in *4QCantᵇ* (see below section 6, and figs. 12.1, 12.2, 12.4, and 12.5) probably draw attention to certain matters or passages of special interest. These symbols, like all other symbols in the Qumran manuscripts, were probably inserted in the text after the writing was completed.

The decision whether a certain letter belongs to either the Cryptic A script (as reflected by *4Q186, 4Q249, 4Q298,* and *4Q317*) or the paleo-Hebrew script is sometimes difficult, in particular since some of the letters are ornamented or stylized. Nevertheless, for the sake of the description, a distinction between these two scripts is made here, although letters of both types were used together in the text of *4QHoroscope (4Q186)* and in the margin of *1QIsaᵃ*. The use of the paleo-Hebrew letters, with the exception of the use of the paleo-Hebrew *waw* as a paragraph sign, probably reflects the same background as the use of letters of the Cryptic A script.

Although the existence of scribal marks in the margins of some manuscripts has been known for some time, no satisfactory solution for their occurrence has been suggested, and today some of them remain enigmatic. These signs probably direct attention to certain details in the text or to certain pericopes, but they may also refer to the reading by the Qumran covenanters of certain passages. The letters in *4QCantᵇ* are probably a special type of line-filler.

a.   Several paleo-Hebrew letters are recognized in the margin of *1QIsaᵃ*, occurring in that scroll without any recognizable pattern, and not more than once.

The sign in *1QIsaᵃ* in the margin to the right of col. VI, 22 (fig. 5.4) referring to Isaiah 7:8[47] represents a *waw* in the paleo-

---

[47]   Trever, "The Isaiah Scroll," fig. 1.

Hebrew script (cf. especially the shape of the *waw* in the patch in *4QpaleoExod^m*, col. VIII; fig. 5.1). This sign should be compared with the similar use of the paleo-Hebrew *waw* in the margin of *1QS* (see fig. 5.5), and in a different way in the margin of *4QPs^b* (fig. 5.2), as well as in the texts of *4QpaleoExod^m* and *11QpaleoLev^a* (figs. 5.1 and 5.3). This paleo-Hebrew *waw*, like other ones (see section 1g), could indicate a new paragraph, but there is no indication in the spacing or context that this is the case.

1QIsa^a col. XXII, 10 (Isaiah 28:9).[48] This sign (fig. 11.1) is an embellished representation of the *zayin* in the paleo-Hebrew script (like fig. 11 referring to *1QS* VII) with an ornamented vertical line on top. This sign appears at the beginning of a paragraph.

b. The two signs in *1QS* in col. VII and col. IX, 3 (figs. 11 and 11.2) possibly seal off a content unit. Both are composite signs, and they resemble in character, though not in shape, the *koronis* used in the Greek scribal tradition. The *koronis*, written at the end of literary units, was likewise shaped as a Greek paragraph sign with ornaments above and below it.[49] The character of the Greek sign thus resembles that of *1QS* IX, 3 (fig. 11.2), of which the top element is likewise a paragraph sign.

The sign occurring at the bottom margin of *1QS* VII (fig. 11) is composed of a paleo-Hebrew *zayin* with an ornamental line on top (similar to *1QIsa^a* XXII, 10 [fig. 11.1]) and a triangular form below.[50] It could indicate the end of a content unit, since a new unit starts at the beginning of the next column. On the other hand, the sign could also be taken to denote a numbering system (see section 8).

The composite sign in *1QS* col. IX, 3 (fig. 11.2) (with elements in common with the sign in *1QIsa^a* XXII, 10; see fig.

---

[48] Ibid., fig. 7.

[49] Cf. Turner, *Greek Manuscripts,* 12, 12 n. 59.

[50] Puech, "Une Apocalypse," 482, explains the triangular form as an ʿayin and the two signs together as (עור)(ה)ז.

1.7)[51] is composed of the paragraph sign above a paleo-Hebrew *zayin* and a *samekh*[52] similar to the one found in the Cryptic A letters in *4QHoroscope (4Q186)*. The paragraph sign indicates a new section, while the letter combination may convey a sectarian message.

The paleo-Hebrew *waw* in *1QS* V, 1 (fig. 5.5) appears at the beginning of a major content division. It probably indicates this major division, since almost all other paragraphs in this scroll are indicated with a regular paragraph sign. See the discussion of fig. 5.4 (*1QIsaᵃ* VI, 22) above.

c. The sign in the bottom margin of *5QLam*ᵃ col. II (fig. 11.3) resembles a truncated *waw* in the paleo-Hebrew script or a *waw* in the Aramaic script of the sixth century B.C.E.[53] For the writing of this letter in the margin, compare *4QPsᵇ* (fig. 5.2).

d. Several signs in the margin of *4QpIsa*ᶜ frgs. 4–7, col. ii resemble either paleo-Hebrew letters or letters in the Cryptic A script. Fig. 4a probably is a paleo-Hebrew *waw*. It is written in the margin, after a blank line, at the beginning of a new paragraph, just like the position of the sign in *1QIsa*ᵃ VI, 22 (fig. 5.4) and in *1QS* V, 1 (fig. 5.5; see section 4b above). Fig. 11.4 probably represents a stylized paleo-Hebrew *sin/shin*, almost of the Samaritan type, introducing a scriptural quotation in the *pesher*.

e. The sign in the margin of *4Q398*, 14–17, i, 4 is explained by the editors as a single cursive *ʾaleph* (fig. 11.5). It is not impossible that this is a reference to the books of scripture mentioned in the text.

---

[51]   Trever, "The Isaiah Scroll," fig. 7.

[52]   John M. Allegro, "An Astrological Cryptic Document from Qumran," *JSS* 9 (1964): 291–94, reads the letter as a *waw*, but it is identified as a *samekh* by Jean Carmignac, "Les horoscopes de Qumrân," *RQ* 5 (1965): 199–206, and John Strugnell, "Notes en marge du volume V des 'Discoveries in the Judaean Desert of Jordan,' " *RQ* 7 (1970): 163–276, esp. 274.

[53]   Suggested orally by Émile Puech.

f. The paleo-Hebrew letters at the ends of lines in *4QCantᵇ* (figs. 12.1, 12.2, 12.4, 12.5, and 12.6), described in sections 3a and 4 above as possible line-fillers, could also denote matters of special (sectarian) interest since their use as line-fillers is not consistent.

5. Marks Drawing Attention to Certain Matters in the Text

Some signs, probably written by readers, were meant to draw attention to certain issues or passages, possibly passages of sectarian interest. Of these, the function of the X sign is the most easily understandable.[54]

While the X sign is probably used in *1QpHab* as a line-filler (see section 6 below), referring to the text to the right of the sign, in *4QCatenaᵃ (4Q177), 1QS* IV, 15, and *1QIsaᵃ* it is used differently, drawing attention to certain lines, sections, or issues. In *4QCatenaᵃ* the use of the X cannot be judged in two passages because of their fragmentary context,[55] but in one case[56] it coincides with the beginning of the *pesher*. In *1QIsaᵃ*, the sign is written eleven times between the columns, referring to the text to the left, although occasionally it seems to refer to the text to the right (col. XLVI, 23). In that scroll the X sign

---

[54] No connection was found between the signs found in the texts from the Judean Desert and the ones mentioned by Epiphanius in his *Treatise on Weights and Measures*, although some signs have a similar shape. Note the X sign, which according to Epiphanius denotes the Messiah, another sign marking obscure passages in the scriptures, and a third sign (fig. 14) denoting the "promises to the ancient people"; cf. James E. Dean, ed., *Epiphanius' Treatise on Weights and Measures: The Syriac Version* (Chicago: University of Chicago Press, 1935), 15. The latter sign (cf. fig. 11.1) is mentioned here since it comes closest to the signs and letters under discussion.

[55] *4QCatena* 12–13, II, line 9, and 29, line 2, in both cases in an indented space.

[56] *4QCatena* 12–13, I, 8, in the text itself above the line between words.

usually occurs at the beginning of a new section after the previous one ended with an open section (e.g., col. XLI, 5 [Isaiah 39:4]; XLVI, 10 [Isaiah 56:1]; XLVI, 13 [Isaiah 56:3]), probably drawing attention to the section as a whole. That this sign does not indicate the division into content units is clear from col. XXXVIII, 6, in which it occurs in conjunction with a complex *paragraphos* sign, so that the X sign, probably added secondarily, must have had a different meaning. A similar use of X indicating noteworthy passages is evidenced in the Greek scribal tradition, both as the single Greek letter χ and in the combination of two letters—ρ above a χ (both denoting χρηστόν)—in Greek papyri,[57] from which this custom may have been transferred to Semitic sources.[58]

6. Marks Written at the Ends of Lines as Line-fillers

The notion that some of the signs in the Qumran manuscripts served as line-fillers reflects a sound assumption, since such a practice can be well demonstrated from pap *5/6Ḥev44*.[59] In this text the X sign is written at the ends of lines 2 and 5, which are somewhat shorter than the remainder. In line 5 it occurs after בעין, while the next line starts with גדי, so that the function of the X can only be that of a line-filler. Line-fillers are also known

---

[57] Cf. Turner, *Greek Manuscripts*, 15.

[58] Teicher linked the X sign, which according to him was used especially with reference to passages of messianic content in the Isaiah scroll, with the Christian abbreviation Χ of Χριστός. See Jacob L. Teicher, "The Christian Interpretation of the Sign X in the Isaiah Scroll," *Vetus Testamentum* 5 (1955): 189–98. However, many passages in the Isaiah scroll and elsewhere do not allow for such an interpretation, and besides, most scrolls were written before the beginning of Christianity. Against Teicher, see Isaiah Sonne, "The X-Sign in the Isaiah Scroll," *Vetus Testamentum* 4 (1954): 90–94.

[59] See Yigael Yadin, "Expedition D—'Cave of the Letters,'" *The Judean Desert Caves—Archaeological Survey 1961* (in Hebrew) (Jerusalem: Israel Exploration Society, 1962), 204–36, esp. 228–32.

from ancient Greek sources[60] and from the medieval tradition of the MT and the Samaritan Pentateuch. It seems that in some Qumran texts they were used with a very specific purpose to indicate that a space at the end of the line should not be mistaken as an open section, which has a definite contextual meaning. This explanation fits the occurrences of X in *1QpHab*, e.g., col. IX, lines 1, 13 (but not the X signs in *1QIsaᵃ* (see section 5). In *1QpHab* these X signs are always written to the right of, and flush with, the vertical ruled line. This also pertains to the single *ʾaleph* in col. II, 5, which must reflect a wrongly copied X sign.[61] Likewise, in *11QTᵇ* the X sign serves as a line-filler in frgs. 6 and 8 (PAM 43.975, 43.977).[62]

This description probably also fits the markings in *4QCantᵇ* (best visible on photograph PAM 40.604), which are, however, of a different nature.[63] That scroll contains five different scribal marks in frg. 1, at the ends of lines 4 (fig. 12.1; paleo-Hebrew *zayin*?), 7 (fig. 12.2; paleo-Hebrew *ʿayin*?), 9 (fig. 12.3, cf. also fig. 15; *epsilon*?), 11 (fig. 12.4; paleo-Hebrew *shin/sin* with a 90-degree rotation, or *sigma*?), 13 (fig. 12.5; paleo-Hebrew *bet*?), and probably also in frg. 2, col. I, line 4, and at the left edge of the last line of frg. 3 (fig. 12.6; *gamma*? or a

---

[60]   See Gardthausen, *Griechische Palaeographie*, 406–7.

[61]   See n. 5 above.

[62]   See Yigael Yadin, *The Temple Scroll*, vol. 3, *Supplementary Plates* (Jerusalem: Israel Exploration Society, 1977), pl. 37*, and Florentino García Martínez, "*11QTempleᵇ*: A Preliminary Publication," in *The Madrid Qumran Congress: Proceedings of the International Congress on the Dead Sea Scrolls, Madrid, 18–21 March 1991*, ed. Julio Trebolle Barrera and Luis Vegas Montaner, 2 vols. (Leiden: Brill, 1992), vol. 2, pl. 10–11.

[63]   They appear in the spaces at the ends of lines that were shorter than the surrounding ones. If they were used as line-fillers, their use is not consistent. In three of the five occurrences in frg. 1 they could be line-fillers in spaces left uninscribed (lines 4, 9, 11), but in lines 7 and 13 they occur in open sections. The possible signs in frgs. 2 and 3 are of an unclear nature. It is less likely that the signs somehow referred to the content of the manuscript, since they occur in the middle of sentences.

sign similar in shape to a *diple obelismene*[64]?). These markings probably represent letters in the paleo-Hebrew script or the Cryptic A script (as in *4Q249, 4Q298, 4Q317*), or a combination of several scripts, including Greek (for the latter, cf. figs. 12.3 and 12.6). Since the Cryptic A script is used for Qumran sectarian writings (and is indeed regarded by Pfann as an "Essene esoteric script"),[65] the appearance of these letters in *4QCant^b* would point either to a sectarian scribal background or to the use of these texts by the Qumranites.

Possibly the two dots at the end of the lines in *1QIsa^a* col. III, 6 and col. XX, 10 (fig. 13) are line-fillers as well. The inverted *paragraphos* at the end of the line in *4Q324* (fig. 11.6) may also represent a line-filler.

7. Separation Dots between Words

In two instances a dot, written even with the tops of the letters, is meant to separate two words lest they be understood as one continuous word: *4QM^c (4Q493),* line 2: ואחר̇כן and *4QOrd^c (4Q514)* 1 i 2: לכל̇הט[מ]אים.

8. Marks Numbering Content Units and Sheets

There is some evidence for the numbering of sheets. Two examples were provided by Milik:[66] a *gimel* in *4QS^b (olim 4QS^d)* on photographs PAM 42.372 and 43.250 in the upper right margin, above the first letter of the column, and a letter (*aleph* ?) in *4QD^a (olim 4QD^b)* in the margin to the right of the column. Further examples:

• *4QExod^k*, of which merely one fragment has been preserved, displays in the upper right corner, above the center of

---

[64]   A paragraph sign used in the Greek scribal tradition for separating different sections in tragedies and comedies.

[65]   Pfann, "4Q298," 207, 213.

[66]   Jozef T. Milik, "Numérotation des feuilles des rouleaux dans le scriptorium de Qumrân (Planches X et XI)," *Semitica* 27 (1977): 75–81.

the first word, a sign (fig. 10.11) that resembles the *lamed* in the Cryptic A script of *4Q317*.

* In *4QVisions of Amram*[b] *(4Q544),* in the top margin above the first word, a slightly curved diagonal line is written, possibly indicating the relative position of the sheet.

* In *MasSir*, col. V (fig. 15), the sign resembling an *epsilon* in the top right margin above the beginning of the column could represent a numbering device, although other columns in that scroll have not been numbered. The slant of the sign very much resembles that of an *ancora (inferior)* mark (denoting omission or addition) in the Greek scribal tradition (fig. 15.1) although the latter has a longer middle stroke. Compare also the *epsilon*-like sign in *4QCant*[b] (fig. 12.3). *Mur* 17B contains a very similar sign which has been explained by its editor as denoting the *seah* occurring in that text together with number signs.[67]

* In *1QS* VII, the composite sign occurring in the bottom margin, immediately under the right edge of the column, is a combination of a paleo-Hebrew *zayin* and a triangular shape (fig. 13). The sign could denote a number,[68] and in that case it should be pointed out that this *zayin* occurs in col. VII (coincidence?). However, this sign probably refers to a major subdivision of the text, as suggested in section 1.

An Additional Note on the Distribution of the Scribal Signs

This descriptive paper devoted to the scribal habits reflected in the texts from the Judean Desert focuses on scribal markings. One issue on which we have not focused, but which nevertheless is central to several descriptions, is the distribution of the signs in the Qumran documents. Although our detailed discussion may create the impression that these scribal markings are

---

[67] Jozef T. Milik, in *Les grottes de Murabba'ât, DJD* 2:97.

[68] In *1QS* columns V and VIII are not denoted with any signs, while the bottom right margin of the other columns has not been preserved.

widely used in the Qumran texts, their use is almost exclusively limited to the texts written according to the Qumran scribal practice.

The research was not carried out to prove this or any other point, since the issues described here are significant enough to be discussed in their own right. But it so happens that as more is known about the scribal habits, support for the assumption that there was indeed a Qumran scribal school grows. In my previous work on the Qumran scribal school, I started from the assumption of the existence of a special orthography, a unique morphology, and scribal practices characterizing certain Qumran scrolls, which in my view have been written by the Qumran scribal school.[69] Some criticisms have been raised against the orthography part of that theory, and I now realize that one may also start the description from the other end, from the scribal practices, as we have done in this paper. In that case one can tabulate all the Qumran texts that use scribal marks of some sort. It will then be seen that most of these texts are written in what I call the Qumran orthography and morphology, and most of them have a Qumran sectarian background. This connection between the distribution of the scribal signs on the one hand and the use of a specific orthography and morphology on the other cannot be coincidental.

---

[69] Emanuel Tov, "The Orthography and Language of the Hebrew Scrolls Found at Qumran and the Origin of These Scrolls," *Textus* 13 (1986): 31–57; "Hebrew Biblical Manuscripts from the Judaean Desert: Their Contribution to Textual Criticism," *JJS* 39 (1988): 5–37; "Scribal Practices Reflected in the Documents from the Judean Desert and in the Rabbinic Literature—A Comparative Study," in *Texts, Temples, and Traditions—A Tribute to Menachem Haran,* ed. Michael V. Fox et al. (Winona Lake, Ind.: Eisenbrauns, in press); "*Tefillin* of Different Origin from Qumran," in *J. Licht Memorial Volume* (in press).

Table

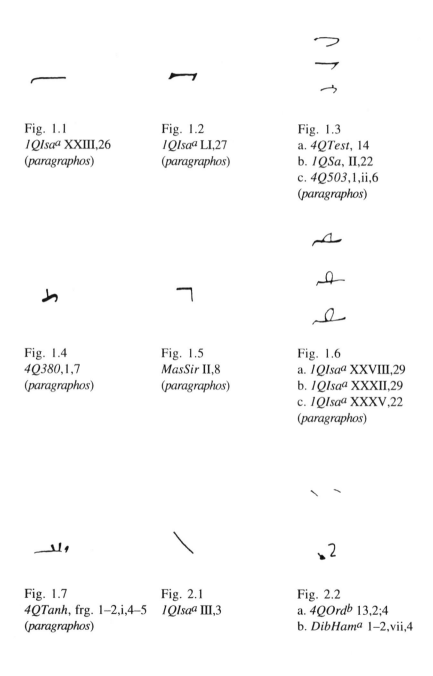

Fig. 1.1
1QIsaa XXIII,26
(*paragraphos*)

Fig. 1.2
1QIsaa LI,27
(*paragraphos*)

Fig. 1.3
a. *4QTest*, 14
b. *1QSa*, II,22
c. *4Q503*,1,ii,6
(*paragraphos*)

Fig. 1.4
4Q380,1,7
(*paragraphos*)

Fig. 1.5
MasSir II,8
(*paragraphos*)

Fig. 1.6
a. *1QIsaa* XXVIII,29
b. *1QIsaa* XXXII,29
c. *1QIsaa* XXXV,22
(*paragraphos*)

Fig. 1.7
4QTanh, frg. 1–2,i,4–5
(*paragraphos*)

Fig. 2.1
1QIsaa III,3

Fig. 2.2
a. *4QOrdb* 13,2;4
b. *DibHama* 1–2,vii,4

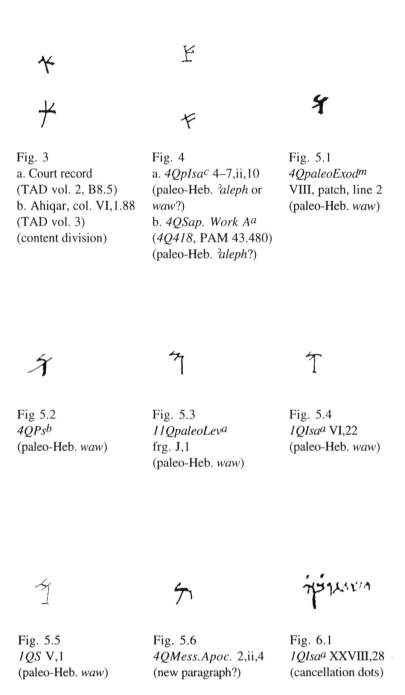

Fig. 3
a. Court record
(TAD vol. 2, B8.5)
b. Ahiqar, col. VI,1.88
(TAD vol. 3)
(content division)

Fig. 4
a. *4QpIsa^c* 4–7,ii,10
(paleo-Heb. *ʾaleph* or
waw?)
b. *4QSap. Work A^a*
(*4Q418*, PAM 43.480)
(paleo-Heb. *ʾaleph*?)

Fig. 5.1
4QpaleoExod^m
VIII, patch, line 2
(paleo-Heb. *waw*)

Fig 5.2
4QPs^b
(paleo-Heb. *waw*)

Fig. 5.3
11QpaleoLev^a
frg. J,1
(paleo-Heb. *waw*)

Fig. 5.4
1QIsa^a VI,22
(paleo-Heb. *waw*)

Fig. 5.5
1QS V,1
(paleo-Heb. *waw*)

Fig. 5.6
4QMess.Apoc. 2,ii,4
(new paragraph?)

Fig. 6.1
1QIsa^a XXVIII,28
(cancellation dots)

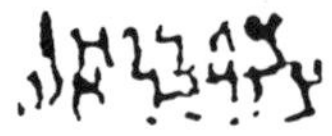

Fig. 6.2
1QIsa^a XXXIII,7
(cancellation dots)

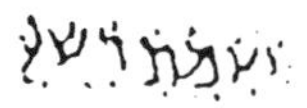

Fig. 6.3
1QIsa^a X,23
(cancellation dots)

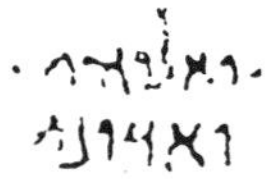

Fig. 6.4
1QIsa^a XLI,14
(cancellation dots)

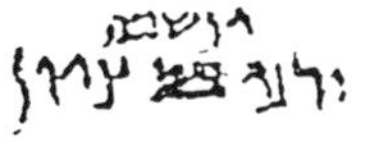

Fig. 7
1QIsa^a XI,10
(crossing out)

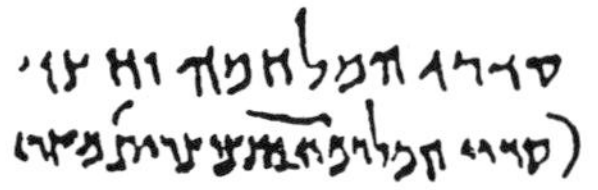

Fig. 8.1
1QM III,1
(parentheses used for
omission)

Fig. 8.2
4QQoh^a II,1 (top ma.)
Qoh 6:4 (parentheses
for insertion)

Fig. 8.3
4QEn^a col. II,1
PAM 41.360
(omission or insertion)

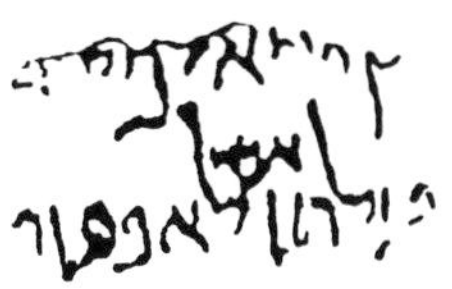

Fig. 9
4QTob^a
3:13 (frg. 6, 1.8)
(insertion)

Fig. 10.1
a. *1QIsa^a* VIII,7–8
b. *4Q298*, 3–4,ii,5
(*resh*)

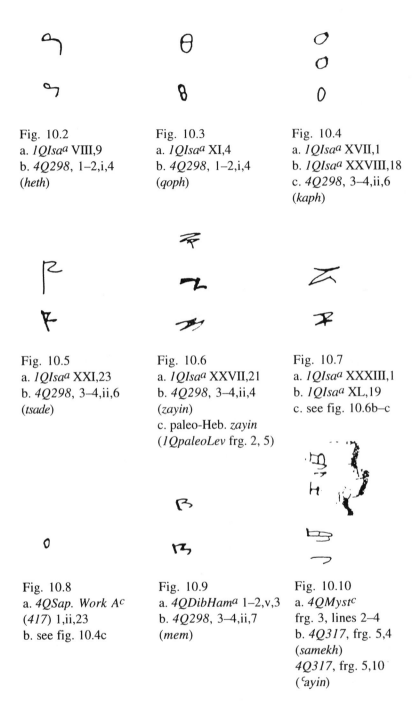

Fig. 10.2
a. *1QIsaᵃ* VIII,9
b. *4Q298*, 1–2,i,4
(*heth*)

Fig. 10.3
a. *1QIsaᵃ* XI,4
b. *4Q298*, 1–2,i,4
(*qoph*)

Fig. 10.4
a. *1QIsaᵃ* XVII,1
b. *1QIsaᵃ* XXVIII,18
c. *4Q298*, 3–4,ii,6
(*kaph*)

Fig. 10.5
a. *1QIsaᵃ* XXI,23
b. *4Q298*, 3–4,ii,6
(*tsade*)

Fig. 10.6
a. *1QIsaᵃ* XXVII,21
b. *4Q298*, 3–4,ii,4
(*zayin*)
c. paleo-Heb. *zayin*
(*1QpaleoLev* frg. 2, 5)

Fig. 10.7
a. *1QIsaᵃ* XXXIII,1
b. *1QIsaᵃ* XL,19
c. see fig. 10.6b–c

Fig. 10.8
a. *4QSap. Work Aᶜ*
(*417*) 1,ii,23
b. see fig. 10.4c

Fig. 10.9
a. *4QDibHamᵃ* 1–2,v,3
b. *4Q298*, 3–4,ii,7
(*mem*)

Fig. 10.10
a. *4QMystᶜ*
frg. 3, lines 2–4
b. *4Q317*, frg. 5,4
(*samekh*)
4Q317, frg. 5,10
(*ᶜayin*)

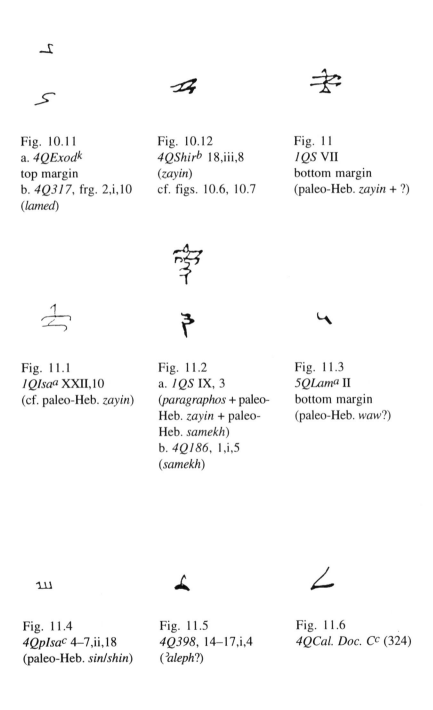

Fig. 10.11
a. *4QExod^k*
top margin
b. *4Q317*, frg. 2,i,10
(*lamed*)

Fig. 10.12
4QShir^b 18,iii,8
(*zayin*)
cf. figs. 10.6, 10.7

Fig. 11
1QS VII
bottom margin
(paleo-Heb. *zayin* + ?)

Fig. 11.1
1QIsa^a XXII,10
(cf. paleo-Heb. *zayin*)

Fig. 11.2
a. *1QS* IX, 3
(*paragraphos* + paleo-
Heb. *zayin* + paleo-
Heb. *samekh*)
b. *4Q186*, 1,i,5
(*samekh*)

Fig. 11.3
5QLam^a II
bottom margin
(paleo-Heb. *waw*?)

Fig. 11.4
4QpIsa^c 4–7,ii,18
(paleo-Heb. *sin/shin*)

Fig. 11.5
4Q398, 14–17,i,4
(*ʾaleph*?)

Fig. 11.6
4QCal. Doc. C^c (324)

Fig. 12.1
4QCant^b 1,4
(paleo-Heb. *zayin?*)

Fig. 12.2
4QCant^b 1,7
(paleo-Heb. *ʿayin?*)

Fig. 12.3
4QCant^b 1,9
(*epsilon?*)

Fig. 12.4
4QCant^b 1,11
(paleo-Heb. *sin/shin?*;
sigma?)

Fig. 12.5
4QCant^b 1,13
(paleo-Heb. *bet?*)

Fig. 12.6
4QCant^b 3, last line
(*gamma* or *diple
obelismene?*)

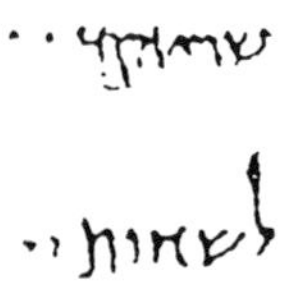

Fig. 13
a. *1QIsa^a* III,6
b. *1QIsa^a* XX,10
(line-fillers?)

Fig. 14
Epiphanius,
*On Weights and
Measures*, p. 47b of
the Syriac ms.

Fig. 15
MasSir V, top margin

Fig. 15.1
ancora (inferior)
(omission, addition)

Fig. 16
1QIsaᵃ XXXII
bottom margin
(scribble?)

Fig. 17
1QS XI,15
(colon)

Multiple Literary Editions: Reflections toward a Theory of the History of the Biblical Text

EUGENE ULRICH

University of Notre Dame

Perennially fascinating to the human mind are questions regarding the genesis and development of important elements that constitute our world, our existence, our physical, psychological or spiritual life. The historical-critical study of the Bible is one such attempt to explore the origins and development of a predominant influence on Western culture and Jewish-Christian values and traditions.

Various new forces provide stimuli for reconsidering and rethinking current perspectives on origins, such as a new invention with wide-ranging possibilities, a new Zeitgeist with fertile potencies for seeing familiar subjects from a fresh viewpoint, or the discovery of a new body of evidence that offers a fresh coign of vantage for reevaluation of traditional theories.

The two hundred biblical manuscripts[1] discovered at Qumran offer, among many other benefits, the possibility of a great

I am especially grateful to Professors Noel B. Reynolds and Donald W. Parry, the Foundation for Ancient Research and Mormon Studies, and the Jerusalem Center for Near Eastern Studies of Brigham Young University for the invitation to contribute to their Judean Desert Scrolls Conference 1995 and for their gracious hospitality.

[1] For a list and discussion of the biblical scrolls from Cave 4, see Eugene Ulrich, "The Biblical Scrolls from Qumran Cave 4: An Overview

advance in the area usually labeled "the history of the biblical text." Discussions of this topic are usually confined to the closing centuries of the Second Temple period, and understandably so, since we have no textual evidence before about the middle of the third century B.C.E. But such constriction tends to distort the picture and even to distort approaches to the picture. Moreover, lack of extant evidence, though regrettable and daunting, should not excessively intimidate us, for history is essentially a process and an art of reconstruction. Lack of extant evidence should certainly cause us to proceed cautiously, but that lack should not prevent us from proceeding. On the one hand, frequent and widespread archaeological discoveries of large depositories have documented highly developed literary activity throughout the ancient Near East in the second and first millennia B.C.E. On the other hand, intense and voluminous literary and historical-critical study of the biblical literature over several centuries has solidly grounded the assumption of a rich and continuous literary history of Israel spanning more than a millennium. And, although it was in existence, it was not until this generation that the documentation of that amazingly large cache of literary remains found near the tiny commune of Qumran happened to become available.

---

and a Progress Report on Their Publication," *RQ* 14/2, no. 54–55 (December 1989): 207–28. For updates of that list plus a list of MSS from the other caves and their publication data, see Emanuel Tov et al., eds., *The Dead Sea Scrolls on Microfiche: A Comprehensive Facsimile Edition of the Texts from the Judean Desert, Companion Volume*, 2nd ed. (Leiden: Brill, 1995). For publication of the Cave 4 biblical scrolls, see *DJD* 9 (MSS in paleo-Hebrew or Greek), 12 (Genesis–Numbers), and 14 (Deuteronomy–Kings), plus the forthcoming *DJD* 15 (Isaiah–Minor Prophets), 16 (Psalms–Chronicles), and 17 (Samuel). For an index of the biblical passages preserved in these MSS, see Eugene Ulrich, "An Index of Passages in the Biblical Manuscripts from the Judean Desert (Genesis–Kings)," *DSD* 1 (1994): 113–29; and "An Index of Passages in the Biblical Manuscripts from the Judean Desert (Part 2: Isaiah–Chronicles)," *DSD* 2 (1995): 86–107.

Thus the scope of the discussion about the history of the biblical text should not be limited to the evidence that we happen to have available, or we will not succeed in the task of reconstructing that history, since all the evidence and all logic points to a much larger scope of biblical literary activity throughout the monarchic and postexilic periods. The following proposal will attempt to situate the discussion in the larger context of the history of the composition of the biblical books. After a review of some of the evidence from Qumran, I will attempt an exposition of variant literary editions as a key to the history of the biblical text.

I. The Evidence from Qumran

Before examining the Qumran evidence, it is helpful to recall that before the Qumran discoveries we had the primary clues necessary for outlining the following proposal, namely, the Samaritan Pentateuch (𝔐) and the Septuagint (𝔊) alongside the Masoretic Text (𝔐). By reconsidering scholarly use of the Samaritan and Septuagint evidence, we may also gain valuable insight for today.

Ever since its rediscovery in 1616, the Samaritan Pentateuch has provided us with examples of an alternate edition of the traditional biblical text. In the books of Exodus and Numbers[2] it displays an only slightly altered version of an edition that is similar to, derived from, and more developed than our traditional text. It tells us a great deal about the Jewish texts of the scriptures at the time of Jesus and Paul, Hillel and Shammai, and Qumran's Teacher of Righteousness. This valuable information was available, but we simply paid little or no attention to it because of religious prejudice against the marginalized Samari-

---

[2]   For the books of Genesis, Leviticus, and perhaps Deuteronomy 𝔐 and 𝔐 share the same literary edition, although in Genesis 5:18–32 and 11:10–32 𝔐, 𝔊, and 𝔐 appear to have intentionally variant forms of the numerical schemata; for further references see Emanuel Tov, *Textual Criticism of the Hebrew Bible* (Minneapolis: Fortress, 1992), 337–38.

tans. Those variant editions were viewed simply as the product of the perverse Samaritans, and, as in racist or other prejudiced groups, scholars colluded, collectively agreeing, without real thought, that the evidence was of little worth.

Similarly, ⅌ preserves editions of some biblical books and passages that are different from those found in 𝔐. ⅌ is the earliest translation of the Hebrew Bible, a translation that started with the Torah probably around 280 B.C.E. and was gradually completed over the next two centuries or so. But the function of ⅌ in biblical scholarship until the middle of this century was often polemical. Catholics tended to use it because it had been the Bible of the Church from the beginnings, until the Vulgate replaced it. Jews tended to ignore it in favor of the traditional Hebrew, and Protestants tended to dismiss it in view of the renewed interest in the "original Hebrew," partly as a result of the Renaissance return to the original languages for all classics. Thus major differences between the text of ⅌ and that of the "original" Hebrew were mainly seen as corruptions or deliberate changes from the inspired text. ⅌ was charged with being a poor translation or a loose paraphrase, and its witness, along with that of 𝔪, lay dormant because it was marginalized. However, the Qumran scrolls are a thousand years older than what was known in the fifteenth century as the "original Hebrew" text, and the scrolls demonstrate that in fact multiple forms of the "original Hebrew" text existed, and that the various books of ⅌—far from being corrupt translations or poor paraphrases— should be viewed as generally faithful translations of ancient, alternate Hebrew forms of texts unknown throughout the Middle Ages but now rediscovered and fragmentarily attested at Qumran.

Perhaps the modern recognition both of the value of 𝔪 and ⅌, and of the scholarly misjudgment due to preconceived denominational loyalties, can provide us with an instructive lesson. We should first pay serious attention to our new data, try creatively to allow various possible interpretations to emerge and be sufficiently explored, and only then come to a judgment between competing interpretations. In other words, we should let our judgments flow logically from the data and not superimpose an interpretation prompted by "what we already know" from traditional theological systems.

Turning now to the Qumran evidence, I would like to begin by presenting an illustration (see fig. 1) that may serve as a point of reference in the ensuing discussion: four lines from *4QpaleoExodᵐ*. Although the full column that begins with this text was published by Patrick Skehan in 1955,[3] to my knowledge no one has made the detailed points and distinctions that follow.

The primary feature to notice is that the scroll exhibits the same basic textual form as ɯ (see lines 1–2). After an examination of the larger patterns of *4QpaleoExodᵐ*, ɯ, ᴍ, and ₢, it becomes clear that this textual form is a revised and expanded *variant edition* of the base text generally shared by all four. Thus *4QpaleoExodᵐ* and ɯ share the same literary edition of Exodus, a secondary edition expanded (in this case from Deuteronomy 9:20) beyond the earlier edition exhibited by ᴍ and ₢. Although the picture gets more complicated, it should be mentioned that for Exodus 35–39 ᴍ probably contains an edition that, in comparison with the earlier edition of ₢, was secondarily revised and rearranged. If we also decide that the final text of the Samaritans qualifies as yet another variant edition of Exodus—not because of quantitative mass but because of the significance of the two kinds of change introduced[4]—then we have isolated

---

[3]   Patrick W. Skehan, "Exodus in the Samaritan Recension from Qumran," *JBL* 74 (1955): 182–87; for full publication, see Patrick W. Skehan, Eugene Ulrich, and Judith E. Sanderson, *Qumran Cave 4, IV: Palaeo-Hebrew and Greek Biblical Manuscripts*, DJD vol. 9 (Oxford: Clarendon, 1992), 53–130.

[4]   The two major changes marking the specifically Samaritan Torah are the commandment to build an altar at Shechem and the use of the perfect בחר "has chosen" [Shechem] in contrast to the future יבחר "will choose" [Jerusalem] to designate the central shrine.

4QpaleoExod^m (Exodus 32:10–11)

1 אֹו\[תך\] לגוי גדול \[ובאהרון התאנף יה\]וה מאד להשמידו\] [

2 וֹ\[י\]תפלל משה בעד אֹ\[הרון \[ ] \[ו ^11] [[

3 י\[חל\] משה את \[פנ\]י \[יהוה אלהיו ויאו\]מר למֹ\[ה \]יהוה יחֹר אֹ\[פך\]

4 בעמֹ\[ך \]אשר \[הו\]צֹ\[א\]את מארץ מצרים בכח גדול ו\[בזרוע חזקֹה\]

Samaritan Pentateuch

1 אתך לגוי גדול ובאהרן התאנף יהוה מאד להשמידו

2 ויתפלל משה בעד אהרן

3 ^11ויחל משה את פני יהוה אלהיו ויאמר למה יהוה יחַר אפך

4 בעמך אשר הוצאת ממצרים בכח גדול ובזרוע נטויה

Masoretic Text

1 אֹותך לגוי גדול:

2

3 ^11ויחל משה את פני יהוה אלהיו ויאמר למה יהוה יחַרה אפך

4 בעמך אשר הוצאת מארץ מצרים בכח גדול וביַד חזקה:

Translation (Exodus 32:10–11; cf. Deuteronomy 9:20)

1 (. . . but I will make) you a great nation. But against Aaron
   the LORD was very angry, (enough) to destroy him;

2 so Moses prayed on behalf of Aaron.

3 ^11Moses entreated the LORD his God and said,
   "Why, O LORD, does your anger burn

4 against your people whom you have brought out of
   the land of Egypt with great power and a mighty arm?"

Figure 1

four variant editions of the book of Exodus that are extant, beyond the many creative new editions that preceded our surviving textual witnesses.

A second feature to notice in the example is the variety in patterns of agreement and disagreement between the three texts in *individual textual variants*: *4QpaleoExodᵐ* and ⅏ agree against 𝔐 in one individual variant, the verb יחר in line 3; in contrast, *4QpaleoExodᵐ* and 𝔐 agree against ⅏ in a second individual variant, מארץ מצרים in line 4; whereas in the final variant all three texts disagree among themselves.

A third feature to notice is that *4QpaleoExodᵐ* and 𝔐 agree in *orthography* against ⅏ with respect to the first word את(ו)ך, whereas they presumably differ regarding אהר(ו)ן, since the scroll habitually has אהרון elsewhere, while 𝔐 and ⅏ habitually have אהרן.[5]

It is easy to understand why one could view this and numerous analogous examples as simply "independent" or "nonaligned" texts;[6] but we should never assume that any particular text encountered is a "pure form" of the literary edition or texttype. Individual variants arise spontaneously or influence other texts *ad hoc*, without regard to literary editions. Moreover,

---

[5]   See another example of the variety of patterns for literary edition vs. individual textual variants vs. orthography in the book of Daniel illustrated in Eugene Ulrich, "Orthography and Text in 4QDanᵃ and 4QDanᵇ and in the Received Masoretic Text," in *Of Scribes and Scrolls: Studies on the Hebrew Bible, Intertestamental Judaism, and Christian Origins Presented to John Strugnell on the Occasion of His Sixtieth Birthday*, ed. Harold W. Attridge, John J. Collins, and Thomas H. Tobin (Lanham, MD: University Press of America, 1990), 29–42.

[6]   Emanuel Tov, "Hebrew Biblical Manuscripts from the Judaean Desert: Their Contribution to Textual Criticism," *JJS* 39 (1988): 5–37, has correctly stated that the Qumran texts have "taught us no longer to posit MT at the center of our textual thinking" (p. 7). He does, nonetheless, continue to use the term *nonaligned* in *Textual Criticism*, 116–17. Perhaps we should rethink the use of such terms, since 𝔐, ⅏, and 𝔊 are not "texts" or "text-types," and thus are not consistent standards by which other manuscripts of individual books are to be measured for proper "alignment."

orthography was expanding generally in Palestine in the latter Second Temple period; expanded use of *matres lectionis* was the tendency, and it would be a healthy assumption that the practice of introducing *matres lectionis* into a text for greater clarity happened independently of text-type.[7]

As additional data for the theoretical considerations that follow, I would like to offer a few more examples from Qumran biblical manuscripts—focusing on the Former Prophets or Deuteronomistic history, mainly because, as I write, those are the books that happen to be in the final process of publication in *Discoveries in the Judaean Desert.*

4QJosh^a possibly provides an example of a variant literary edition of the book of Joshua.[8] The quantity and scope of the evidence is small, and so it is uncertain whether this scroll represents a variant edition of the full book of Joshua or only of the extant passages. However, the sizable extent of the differences between 𝕸 and 𝕲 make it plausible that multiple editions of the full book did exist.[9] At any rate, the scroll presents the narrative of Joshua's building of the first altar in the newly entered promised land in a sequence quite different from that found in 𝕸 and 𝕲. In the traditional text the first altar is built curiously on

---

[7]   See, e.g., the supralinear insertion of *matres lectionis* in *4QSam^c* in Eugene Ulrich, "4QSam^c: A Fragmentary Manuscript of 2 Samuel 14–15 from the Scribe of the *Serek Hay-yahad* (1QS)," *Bulletin of the American Schools of Oriental Research* 235 (1979): 1–25. Note also the expanded orthography of *4QDan^b* in contrast to that of *4QDan^a*, though the two apparently both share the same text-type and share the same individual variants; see Ulrich, "Orthography and Text in 4QDan^a," 41–42.

[8]   See Eugene Ulrich, "4QJoshua^a and Joshua's First Altar in the Promised Land," in *New Qumran Texts and Studies: Proceedings of the First Meeting of the International Organization for Qumran Studies, Paris 1992*, ed. George J. Brooke with Florentino García Martínez (Leiden: Brill, 1994), 89–104, plates iv-vi; and Eugene Ulrich, "47. 4QJosh^a," in *DJD* 14:143–52.

[9]   See Lea Mazor, "The Septuagint Translation of the Book of Joshua," *Bulletin of the International Organization for Septuagint and Cognate Studies* 27 (1994): 29–38.

Mt. Ebal (Joshua 8:30–35 [ᵴ 9:3–8]) after the fall of Jericho and
the destruction of Ai. In *4QJosh^a*, however, Joshua apparently
builds the first altar at Gilgal immediately after crossing the
Jordan. The scroll's narrative, seemingly supported by
Josephus,[10] may well be an earlier form of the story, in contrast
to a revision in 𝔐 based on cultic polemics.[11]

   4QJudg^a, to my knowledge the oldest manuscript of the
book of Judges, dating from about 50–25 B.C.E., survives in
only a single fragment, measuring 7.6 cm high and 4.8 cm wide
(or roughly half the size of the palm of one's hand).[12] It contains
bits of text from Judges 6:2–6, followed directly by verses 11–
13. In other words, what our traditional Bible lists as Judges
6:7–10 is not present. Two explanations are possible: first,
either the scribe made a mistake and accidentally omitted four
verses that were in the text from which he was copying; or second, this ancient manuscript contains an early form of the text,
which was secondarily expanded by a late addition attested in
our surviving manuscript tradition.

   With reference to the second possibility (i.e., that the scroll
witnesses to an earlier form of the text, while 𝔐 and ᵴ transmit a
subsequent enrichment of the tradition), all the evidence points
to this explanation. First, Judges 6:7–10 forms a cohesive unit
in a style different from what precedes and what follows; second, it is introduced by a resumptive clause (repeating Judges
6:6), just as many secondary additions are introduced—and
some 𝔐 MSS, ᵴ, the Peshitta, and the Vulgate all lack this
resumptive clause; third, it has for more than 100 years been
regarded as a secondary addition in the text by scholars such as

---

   [10]   Josephus, *Antiquities* V, 20; cf. V, 45–57.
   [11]   Ulrich, "47. 4QJosh^a," in *DJD* 14:145–46.
   [12]   See Julio Trebolle Barrera, "49. 4QJudg^a," in *DJD* 14:161–64; and
"Textual Variants in 4QJudg^a and the Textual and Editorial History of the
Book of Judges," in *The Texts of Qumran and the History of the Community: Proceedings of the Groningen Congress on the Dead Sea Scrolls (20–
23 August 1989)*, 1. *Biblical Texts*, ed. Florentino García Martínez (Paris:
Gabalda, 1989), 229–45.

Wellhausen, Gray, Bodine, and Soggin; and fourth, it is set off within 𝔐 by major paragraph markers (*petuhot*) as a separate unit.

Thus *4QJudg^a* is probably a witness to an earlier, shorter form of the text, and the other witnesses attest to a secondarily expanded and enriched form of the text. Since this is all that survives of this oldest MS of Judges, we cannot be sure whether this is a singular phenomenon or whether it represents an earlier complete edition of the book, but Trebolle presents additional evidence from the Old Greek and the Vetus Latina supporting a variant edition of the book.

4QSam^a, in contrast, provides a dramatic paragraph that is not found in any other biblical text, though it was present in the text used by Josephus.[13] This paragraph does not appear to be related to any other variants in the MS, but was probably lost through a single error, and thus it does not constitute a variant *edition*. The omission of it, however, does create an alternate text-type, insofar as subsequent MSS will either have the reading or lack it.

---

[13]   This paragraph was first described in the private notes of Frank Moore Cross and was heralded in the footnotes to the *New American Bible* by Patrick W. Skehan. See the textual and literary discussion in Eugene Ulrich, *The Qumran Text of Samuel and Josephus* (Missoula: Scholars Press, 1978), 69 and 166–70. The fragment was published by Frank Moore Cross, "The Ammonite Oppression of the Tribes of Gad and Reuben: Missing Verses from 1 Samuel 11 Found in 4QSamuel^a," in *History, Historiography, and Interpretation*, ed. H. Tadmor and M. Weinfeld (Jerusalem: Magnes, 1983), 148–58. It has subsequently been adopted into the *NRSV* translation.

For my present purposes it would not matter whether the longer passage is original or, as Alexander Rofé, "The Acts of Nahash according to 4QSam^a," *Israel Exploration Journal* 32 (1982): 129–33, has suggested, a secondary midrashic addition, since in either case we would have two significantly different forms of the text. Although I disagree with my friend in this instance, he is surely correct that numerous sections of the biblical text arose in precisely the manner he describes.

II. Variant Literary Editions as a Key to the History of the Biblical Text

The view that I proposed at the Madrid Congress in 1991, and have been gradually developing since, is a theory of "new editions" of biblical books or passages.[14] Two preliminary steps are necessary to understand the main lines of the history of the text. These two steps are designed to dispel the sense of "chaos" engendered when confronted with a variety of manuscripts. First, it is helpful to sift out the orthographic differences between texts (these are usually relatively insignificant); and then second, to study, but then also sift out for a moment, the individual textual variants that populate every manuscript (they should be studied first and brought back into consideration after the next step). Then, with the distracting orthographical and minor variants out of the way, the larger picture becomes more clear. The three different categories of variation arise at different moments or different stages in the history of the text, because of different causes.

Thus I propose that the main lines in the picture of the history of the biblical text are formed by the deliberate activity of a series of creative scribes who produced the new or multiple literary editions of the books of the Bible. These multiple literary editions have been demonstrated for us over the past forty-five years in the biblical manuscripts from Qumran; they have been under our noses for centuries in the new literary editions preserved in 𝔐 and 𝔊 or attested in Josephus; and they have been described for us by literary and historical critics since the Enlightenment as the successive literary editions constituting the history of the very composition of the scriptures from the beginning.

---

[14]   See Eugene Ulrich, "Pluriformity in the Biblical Text, Text Groups, and Questions of Canon," in *Proceedings of the International Congress on the Dead Sea Scrolls, Madrid, 18–21 March 1991*, ed. Julio Trebolle Barrera and Luis Vegas Montaner (Leiden: Brill, 1992), 37–40.

After the main lines become clear through sorting out variant literary editions, study then moves back to the individual variants in order further to delineate text-types, text-traditions, and text-families, and even to orthography, which can possibly give detailed clues concerning text-families. The proposal presented here follows those three main levels.

1. Variant Literary Editions

As usual, it will be helpful to begin by defining terms:

> By multiple literary editions I mean a literary unit—a story, pericope, narrative, poem, book, etc.—appearing in two or more parallel forms (whether by chance extant or no longer extant in our textual witnesses), which one author, major redactor, or major editor completed and which a subsequent redactor or editor intentionally changed to a sufficient extent that the resultant form should be called a revised edition of that text. . . . In fact we seldom have more than two parallel forms of subsequent editions of biblical passages; but that is chiefly an accident of history, and the process I am intending to describe was a much richer and more frequent process.[15]

The fundamental principle guiding this proposal is that the scriptures, from shadowy beginnings until the final, perhaps abrupt, freezing point of the Masoretic tradition, arose and evolved through a process of organic development. The major lines of that development are characterized by the intentional, creative work of authors or tradents who produced new, revised editions of the traditional form of a book or passage.

---

[15] Eugene Ulrich, "The Canonical Process, Textual Criticism, and Latter Stages in the Composition of the Bible," in *Sha'arei Talmon: Studies in the Bible, Qumran, and the Ancient Near East Presented to Shemaryahu Talmon*, ed. Michael Fishbane and Emanuel Tov with Weston W. Fields (Winona Lake, Ind.: Eisenbrauns, 1992), 278.

It is well known that many parts of scripture began as small, oral units and were told and retold, grouped into small collections of related material, and gradually written down. The oral and written forms were occasionally reformulated to meet the varied needs of the times and were handed down and repeated faithfully for generations.

But every once in a while, an occasion arose that sparked reflection on the traditional literature and readaptation of its traditional thrust in order to illuminate the current situation with its dangers or possibilities, to help the people see the situation more clearly and to motivate them to act in the way the tradent-authors considered necessary or proper.

Equally well known is the evolutionary development of the principal literary works that comprise the scriptures: the Pentateuch, with its several sources interwoven, each of which was itself a quilt of earlier materials; the Deuteronomistic history, a large redactional unit compiled from variegated national sources and itself reedited during the Exile; the prophetic collections, many of which have a multilayered compositional and redactional history; the Psalter and Proverbs, both magnets which attracted numerous individual units and small collections over the centuries. This process had already started in Israel's early existence and continued over the centuries until the Roman threat and the growing division between the Rabbinic Jews and the Christian Jews finally brought a halt to the process. By then new anthologies of religious literature in new forms had begun to emerge: the New Testament and the Mishnah.

The emergence of each fresh literary edition occasioned variant versions of the literature that would coexist for some time. Variant text-types were thus caused by revised literary editions.

When we turn to the textual transmission level, we must always remember that we have lost most of the ancient evidence. The witnesses that have survived attest to the continuation of this process of faithful transmission occasionally punctuated by evolutionary leaps to a new, revised, and expanded edition of biblical books. Our extant witnesses are the scrolls from the

Judean Desert, 𝔐, 𝔴, 𝔊, and the versions (not necessarily the specific manuscripts but the text forms they transmit), and all apparently derive from the last four hundred years—roughly the last one-third—of Israel's major period of literary formation from national literature to sacred scriptures.

We do, and we do not, see serious movement in the growth of the text. The base text of most books is relatively stable, although new, variant editions were being produced or handed on side-by-side with the older editions. Some variant editions may well go back several centuries—we have little or no criteria or data for determining this—but it also appears that others were created within the late Second Temple, or Qumran, period. The further back, the more important this phenomenon is, because it is a more deeply established and accepted aspect of their "authoritative books" consciousness that will eventually emerge into canonical decisions.

For example, the edition of Exodus transmitted in 𝔐 and 𝔊 and the revised and expanded edition exhibited in *4QpaleoExod^m* could both conceivably go back to the fifth century; it is unlikely that the edition in 𝔊, perhaps revised in 𝔐 for Exodus 35–39, is much later than the fifth century. But the edition in *4Qpaleo-Exod^m* could be as late as the early second century B.C.E., though not later, because it was apparently sufficiently known and accepted in Judaism that it was the form of that scriptural book taken and used by the conservative Samaritans, with only a handful of changes, for their scriptures.

2. Individual Textual Variants

Although the primary lines in the history of the text are determined by variant literary editions, another significant determining factor can be major individual variants. The smaller lines are caused by the introduction, frequently intentional, of individual expansions, clarifications, interpretations, and even errors.[16] Major variants, such as those discussed earlier—the passage involving the first altar in *4QJosh^a* suggesting a transposition in 𝔐, the lack of the Deuteronomistic passage in *4QJudg^a*, the Nahash passage in *4QSam^a*—could theoretically be either part of a pattern constituting a revised literary edition or simply an isolated variant. If simply individual variants, they would certainly give rise to variant text-families in the subsequent transmission. The individual textual variants of an entire book or section must be studied both singly and synoptically in order to determine whether they are truly "individual" textual variants or part of the pattern constituting a variant edition. For example, Goliath's height (1 Samuel 17:4) was four cubits in one text group (*4QSam^a*, 𝔊, Josephus),[17] five cubits in another (𝔊^N), and six cubits in yet another (𝔐, 𝔊^O, σ'). Most textual critics, viewing that evidence alone, would probably judge that "four cubits" was the earlier reading and the height was exaggerated in subsequent recitations. But is that an isolated variant or part of the larger pattern in which 𝔊 of 1 Samuel 17–18 displays an earlier, shorter form of the narrative and 𝔐 and 𝔊^O display a secondary, expanded variant edition?[18] But again, texts

---

[16]   The errors, of course, are usually unintentional; but sometimes they are intentional—not as errors but as changes which happen to involve error. An example of an intentional change that is in fact erroneous is the introduction of the king's name in 𝔐^L Jeremiah 27[34𝔊]:1. The earlier Greek edition has no elaborate introduction, but the expanded edition 𝔐^L has added an introduction similar to that in Jeremiah 26:1, complete with the name Jehoiachim. The correct name, however, is Zedekiah, as 27:3, 12 and 28:1 [𝔊 34:2, 10; 35:1] indicate, and as three 𝔐 MSS attest, according to *BH^3*; for illustration and discussion see Tov, *Textual Criticism*, 11, 322.

[17]   Josephus, *Antiquities* VI, 171.

[18]   In their collaborative volume, *The Story of David and Goliath: Textual and Literary Criticism: Papers of a Joint Research Venture* (Fribourg, Switzerland: Éditions Universitaires, 1986), Dominique Barthélemy, David W. Gooding, Johan Lust, and Emanuel Tov split over the question of the variant editions of 𝔊 and 𝔐. Barthélemy and Gooding attempt to demonstrate that the shorter 𝔊 edition of the David-Goliath narrative in 1 Samuel 17–18 is a pruned version of a more original 𝔐 version, but the explanations of Tov and Lust are decidedly more persuasive. Texts

and their variants have a rich life, and individual variants can and do cross the boundaries between variant editions. Thus those who say simply that texts exhibiting different editions should not be used to correct individual variants in the other begin with a good premise but are also likely to be mistaken as often as they are correct.

3. Orthographic Differences

Similarly, the orthographic profile of a manuscript generally appears to be unrelated or incidental to its textual character.[19] Although orthographic differences are sometimes significant for identifying stemmatic relationships, this does not usually seem to be the case. Attention to and study of orthography helps sort out the "chaos of texts," but often more through removing the orthographic factor temporarily from cluttering the textual variants.

The Qumran scrolls have taught us much about orthography in the late Second Temple period. One area especially attracts discussion, if only to urge greater clarity and less uncritical adoption by others. Emanuel Tov speaks of a "Qumran practice"[20] of orthography and morphology that is "unique" and claims that "it appears that the texts belonging to this group were

---

are usually foreshortened through error, often by parablepsis, the loss of material through inadvertent skipping from one occurrence of a word or phrase to another; in contrast, it is usually intentional change that lies behind either expansions or quantitatively equal substitutions of a preferable word for a less preferable.

[19] See Ulrich, "Orthography and Text in 4QDan^a," and Eugene Ulrich, "The Palaeo-Hebrew Biblical Manuscripts from Qumran Cave 4," in *Time to Prepare the Way in the Wilderness: Papers on the Qumran Scrolls by Fellows of the Institute for Advanced Studies of the Hebrew University, Jerusalem, 1989–1990*, ed. Devorah Dimant and Lawrence H. Schiffman (Leiden: Brill, 1995), 103–29.

[20] Emanuel Tov, "The Orthography and Language of the Hebrew Scrolls Found at Qumran and the Origin of These Scrolls," *Textus* 13 (1986): 31–57; and Tov, *Textual Criticism*, 107–9.

copied by the Qumran covenanters themselves."[21] He concedes
that the term "is somewhat misleading" and that it "merely indicates that as a scribal system it is known mainly from a number
of Qumran scrolls, without implying that this orthography was
not used elsewhere in Palestine."[22]

I think the term is sufficiently misleading that it should be
abandoned, for at least two reasons. First, the features noted are
encountered only erratically in the scrolls, and most of them are
not unique to Qumran but are also found either in 𝔐 itself or in
other texts, often biblical. For example, for the pleonastic א in
כיא note the same double marking in נקיא in 𝔐 at Joel 4:19 and
Jonah 1:14; the Targums also attest analogous forms such as
איתי- (e.g., ואיתגלי) for את-. For *waw* to mark short *o* or *u*, note
לכול in 𝔐 at Jeremiah 33:8 (though a *qĕrê* also attests a variant
לכל) as well as forms such as גוברא and מגובר in the Targums;
כול also occurs in both absolute and suffixal forms in an Aramaic inscription from Hatra.[23] לוא appears in the Nash Papyrus
from Egypt. Further, how is מושה in some scrolls vs. משה in 𝔐
(and some other scrolls) different from דויד in 𝔐 of Chronicles
vs. דוד in 𝔐 of Samuel; or for that matter from יהד on some
coins vs. יהוד on others? Rather, it appears preferable to agree
with E. Y. Kutscher, that "we may assume that many of those
points in which the Scroll [*1QIsaᵃ*] differs linguistically from the
Masoretic Isaiah represent characteristics of the literary Hebrew
of the last centuries of the first millennium B.C.E."[24]

Second, the term in fact misleads. It is increasingly quoted
without Tov's nuance, and is thus proclaimed as established fact
rather than as tentative hypothesis. For example, the most recent
use of it I have seen simply states:

---

[21] Tov, *Textual Criticism*, 107.

[22] Ibid., 108.

[23] Herbert Donner and W. Röllig, *Kanaanäische und Aramäische Inschriften*, Band 1 (Wiesbaden: Harrassowitz, 1966), 49, no. 256.

[24] Eduard Y. Kutscher, *A History of the Hebrew Language* (Jerusalem: Magnes, 1982), 95.

In addition to the three already known text families [𝔐, 𝔰𝔪, and 𝔊], there exist at Qumran biblical manuscripts of a type unique to this collection. Many Qumran manuscripts are written in an orthography (spelling system) and morphology (grammatical form) characteristic of the Qumran sect. This writing method is used in virtually all the documents that can be directly attributed to the sect and that contain its teachings. Texts composed elsewhere but preserved at Qumran do not exhibit the special characteristics of the language of Qumran.

It stands to reason that the biblical texts written in the unique Qumran style were copied by the sectarians, perhaps at Qumran, although the geographic location cannot really be proven and is not of great importance.[25]

We may presume that some biblical and some nonbiblical MSS were copied at Qumran, but we may also presume that many or most were penned outside Qumran. Very little evidence exists to demonstrate that any specific biblical MS was copied there. The text represented in *4QpaleoExodᵐ*, for example, was a Jewish text, known outside Qumran, for we may be confident that the Samaritans did not come to Qumran to acquire it for their base text.

Nonetheless, some biblical texts were probably copied at Qumran. On the one hand, it is virtually certain that the manuscript *4QSamᶜ* was indeed copied there, because it is very likely that the distinctively inexpert scribe who copied it also copied the *Community Rule (1QS)*, one of the community's "Foundation Documents." But on the other hand, there is no reason to suspect that the text presented in *4QSamᶜ* does not reflect its *Vorlage* from Jerusalem or elsewhere in Palestine. In fact, *4QSamᶜ* is textually closer than 𝔐 is to 𝔊 and Josephus, which have nothing to do with Qumran.

---

[25]   Lawrence H. Schiffman, *Reclaiming the Dead Sea Scrolls: The History of Judaism, the Background of Christianity, the Lost Library of Qumran* (Philadelphia: Jewish Publication Society, 1994), 171.

The orthography and morphology of the scrolls (and of 𝔐)
do indeed exhibit intriguing aspects, but it is far more likely that
the range of tendencies (neither "method" nor "characteristic")
observed in the scrolls is generally typical of contemporary Pal-
estinian copyists rather than specific to the copyists at Qumran.
Even if this were not so, I would still argue that orthographic
style is usually unrelated to the textual character of a biblical
book, and therefore that the orthography displayed in the
Qumran biblical scrolls tells us little about the nature of the text
in those scrolls.[26]

Returning to consideration of the main lines of the history of
the text, we may again temporarily bracket orthography and
individual variants to focus on what may be called the base
text.[27] The base text may be thought of as the form of the text,
or the literary edition, of any particular book that was current
(during any given period) before a new, creatively developed
literary edition.

The base text functions with respect to subsequent variant
editions in a manner analogous to an original or correct reading
in relation to variant readings, whether expansions, revisions, or
errors. That is, it is what one expects to find—the "default
reading"—and so its occurrence is unremarkable. In a sense, all
witnesses of a given book exhibit the base text; the material that
indicates a variant literary edition is the coordinated pattern of
intentional variants intended by a creative author. Thus, again,
one can see why the key to seeing the stemma properly is not to
use 𝔐, 𝔪, and 𝔊 as the three principal lines. Those three are not
properly "texts" or "text-types" or "recensions." The only one
that possibly comes close is 𝔪, and that is because 𝔪 is
restricted to only the five books of the Torah, and because it
used texts containing the expanded editions for the two books,

---

[26]   See Ulrich, "The Palaeo-Hebrew Biblical Manuscripts," and Ulrich,
"Orthography and Text in 4QDan^a."

[27]   The term *base text* may advance the discussion beyond what is
sometimes referred to as the *Urtext*, which gives the impression of a single,
static entity.

Exodus and Numbers, for which seriously expanded editions were circulating. Neither 𝔐, nor 𝔰𝔪, nor 𝔊 is properly "a text" in the sense that the nature of their text has any consistency or related character from book to book. Nor are they "text-types" or "recensions" in the sense that they were planned and designed or carefully edited according to textual principles or textual criteria. They are rather *collections* of individual scrolls, the nature of whose text varies from scroll to scroll, apparently quite without regard to any criteria. This is not a problem as long as one recognizes the phenomenon and does not treat the collections as though they were unities.

It may prove helpful to pause and remember two things. First, the shape of all collections of scripture until around the third century C.E. was a collection of individual scrolls, not a codex or book. Second, 𝔐 is a nonunified collection of texts, the nature of which varies from book to book. Scholarship has gained considerable clarity in our century by recognizing the aggregate or collection aspect of the texts that constitute the anthology labeled 𝔊; many problems have been clarified by understanding that the text of 𝔊 varies from book to book. We can expect similar gains in clarity if we realize that the text of 𝔐 also varies from book to book. Clearly the books were copied with a care and fidelity that fills us with awe and admiration, but no evidence before 135 C.E. has been forthcoming that intentional consideration was given to the precisely textual criteria governing the selection of individual texts.[28]

If we can work with the supposition that proto-𝔐 was a collection of texts whose textual character varied from book to book, then we may have advanced a step in focusing with increased acuity on the history of the biblical text. We should not look to 𝔐 as the standard by which to judge the text of the various books, but to the base text, or earliest available literary

---

[28] Evidence against such consideration is the problematic state of texts such as 𝔐 of Samuel and Hosea; if the texts had been compared and selected on the basis of superior text form, it is dubious that the texts of those two books would have been selected.

edition of each. The base text of each book, i.e., the earliest edition of that book attested in our extant witnesses, must be individually assessed and determined. It already stands late in the succession of reworked editions of that book, but for the sake of general applicability we can call the first extant edition of each book the base text. For some books only one edition appears to be attested, and for those books one can skip to the level of individual textual variants to refine the interrelationship of preserved MSS. But for many books our witnesses document variant literary editions. Normally, the interrelationship of variant editions can be determined somewhat easily, since the barometer of quantity seldom fails. That is, the tendency was to expand the scriptural text, not to remove anything that had come to be considered God's word, though of course this barometer must be used cautiously.[29]

Thus I would propose for consideration that the goal of textual criticism is not 𝔐, as Emanuel Tov proposes, i.e., the text of that edition of each book which Rabbinic Judaism eventually chose, but rather the ancient Hebrew text which was in fact a developing text, not a static, fixed text. It is certainly legitimate, for religious or historical purposes, to decide to focus a specific text-critical project on 𝔐, but I propose that the goal of the general project labelled "textual criticism of the Hebrew Bible" is exactly that—textual criticism of the ancient Hebrew Bible, not of the Masoretic or, more accurately, the proto-Masoretic texts. And it must focus on the text of the ancient Hebrew Bible such as it was, namely, diachronic and pluriform. Thus the target of "textual criticism of the Hebrew Bible" is not a single text. The purpose or function of textual criticism is to reconstruct the history of the texts that eventually become the biblical collection in both its literary growth and its scribal transmission; it is not just to judge individual variants in order to determine which were "superior" or "original." "The original text" is a distracting con-

---

[29]   See n. 16.

cept for the Hebrew Bible;[30] in a very real sense, there was no "original text," at least none accessible, except for those relatively late parts contributed by redactors. Late layers or additions often have as much claim to being important tessarae in the biblical mosaic as do "original" or "early" elements of the developed text, since this cumulative aspect founds the nature of the biblical text from its very beginnings.

It is important to see the distinctions in the gradual development of Israel's "literature" into its becoming "scripture" and then its becoming "bible" or canon of scripture. And this development was different for the various books, or at least for various groups of books. In its early stages Israel's national religious literature was probably treated not very differently from the way other peoples treated their own national religious literature. Near the closing of the creative period, the Torah and the main Prophets had long since become "scripture," i.e., sacred and authoritative works, but their individual texts were still in a somewhat creative stage. The Writings were still mainly "literature" though some books would have been considered by some Jews as "scripture." The debates over Qoheleth and the Song highlight the important transition being made.

Recently, Lawrence Schiffman has proposed an alternate view of the nature of the biblical manuscripts from Qumran. His interpretation of the data leads to serious differences in judgments about the Qumran evidence: are "the biblical scrolls" truly biblical in our sense of the term, or are they only biblically related, or were they considered biblical by only one insignificant "sect"?

Here we have space to focus only on one example, *11QPs^a*.[31] This beautiful and extensive scroll from Cave 11 is regarded by Schiffman, following noted authorities in the earlier

---

[30]   The term is, of course, a valuable concept for works entirely composed by a single author, as is often the case in classical studies.

[31]   See the forthcoming treatment of the Psalms scrolls by Peter W. Flint, *The Dead Sea Psalms Scrolls and the Book of Psalms* (Leiden: Brill, 1995), which discusses *11QPs^a* more extensively.

generation of Qumran scholars, as nonbiblical.[32] He considers
11QPs^a a "liturgical" scroll, denying its biblical status. Earlier
scholars had rejected its biblical status for the following reasons:

a. It presents the biblical psalms in an order notably different from 𝔐, the *textus receptus.*

b. It has additional psalms not contained in 𝔐.

c. Within one biblical psalm (Psalm 146) it repeatedly adds
an antiphon not found in the 𝔐 version.

d. It has a prose composition near, but not at, the end of the
scroll.

e. The divine name is inscribed, not in the normal Jewish
("square") script, but in the paleo-Hebrew script.

In response I would say that the 𝔐 Psalter is by its very
nature a liturgical scroll and that all the above features are contained either in 𝔐 at other loci or in other manuscripts which are
undeniably biblical.

a. The 𝔐 text of Jeremiah is generally recognized as a secondarily revised edition of the book as found in 𝔊, and it presents major blocks of the book in a variant order.[33]

b. The Greek and especially Syriac Psalters include psalms
that were clearly originally Hebrew psalms but are not contained
in 𝔐.

c. The antiphon "Blessed be the Lord and blessed be his
name forever and ever" is totally derived from verse 1 of Psalm
146 and is systematically repeated in the identical manner in
which the antiphon "For his faithfulness endures for ever" is
repeated in Psalm 136 in 𝔐.

d. The prose composition, called "David's Compositions,"
is an explicit claim to scriptural status for the Psalter and may
have functioned as a colophon found at the end of this collection
at an earlier stage. It records that David composed all his psalms

---

[32] Schiffman, *Reclaiming the Dead Sea Scrolls*, 165–69, 178–80.
[33] See the commentaries and Emanuel Tov, "Some Aspects of the
Textual and Literary History of the Book of Jeremiah," in *Le livre de
Jérémie: Le prophète et son milieu, les oracles et leur transmission*, ed.
P.-M. Bogaert (Leuven: Leuven University Press, 1981), 145–67.

"by prophecy that was given to him from before the Most High,"[34] and it is through "prophecy" that it makes the transition from being the hymnbook of the Temple to being scripture, i.e., an integral part of the "Law and the Prophets." This passage follows the song (also found in 2 Samuel 23:[1–]7), the "Last Words of David," which speaks of "the man raised on high, the anointed of the God of Jacob, and the sweet singer of Israel." In turn, the "Last Words of David" follows Psalms 149 and 150 and the closing "Hymn to the Creator." Later, a few more related passages were added (as happened at the end of the books of Samuel, Isaiah, Amos, etc.). And in fact, *11QPs^a* ends with the same extra Psalm 151 with which the ⑥ Psalter ends. In sum, the problem with Schiffman's conclusions is that current evidence challenges earlier judgments about the character of biblical texts.

e. The use of the paleo-Hebrew script for the divine name in a text principally written in the Jewish script had earlier been viewed as a sign that the text was not biblical. As with the previous points, that view was understandable in light of the early evidence, but it should be laid to rest now that a number of scrolls, all judged to be biblical, and one (*4QIsa^c*) indisputably biblical, have attested the practice. I will close by describing several of these scrolls (see plates 1 and 2):[35]

1. *11QPs^a*: The top two lines contain the end of Psalm 134. After a paragraph break Psalm 151 begins; the empty leather to the left shows that the manuscript ended with the same "extra" psalm with which the Greek Psalter concludes. The first word at the top right corner is the Tetragrammaton written in the ancient paleo-Hebrew script, found also three words to the left, as well as the third and fifth words in the next line, and the second word in the last line shown.

---

[34]   *DJD* 4:48 and pl. XVI.

[35]   Photographs courtesy of the Palestine Archaeological Museum, the Israel Antiquities Authority, Oxford University Press, Professor John C. Trever, and the American Schools of Oriental Research.

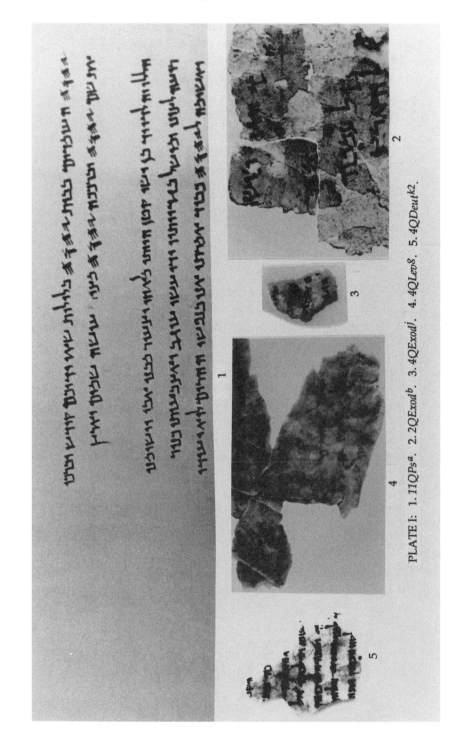

PLATE I: 1. 11QPs[a]. 2. 2QExod[b]. 3. 4QExod[j]. 4. 4QLev[g]. 5. 4QDeut[k2].

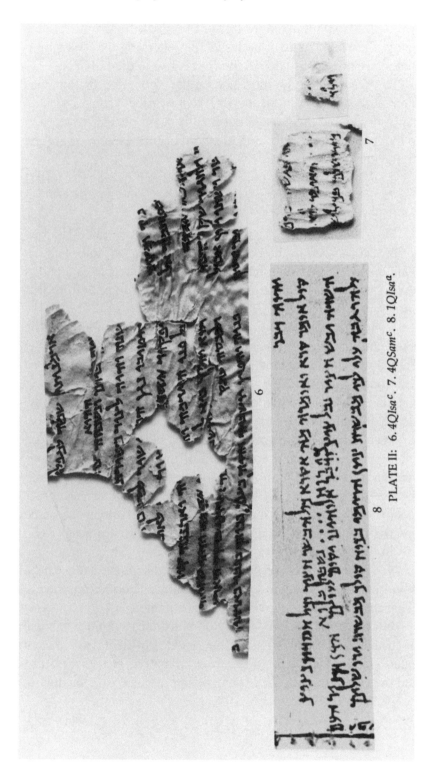

PLATE II: 6. 4QIsa^c. 7. 4QSam^c. 8. 1QIsa^a.

2. *2QExod^b*: In the third line of this small fragment (the line below the blank space), the last three letters of the Tetragrammaton are preserved, though the first is lost in the hole.

3. *4QExod^j*: In the third line, at the right edge of the fragment, only the left side of the final letter of the Tetragrammaton is preserved, but the three horizontal lines are distinctive enough to make the letter certain, and the word occurs exactly where the divine name is expected.

4. *4QLev^g*: This MS is difficult to read, but in the next-to-last line (above the number "4") the Tetragrammaton can be seen in the paleo-Hebrew script.

5. *4QDeut^{k2}*: The Tetragrammaton in the paleo-Hebrew script can be seen in the center of the next-to-last line. This MS contains text from Deuteronomy 19–26, which indicates that it is a MS of the book of Deuteronomy, not merely excerpts from that book.

6. *4QIsa^c*: At the end of the third line in the column to the right, and in lines seven and nine in the column to the left, the Tetragrammaton is written in the paleo-Hebrew script. This is a generously preserved MS, with portions of chapters 9–55 extant, and parts of two contiguous columns are displayed to show clearly that this is indeed a full biblical MS.

7. *4QSam^c*: The scribe of this biblical MS employed an analogous device—four dots in lieu of the four letters—for preventing the pronunciation of the divine name. In the small fragment at the right three of the dots can be seen before the fragment breaks off, losing the fourth, and further along the same line the phenomenon recurs, though here the first dot has been lost in the lacuna, and so again only three dots can be seen.

8. *1QIsa^a*: Above the third line pictured here the same scribe who penned *4QSam^c* inserted a supralinear correction, clearly using the four dots to replace the divine name.

In conclusion *4QIsa^c* clearly demonstrates within a biblical MS in the regular Jewish script the practice of using the ancient paleo-Hebrew script for the Tetragrammaton, just as *4QSam^c* and the correction in *1QIsa^a* demonstrate the use of four dots in biblical ᴍss. This and the arguments above press for the revision of earlier views and the acceptance of *11QPsᵃ* as a truly biblical manuscript, though a variant edition, of the Psalter. *11QPsᵃ* and the other manuscripts described above should be viewed as variant forms of the multiple literary editions of the biblical books which had full claim to being authoritative scripture.

4QSam^a and the Tetragrammaton

DONALD W. PARRY

Brigham Young University

During the past four decades students of the Dead Sea Scrolls have witnessed a fair amount of activity with regard to divine names in the texts of the Judean desert. It is generally well known, for instance, that the Qumran sectarians employed various surrogates for the Tetragrammaton to set it apart from common words, to protect it from erasure, or to alert a reader lest he pronounce the divine name while reading it.[1] Surrogates

---

I am most thankful to Professor Eugene Ulrich for reviewing this paper in its final stages and to Professor Frank Moore Cross for permitting me to assist him with the *4QSam* texts, to be published in *DJD* 17. This paper is an outgrowth of my study of *4QSam*. I alone, however, am responsible for the contents of this article.

[1]   See for instance, Lawrence H. Schiffman, "The Use of Divine Names," in Schiffman, *Sectarian Law in the Dead Sea Scrolls* (Chico, Cal.: Scholars Press, 1983), 133–54; Jonathan P. Siegel, "The Employment of Palaeo-Hebrew Characters for the Divine Names at Qumran in the Light of Tannaitic Sources," *HUCA* 42 (1971): 159–72; George Howard, "The Tetragram and the New Testament," *JBL* 96 (1977): 63–83; Patrick W. Skehan, "The Qumran Manuscripts and Textual Criticism," in *Supplements to Vetus Testamentum IV* (Leiden: Brill, 1957), 148–60; Joseph M. Baumgarten, "A New Qumran Substitute for the Divine Name and Mishnah Sukkah 4.5," *Jewish Quarterly Review* 83 (July–October 1992): 1–5; Gerhard-Wilhelm Nebe, "Psalm 104, 11 aus Höhle 4 von Qumran (4Q Ps^d) und der Ersatz des Gottesnamens," *ZAW* 93 (1981): 284–90; Patrick W. Skehan, "The Divine Name at Qumran, in the Masada Scroll, and in the Septuagint," *Bulletin of the International Organization for Septuagint and*

used by the sectarians included dots in various settings; for example, two dots are located before the divine name in *4Q139*; and four dots indicate the presence of the Tetragrammaton at the quotation of Isaiah 40:3 in the *Community Rule*, in *4QTanhumim (4Q176), 1QIsa^a* at 40:7, *4QTest (4Q175),* and elsewhere.[2]

Hebrew characters have also been used as surrogates for the divine name (e.g., the characters אונ הו, located at the end of *4Q266*, are "clearly a substitution for the divine name," says Baumgarten).[3] Additionally, the strange combination of characters/surrogate הואהא, located in the *Community Rule* at 8:13, may represent an abbreviation for "He is the God."[4] A third and equally strange apparent surrogate is found in Ben Sira MS B, at 42:17, which reads נפלאות ייי, against the Masada scroll which

---

Cognate Studies 13 (1980): 14–44; H. P. Rüger, "הואהא-Er zur Deutung von 1QS 8 13–14," *Zeitschrift für die neutestamentliche Wissenschaft* 60 (1969): 142–44.

[2] See Howard, "The Tetragram and the New Testament," 67. Connected with this, Siegel, "The Employment of Palaeo-Hebrew Characters," 162, points out that the scribe of *11QPs^a* twice superfluously wrote the divine name, but then placed dots above and below, apparently canceling "them from reading, but not from existence, which would have been the case with erasure."

[3] Baumgarten, "A New Qumran Substitute," 3.

[4] Two curious surrogates for the divine name occur in the quotation of Isaiah 40:3 located at 8:13 of the *Community Rule*. The Isaiah passage reads "to go into the wilderness to prepare there the way of him"; *him* is spelled הואהא and may be an abbreviation of הוא האלהים, influenced by Isaiah 45:18. See Millar Burrows, *The Dead Sea Scrolls* (New York: Viking, 1955), 383, in which he translated הואהא as "the Lord." See also Sigmund Mowinckel, "The Name of the God of Moses," *HUCA* 32 (1961): 132; William H. Brownlee, *The Dead Sea Manual of Discipline: Translation and Notes* (New Haven, Conn.: BASOR, 1951), 33 n. 29; A. R. C. Leaney, *The Rule of Qumran and Its Meaning* (London: SCM, 1966), 222; Rüger, "הואהא-Er zur Deutung von 1QS 8 13–14," 142–44; Howard, "The Tetragram and the New Testament," 68.

reads נפלאתיו. According to Howard, "The pronominal suffix (*w*) appears to be a surrogate for the Tetragram."[5]

In a similar manner, the scribes frequently placed divine names in paleo-Hebrew characters,[6] and on occasion the attached suffixes and prefixes were also placed in paleo-Hebrew characters (e.g., *4QIsaᶜ* features the divine names Yhwh, Yhwh of Armies, and Elohenu in paleo-Hebrew script). *4Q161, 171,* and *183* use paleo-Hebrew script for the divine name (however, once in *171*, col. III, 1.5a, the divine name appears in square script) whereas *4Q158, 162, 163, 168, 169, 170, 173,* and *174* use the square script for the divine name. This was true, at times, of both biblical and nonbiblical materials. *4Q171 (4QpPsᵃ)* and *1QpHab* substitute the divine names Yhwh, and at times Elohim, in paleo-Hebrew script. Interestingly, the scribe of Psalm 135 placed Yhwh in paleo-Hebrew, but used the apocopated version Yah (יה) in the so-called Aramaic script. *4Q173,* frg. 5, citing Psalm 118:20, replaces ליהוה with לאל, written in awkward paleo-Hebrew script.[7] According to Gerhard-Wilhelm Nebe (after P. W. Skehan), a paleo-Hebrew *waw* is in one instance substituted for the Tetragrammaton in *4QPsᵈ* at Psalm 104:11.[8] However, Skehan misread this difficult passage, and, in fact, no paleo-Hebrew *waw* is found in this location.[9]

The use of the various divine name surrogates identified above also establishes that several of the scribes or authors of Qumran biblical commentaries (such as *1QpZeph* or *1QpHab*) preferred the name El in the commentary portion of texts, using

---

[5]   Howard, "The Tetragram and the New Testament," 69.

[6]   Siegel, "The Employment of Palaeo-Hebrew Characters," 163–64; Skehan, "The Divine Name at Qumran," 22–24. Writing divine names in paleo-Hebrew characters represents "a late phenomenon at Qumran," Skehan, "The Qumran Manuscripts and Textual Criticism," 151.

[7]   Skehan, "The Divine Name at Qumran," 27.

[8]   Nebe, "Psalm 104, 11 aus Höhle 4 von Qumran (4QPsᵈ)," 284–90.

[9]   I appreciate Eugene Ulrich's pointing this out to me in a private communication.

the Tetragrammaton only in the actual biblical quotations.[10] This is not the case in the legal texts—especially *1QS*, but including *MMT* and others—in which the authors avoided the Tetragrammaton not only in the newly written texts but also in the scriptural proof texts in which the Tetragrammaton normally appears.

In this paper I add to the ongoing discussion of the use of the divine name in the Qumran texts by examining the seventeen occasions[11] that one or more of the divine names Yhwh and Elohim appear as a variant reading in *4QSam^a*[12] (hereafter I will refer to *4QSam^a* as simply *4Q*) compared and contrasted with 𝔐 and 𝔊. I will examine the agreements and disagreements between *4Q* and the other two witnesses as well as the unique readings of divine names in *4Q*. Afterwards I will set forth the possible significance of my findings.

I now introduce and examine the seventeen variant readings of the divine name in *4Q*.

1. 1 Samuel 1:22

4Q [יהוה] וישב לפני

𝔐   וישב

𝔊   וישב

---

[10] See, for example, Howard, "The Tetragram and the New Testament," 66.

[11] In addition to the seventeen instances of variant readings identified in this paper, other divine name variants that belong outside the focus of this work exist. For instance, I will not deal with *plene* spelling versus defective spelling (see, for example, 1 Samuel 5:8, *4Q* אלוהי ישראל, versus 𝔐 אלהי ישראל). Other notable variants that will not be discussed in this paper include: In 1 Samuel 5:11, *4Q* and 𝔊 read "ark of the God of Israel" against 𝔐's reading "the hand of God." In 2 Samuel 6:2=1 Chronicles 13:6, a copiest corrected *4Q* by superimposing a *dalet* between the *waw* and the *he* in the word ליהוה, thus creating ליהו̇ה, producing general agreement between the textual witnesses. Also in the same verse *4Q* reads יהוה against 𝔐 and 𝔊, which read יהוה צבאות (but in 1 Chronicles 13:6, 𝔐 and 𝔊 read יהוה); on this passage see Eugene Ulrich, *The Qumran Text of Samuel and Josephus* (Missoula, Mont.: Scholars Press, 1978), 66.

[12] Notable variant readings of divine names also exist in *4QSam^b* (see 1 Samuel 23:10, in which *4QSam^b* and 𝔊 add the Tetragrammaton) and *4QSam^c* (see 2 Samuel 14:13).

Cross,[13] Tov,[14] and McCarter[15] reconstruct *4Q* to read
[יהוה] וישב לפני. The phrase *before Yhwh* is a well-known formula that is attached to textual pericopes dealing with the Mosaic
Tabernacle and Israelite Temples.[16] Here the phrase, superflu-
ous in its present position, is a secondary expansion, most likely
based on 1 Samuel 1:11 [לפניך *(4Q), ליהוה (𝔐)*]. Hence *lectio
brevior.* Compare 2 Samuel 7:18=1 Chronicles 17:16, where the
record declares, concerning King David, וישב לפני יהוה.

2.   1 Samuel 2:1

4Q   ביהוה

𝔐   ביהוה

𝔊   באלהי (εν θεω μου)

According to Cross, *4Q* "reads ביהוה in the second colon
with 𝔐, though 𝔊 באלהי (εν θεω μου) obviously is original."[17]

3.   1 Samuel 2:10

4Q   [מי ק]דוש כיהוה

𝔐   lacking

𝔊   יהוה קדוש (κυριος αγιος)

The reconstructed reading of *4Q* is influenced by 𝔊, which
reads "Yhwh is holy"[18] (cf. 1 Samuel 2:2, "For there is no holy
one like Yhwh"). *4Q* and 𝔊 likely reflect the original reading;[19]

---

[13]   Frank Moore Cross, "A New Qumran Biblical Fragment Related to
the Original Hebrew underlying the Septuagint," *Bulletin of the American
Schools of Oriental Research* 132 (December 1953): 18.

[14]   Emanuel Tov, *Textual Criticism of the Hebrew Bible*
(Minneapolis, Minn.: Fortress, 1992), 114.

[15]   P. Kyle McCarter, Jr., *I Samuel: A New Translation with Introduction and Commentary* (New York: Doubleday, 1980), 56.

[16]   Menahem Haran, *Temples and Temple Service in Ancient Israel*
(Winona Lake, Ind.: Eisenbrauns, 1985), 26.

[17]   Cross, "A New Qumran Biblical Fragment," 20.

[18]   Compare McCarter, *I Samuel*, 70, and Julius Wellhausen, *Der
Text der Bücher Samuelis* (Göttingen: Vandenhoeck und Ruprecht, 1871),
44.

[19]   It is noteworthy that hymns belonging to the historical books
(i.e., Judges 5; 1 Samuel 2:1–10; 2 Samuel 22; Jonah 2:3–10; 1 Chronicles

𝔐 (also Syr, V) omits the phrase, lost perhaps through haplography. For the interrogation in *4Q* as part of a religious song, cf. the Song of Moses (Exodus 15:11).

4. 1 Samuel 2:25

4Q אל יהוה

𝔐 אלהים

𝔊 אל יהוה (προς Κυριου)

The verse contains several corruptions.[20] It is possible, as McCarter suggests, that in 𝔊 and "so probably *4QSam^a* ʾlhym evidently was read ʾl yhwh (a likely corruption because of the virtual identity of w and y in MSS of the Hasmonaean and Herodian periods)."[21]

5. 1 Samuel 5:11

4Q [מ]המת יהׁוה

𝔐 מהומת מות also 𝔐 𝔊^{OLC} Syr ⅅ ℭ.

𝔊 מהמה 𝔊^B (συγχυσις)

LXX^B presents the shortest reading "panic" (cf. vs. 5:6) while most witnesses (𝔐, Syr, Targ, Vulg) expand this reading to "panic of death." The reading of *4Q* stands alone with its use of the Tetragrammaton, combined with the construct form of מהמה, resulting in "panic of Yhwh." 𝔊, with its shorter reading, may be original, with "panic of death" and "panic of Yhwh" representing secondary expansions. 𝔐 may have accepted the reading "panic of death," influenced by ולא ימית in the immediate context.[22] It is also possible, however, that the reading of *4Q* is original in its presentation of the divine name while 𝔐, for

---

16:8–36) use only the name Yhwh; M. H. Segal, "El, Elohim, and YHWH in the Bible," *Jewish Quarterly Review* 46 (October 1955): 104.

[20] On this see Wellhausen, *Der Text der Bücher Samuelis*, 47, and Otto Thenius, *Die Bücher Samuels* (Leipzig: Hirzel, 1864), 13.

[21] McCarter, *I Samuel*, 82.

[22] Yet another possibility exists with regard to 𝔐's reading. Ulrich, in a private communication dated 29 November 1995, suggested that the phrase מהומת מות may be original, having reference to Mot, the god of death in the Canaanite pantheon of deities (cf. Isaiah 28:15).

theological reasons,[23] dropped the divine name and altered the text. The phrase *panic of Yhwh* is not unique; it is attested in Zechariah 14:13.

6.   1 Samuel 6:3

4Q   [ארון] ברית יהוה אלוהי ישראל

ℳ   ארון   אלהי ישראל

𝕲   ארון ברית יהוה אלוהי ישראל (κιβωτον διαθηκης Κυριου Θεου Ἰσραηλ)

4Q and 𝕲 present the longer reading with the addition of the phrase *covenant of Yhwh*. The entire chain of constructs reads "the ark of the covenant of Yhwh, the God of Israel." A close equivalent of the phrase *the ark of the God of Israel* is unique to Samuel's writings (1 Samuel 5:7–8; 5:10–11; 6:3). The plus of *4Q* and 𝕲 represents a secondary reading.[24]

7.   1 Samuel 6:5

4Q   [ליהוה כבוד]

ℳ   לאלוהי ישראל כבוד

𝕲   ליהוה כבוד (τω Κυριω δοξαν)

The reconstruction of *4Q* is speculative. I have based it on 𝕲 rather than ℳ, because the space on the fragment is insufficient to reconstruct *4Q* to read לאלוהי ישראל כבוד, as attested in the reading of ℳ.

8.   1 Samuel 6:20

4Q   יהוה   הקדוש

ℳ   יהוה האלהים הקדוש

𝕲   יהוה האלהים הקדוש

𝕲[B]   הקדוש

---

[23]   As suggested by Ulrich, *The Qumran Text of Samuel and Josephus*, 123–24.

[24]   However, Ulrich points out that "in addition to the visible plus *brit Yahweh* in common with G, 4Q probably preserves with G the *atem* glaringly absent (by haplography) from M," Ulrich, *The Qumran Text of Samuel and Josephus*, 51.

𝕲ᴮ הקדוש הזה ("this holy thing") presents the shortest reading, with the demonstrative pronoun הזה possibly modifying ארון, a masculine, singular noun. *4Q* expands the phrase to include the name Yhwh ("this holy Yhwh") and 𝔐 and 𝕲 present the longest reading with "this holy Yhwh God." The readings of *4Q*, 𝔐, and 𝕲 are not attested elsewhere in the Hebrew Bible and should be considered secondary readings.

9.   1 Samuel 6:20

4Q   [את ארון יהוה]

𝔐   lacking 𝔐 𝕮 𝕯

𝕲   את ארון יהוה (κιβωτος Κυριου)

Otto Thenius says that the expression on את ארון יהוה, already appearing in 1 Samuel 6:8, 11, 15, 18 (as well as 1 Samuel 6:21; 7:1), is "almost obligatory" in this position.[25]

10.   1 Samuel 10:26

4Q   יה[ו]ה בלבבם

𝔐   אלהים בלבם

𝕲   יהוה בלבבם (Κυριος καρδιας αυτων)

4Q reads with 𝕲, "whose hearts Yhwh had touched," against 𝔐, "whose hearts God had touched." It is likely that the reading of 𝔐 represents the later strand.

11.   1 Samuel 11:9

4Q   מיהוה התש[ו]עה

𝔐   תשועה

𝕲   תשועה (σωτηρια)

"Tomorrow . . . deliverance from Yhwh will be yours." The existence of the Tetragrammaton in *4Q* may indicate an original reading. But, more likely, the divine name represents a secondary plus created by a scribe in anticipation of Samuel's promise recorded in verse 13 that "on this day no man shall be put to death, for today *Yhwh* has brought deliverance to Israel."

---

[25]   Thenius, *Die Bücher Samuels*, 27.

12. 1 Samuel 23:14

4Q   יה[ו]ה

𝔐   אלהים

𝔊   יהוה (κυριος)

𝔐 uses the appellative Elohim in the statement, "and Saul sought [David] continually, but God did not give him over to his hand," against *4Q* and 𝔊, which employ the Tetragrammaton, "but Yhwh did not give him over to his hand." The reading of 𝔐 may indicate a tendency to replace the Tetragrammaton.

13. 1 Samuel 23:16

4Q   ב[יהו]ה

𝔐   באלהים

𝔊   ביהוה (εν κυριω)

4Q and 𝔊 use the divine name in the following sentence: "And Jonathan, the son of Saul, arose and went to David at Horesh, and strengthened his hand by Yhwh." According to 𝔐, Jonathan's hand was strengthened "by Elohim." Similar to 1 Samuel 23:14, 𝔐 reads Elohim against *4Q* and 𝔊, Yhwh.

14. 2 Samuel 5:10=1 Chronicles 11:9

4Q   יהוה צבאות (Sam), יהוה צבאות (Chronicles)

𝔐   יהוה אלהי צבאות

𝔊   יהוה צבאות (Κυριος Σαβαωθ)

𝔐 reads "and David grew greater and greater, and Yhwh, God of Armies was with him." Both *4Q* and 𝔊 lack the term *God* to read "Yhwh of Armies." The shorter reading of *4Q* and 𝔊 is to be preferred, since the reading "Yhwh, God of Armies" is attested only here in Samuel, although the expression is often present elsewhere in the Hebrew Bible.

15. 2 Samuel 6:3=1 Chronicles 13:6

4Q   יהו[ה]

𝔐   האלוהים (Samuel) האלהים (Chronicles)

𝔊   יהוה (Κυριου) (Chronicles 𝔊=אלוהים)

The entire verse is full of uncertainties, and much scribal activity is present throughout. Most textual critics from Thenius to Barthélemy note a dittography of six words in 𝔐 in verses 3b–4a, beginning with חדשה—the final word of verse 3—and continuing to בגבעה of verse 4. In any case, note the use of האלוהים in both Samuel and Chronicles by 𝔐, rather than the יהוה in *4Q* and 𝔊.

16. 2 Samuel 7:23

4Q ואהלים

𝔐 ואלהיו

𝔊 ואהלים (και σκηνωματα)

A transposition of the letters *he* and *lamed* explains the error shared by *4Q* and 𝔊, incorrectly reading "and tents," against 𝔐's reading of "and its gods."[26] The shared error "is again proof of the highest calibre for close textual affiliation" between the two texts.[27]

17. 2 Samuel 12:15

4Q אלוהים

𝔐 יהוה

𝔊 יהוה (κυριος)

4Q, against the reading of both 𝔐 and 𝔊, reads God in the phrase "Nathan went home to his house, and God afflicted the child which the wife of Uriah had bore to David."

This study points out the range of use of the divine name in the texts of Samuel represented in *4Q*, against 𝔐 and 𝔊 (see table 1). The data that I have presented above may be examined in such a way to show agreements and disagreements between *4Q* and the other two textual witnesses, as well as unique readings

---

[26] On this see Thenius, *Die Bücher Samuels*, 177; Ulrich, *The Qumran Text of Samuel and Josephus,* 71, 161–62; McCarter, *I Samuel*, 235; and S. R. Driver, *Notes on the Hebrew Text of the Books of Samuel* (Oxford: Clarendon, 1890), 214.

[27] Ulrich, *The Qumran Text of Samuel and Josephus*, 71.

in any of the three witnesses. The data may be arranged into four groups: *4Q*=𝔊≠𝔐, *4Q*≠𝔊≠𝔐, *4Q*≠𝔊=𝔐, and *4Q*=𝔐≠𝔊.

Table 1. Use of Divine Names in *4QSam*, 𝔐, and 𝔊.

	4QSam	𝔐	𝔊
1 S 1:22	[יהוה] וישב לפני	וישב	וישב
1 S 2:1	ביהוה	ביהוה	באלהי
1 S 2:10	[מי ק]דוש כיהוה]	lacking	יהוה קדוש
1 S 2:25	אל יהוה	אלהים	אל יהוה
1 S 5:11	[מ]המת יהוֹה	מהומת מות	מהמה
1 S 6:3	יהוה אלוהי ישראל	אלהי ישראל	יהוה אלוהי ישראל
1 S 6:5	[ליהוה כבוד]	לאלוהי ישראל כבוד	ליהוה כבוד
1 S 6:20	יהוה הקדוש	יהוה האלהים הקדוש	יהוה האלהים הקדוש
1 S 6:20	[את ארון יהוה]	lacking	את ארון יהוה
1 S 10:26	יהֹ[ו]הֹ בלבבם	אלהים בלבם	יהוה בלבבם
1 S 11:9	מ]יהוה התש[ו]עה	תשועה	תשועה
1 S 23:14	יה[ו]ה	אלהים	יהוה
1 S 23:16	[ביהו]ה	באלהים	ביהו[ה]
2 S 5:10	יהוה צבאות	יהוה אלהי צבאות	יהוה צבאות
2 S 6:3	יהו[ה]	האלוהים (האלוהים Chronicles)	אלוהים L; יהוה OG
2 S 7:23	ואהלים	ואלהיו	ואהלים
2 S 12:15	אלוהים	יהוה	יהוה

4Q=𝔊≠𝔐. On seven occasions *4Q* and 𝔊 read Yhwh against 𝔐, which reads Elohim (1 Samuel 2:25; 6:3; 6:5; 10:26; 23:14; 23:16; 2 Samuel 6:3). On three additional occasions *4Q* and 𝔊 feature Yhwh while 𝔐 lacks a divine name (1 Samuel 2:10; 6:3; 6:20). In one instance, *4Q* and 𝔊 read Yhwh Sebaoth, while 𝔐 presents the longer formula Yhwh Elohay Sebaoth (2 Samuel 5:10). In 2 Samuel 7:23, both *4Q* and 𝔊 share the same error, reading "tents" against the correct reading of 𝔐, which has "its gods."

4Q≠𝔊≠𝔐. In three instances *4Q* reads Yhwh, but 𝔐 and 𝔊 lack a divine name (1 Samuel 1:22; 5:11; 11:9).

4Q≠𝔊=𝔐. In 2 Samuel 12:15, *4Q* reads Elohim, while 𝔐 and 𝔊 read Yhwh.

4Q=𝔐≠𝔊. On one occasion *4Q* and 𝔐 read Yhwh against 𝔊, which reads Elohim (1 Samuel 2:1).

A summary of the agreements, disagreements, and unique reading of the witnesses with regard to the seventeen verses under discussion demonstrates that on twelve occasions *4Q=𝔊≠𝔐*, on three occasions *4Q≠𝔊≠𝔐*, once *4Q≠𝔊=𝔐*, and once *4Q=𝔐≠𝔊*. In other words, *4Q* agrees with 𝔊 twelve times against the reading of 𝔐, *4Q* agrees with 𝔐 once against the reading of 𝔊, and *4Q* stands independent (against 𝔊, 𝔐) with four of its readings.

Conclusions

1. It is most significant that *4Q* provides four independent readings. This attests to the individuality of *4Q* and demonstrates that *4Q* is neither a Masoretic nor a septuagintal text (although *4Q* does stand closer to 𝔊 than to 𝔐; see section 2 below); while *4Q* may share the same family lineage (*Vorlage*) as 𝔊, it is not identical with 𝔊. Three of *4Q*'s four independent readings comprise pluses of the Tetragrammaton not attested in either 𝔊 or 𝔐. The three pluses are almost certainly secondary (see my comments above) and would then indicate a revisional layer on the part of the scroll's editor in which the Tetragrammaton was added for elucidatory purposes, perhaps to clarify the referent or antecedent. Certainly *4Q*'s scribe did not hesitate to use the Tetragrammaton frequently. On three occasions he uses it independently of either 𝔐 or 𝔊, but, in addition, he employs the Tetragrammaton a number of times in agreement with 𝔊, against 𝔐, which prefers the name Elohim (on this, see section 3 below).

It also appears that *4Q*'s scribe permitted his socioreligious background to persuade him to add the Tetragrammaton on the three occasions mentioned above. Note that a common theological concept belongs to each of the three pluses—Yhwh, the God of Israel, takes on an active role in the lives of the Israelite nation, the Israelite prophet, and the enemy of Israel, the Philistines. In the first verse, Samuel is not simply sitting by himself; he is sitting "before Yhwh" (1:22), an expression that recalls the power of the temple experience and Yhwh's presence there. In the second verse, the dreaded panic experienced by the Philistines is not due simply to human frailty; rather, the panic originates from Yhwh (5:11). He is an active force in the defeat of Israel's enemies. In the third verse, it is not simply that deliverance for Israel will come because of chance or the deeds of the arm of flesh, but deliverance comes specifically from Yhwh (11:9). Yhwh, then, as he appears in these three scriptures, is active in the life of the boy-prophet of Israel, Samuel; causes havoc in the lives of the fearful enemies of Israel, the Philistines; and, finally, brings deliverance to Israel.

The fourth independent reading is found in 2 Samuel 12:15, in which *4Q* features Elohim against 𝔊 and 𝔐, which use Yhwh.

2. The fact that *4Q* and 𝔊 are in agreement twelve times in their representation of the divine name lends support to the observation made by Cross more than forty years ago, under the title "A New Qumran Biblical Fragment Related to the Original Hebrew Underlying the Septuagint."[28] In that article Cross wrote: "We conclude that our fragment *(4QSamᵃ)* stands in the same general tradition as the Hebrew text upon which the Septuagint was based. The divergences between *4Q* and 𝔊 are sufficiently explained by the century or so between the translation of Samuel into Greek, and the copying of our MS, during which time some cross-fertilization certainly took place between Hebrew textual traditions current in Palestine."[29] Subsequent

---

[28] Cross, "A New Qumran Biblical Fragment," 15–26.
[29] Ibid., 23.

studies have found general support for this thesis;[30] it is therefore not necessary in this paper to review what has already been
said.

3. One can see certain tendencies in sections of the Hebrew
Bible to favor the epithet Elohim over the Tetragrammaton,[31]
presumably for theological reasons. An examination of the book
of Chronicles reveals that the Chronicler preferred Elohim "even
where his sources (e.g., Samuel and Kings) had employed the
divine name YHWH."[32] The Elohistic psalms (chs. 42–83)
show a marked preference for the divine name Elohim rather
than Yhwh, a noticeably different approach over the remaining
psalms (chs. 1–41; 84–150), which frequently use the Tetragrammaton throughout. It has been suggested on more than one
occasion that a redactor, perhaps connected with the Jerusalem
temple cult, reworked Psalms 42–83 and for pious reasons frequently substituted Elohim for Yhwh.[33]

---

[30] See, for example, Ulrich, *The Qumran Text of Samuel and
Josephus*, passim; Ulrich, "4QSamᵃ and Septuagintal Research," *Bulletin of
the International Organization for Septuagint and Cognate Studies* 8 (1975):
24–39; Emanuel Tov, "The Textual Affiliations of 4QSamᵃ," *JSOT* 14
(1979): 37–53.

[31] I note, however, that not all religious texts prefer the epithet
Elohim. For the author(s) of Proverbs, Yhwh is the preferred name, used
scores of times against Elohim, which is found only three times. In addition, it is clear that the name YHW was the preference of divine names for
the Elephantine Jews, used in its absolute state as well as in a host of theo-
phoric names. Bezalel Porten, *Archives from Elephantine* (Berkeley: University of California Press, Berkeley, 1968), 134–45. Porten asserts that "El
is completely absent from the Elephantine onomasticon," 135.

[32] Segal, "El, Elohim, and YHWH in the Bible," 100; in connection
with this, Alexander Rofé detects that the Chronicler omits the name
Sebaoth in "three otherwise verbatim quotations from Samuel (1 Chronicles
13:6; 16:2; 17:25)," Alexander Rofé, "The Name YHWH Sebaoth and the
Shorter Recension of Jeremiah," *Prophetie und geschichtliche Wirklichkeit
im alten Israel: Festschrift für Siegfried Herrmann*, ed. R. Liwak and S.
Wagner (Stuttgart: Kohlhammer, 1991), 309.

[33] "The preponderance of Elohim in those psalms cannot be original,"
states Segal, "El, Elohim, and YHWH in the Bible," 94, 104–5, because

With two notable exceptions (Job 12:9; 28:28), the poetic sections of Job lack the Tetragrammaton in favor of other divine names.[34] In a similar manner Yhwh is not attested in the book of Daniel with the exception of the prayer of Daniel (Daniel 9); both the books of Daniel and Qohelet prefer the epithet Elohim or ha-Elohim.[35] The tendency to prefer the name Elohim also occurs in the memoirs of both Ezra (Ezra 7:27–10:17) and Nehemiah (Nehemiah 1–6; 12:27–13:31); here it is appropriate to mention that neither of the divine names—Yhwh or Elohim—is used in the Song of Songs or the book of Esther.[36]

Exactly how much credit may be attached to scribal activity for the preference of the epithet Elohim over the name Yhwh in certain Hebrew texts is unclear; neither is it clear why the divine names Yhwh and Elohim are not found in the Song of Songs or Esther. Certainly one can see choices in this regard being made by the hand of the Chronicler as well as by the redactor of the Elohist psalms. The chief purpose for the preference for Elohim is somewhat more evident. Segal summarizes the prevailing view of scholars concerning the avoidance of the Tetragrammaton when he argues that during the postexilic period

> a heightened sense of the sanctity of the deity and of the
> sacredness of its own proper name led to the avoidance
> of a too-frequent employment of the name Yhwh which

---

the Psalmist would not have employed the awkward expressions *Elohim my Elohim* (Psalm 43:4) and *Elohim your Elohim* (Psalm 45:8). On the Elohistic psalms, see also G. H. Parke-Taylor, *Yahweh: The Divine Name in the Bible* (Waterloo, Ont.: Wilfred Laurier University Press, 1975), 8–9; G. F. Moore, *Judaism I* (Cambridge: Harvard University Press, 1930), 424; G. F. Moore, *Judaism III* (Cambridge: Harvard University Press, 1930), 127; cf. Skehan, "The Divine Name at Qumran," 20.

[34]   Skehan, "The Divine Name at Qumran," 20; Robert Gordis, *Poets, Prophets, and Sages: Essays in Biblical Interpretation* (Bloomington, Ind.: Indiana University Press, 1971), 167.

[35]   Parke-Taylor, *Yahweh: The Divine Name in the Bible,* 8; Segal, "El, Elohim, and YHWH in the Bible," 101.

[36]   Skehan, "The Divine Name at Qumran," 20–21; Gordis, *Poets, Prophets, and Sages: Essays in Biblical Interpretation*, 167.

gradually became ineffable, and to its replacement by a synonymous substitute. The first stage in this tendency was the revival of the use of Elohim which appears clearly in the book of Chronicles.[37]

This study adds yet another strand of information regarding the use of the Tetragrammaton in biblical texts. I have juxtaposed two biblical texts (*4Q* and 𝔐's version of Samuel), making contrasts and comparisons. I have also examined 𝔊, a third textual witness, in light of *4Q* and 𝔐. The findings suggest that 𝔐, compared with *4Q* and 𝔊, prefers the epithet Elohim over Yhwh.

Reviewing the seventeen variant readings listed above, 𝔐 lacks the Tetragrammaton on two occasions against *4Q* and 𝔊, which read Yhwh (1 Samuel 2:10; 6:20); 𝔐 prefers Elohim on six occasions against *4Q* and 𝔊, which prefer Yhwh (1 Samuel 2:25; 6:5; 10:26; 23:14; 23:16; 2 Samuel 6:3); 𝔐 (and 𝔊, as discussed above in section 1) lacks the Tetragrammaton on three occasions in which *4Q* reads it (1 Samuel 1:22; 5:11; 11:9); in addition, in the phrase "Yhwh, the God of Israel" attested in 1 Samuel 6:3 (*4Q*, 𝔊), 𝔐 lacks the Tetragrammaton with the reading "the God of Israel." To sum up, of the seventeen variant readings, 𝔐 avoids or lacks the Tetragrammaton on twelve occasions. If one discounts the three secondary pluses belonging to *4Q* in which the name Yhwh appears to have been added, we are still left with nine occasions when 𝔐 either lacks or has substituted for the Tetragrammaton. Compare this with the one occasion where 𝔐 reads Yhwh against *4Q*, which reads Elohim (2 Samuel 12:15).

Does this suggest an avoidance of the Tetragrammaton on the part of 𝔐's version of Samuel? The evidence does not necessarily point to an avoidance, but certainly one can see preferences being made by the textual witnesses for divine names. I have attempted to demonstrate above that 𝔐 often uses the epithet Elohim, against *4Q* and 𝔊's frequent use of Yhwh. My con-

---

[37] Segal, "El, Elohim, and YHWH in the Bible," 100.

clusions, set forth in 1 and 2 above, establish that *4Q* used
Yhwh on three occasions independently of ⅏ or ⅏; also, *4Q* and
⅏ preferred Yhwh on twelve occasions when ⅏ lacked the name
or used Elohim.

One other method of testing my results, knowing that the
texts of *4Q* represent only 10 percent of the extant portions of
the book of Samuel,[38] is to compare the use of the divine names
Elohim and Yhwh in ⅏ and ⅏'s witnesses of the entire text of
Samuel. This I have done below in table 2.[39] A review of the
data shown in the table demonstrates that ⅏ uses the name
Elohim more frequently than ⅏, which in turn seems to show a
preference for the Tetragrammaton. However, this wholesale
approach (without reviewing each attested variant in some detail)
tends to provide imprecise results that can lead to a warped picture.

Table 2. Use of Divine Names in ⅏ and ⅏.

1 Samuel	⅏	⅏
1:6	Κυριος (2 times)	יהוה (1 time)
1:8	Κυριε	lacking
1:9	ενωπιον Κυριου	lacking
1:11	Κυριω	lacking
	lacking	ליהוה
1:14	Κυριου	lacking
1:20	Κυριου Θεου Σαβαωθ	מיהוה
1:21	Σηλαμ	ליהוה
1:24	Κυριου	lacking
2:1	Θεω	ביהוה
	Θεος	lacking
2:8	lacking	ליהוה
2:10	Κυριος (3 times) + Κυριον (1 time)	יהוה (2 times) + משיחו (1 time)

---

[38] On this estimate, see Ulrich, *The Qumran Text of Samuel and Josephus*, 257.

[39] I extend my appreciation to Jeanette W. Miller for her assistance in compiling the data found in table 2.

1 Samuel	𝕲	𝔐
2:14	Κυριω εν Σηλωμ	בשלה
2:23	Κυριου	lacking
2:24	Θεω	יהוה
2:25	Κυριον	אלהים
3:3	lacking	יהוה
3:7	Θεον	יהוה
3:9	lacking	יהוה
3:13	Θεον	lacking
3:21	Κυριος (2 times)	יהוה (3 times)
4:1	Κυριω	lacking
	Κυριου	lacking
4:3	Θεου	יהוה
4:22	Κυριου	האלהים
5:2	Κυριου	האלהים
5:3	Θεου	יהוה
	Κυριου	lacking
6:1	lacking	יהוה
6:2	Κυριου	אלהי
6:5	τω Κυριω	לאלהי ישראל
6:8	lacking	יהוה
6:13	Κυριου	lacking
6:20	Κυριου	lacking
7:13	Κυριος	lacking
10:1	Κυριου	lacking
10:2	Κυριος	lacking
10:26	Κυριος	אלהים
11:6	Κυριου	אלהים
12:14	Κυριον + Κυριου (2 times)	יהוה (2 times) + יהוה אלהיכם
12:23	τω Κυριω (2 times)	ליהוה (1 time)
13:13	Κυριος (2 times)	יהוה + יהוה אלהיך
14:3	Θεου	יהוה
14:15	Κυριου	אלהים
14:18	lacking	האלהים (2 times)
14:26	Κυριου	lacking
14:41	Κυριε ο Θεος (2 times)	יהוה אלהי (1 time)

1 Samuel 𝕲   𝔐

	𝕲	𝔐
14:42	Κυριος	lacking
15:13	τω Κυριω (2 times) + Κυριος	ליהוה (1 time) + יהוה
15:20	Κυριος (1 time)	יהוה (2 times)
15:23	Κυριου + Κυριος	יהוה (1 time)
15:25	Κυριω τω Θεω	ליהוה
16:7	Θεος (2 times)	ויהוה (1 time)
16:8	Θεος	יהוה
16:12	Κυριω	lacking
16:15	Κυριου	אלהים
16:16	lacking	אלהים
16:23	lacking	אלהים
17:47	Κυριος	lacking
18:12	lacking	יהוה
20:13	Θεος	יהוה
20:14	lacking	יהוה
21:2	Θεου	lacking
22:10	Θεου	ביהוה
22:18	Κυριου	lacking
23:9	Κυριου	lacking
23:14	Κυριος	אלהים
23:16	εν Κυριω	באלהים
26:8	Κυριος	אלהים
26:19	Θεος	יהוה
28:10	lacking	ביהוה
29:9	lacking	אלהים
30:23	Κυριον	lacking

2 Samuel 𝕲   𝔐

	𝕲	𝔐
1:12	lacking	יהוה
2:5	Κυριου	lacking
2:27	Κυριος	אלהים
5:10	Κυριος	יהוה אלהי צבאות
5:23	Κυριος	lacking
6:4	lacking	האלהים
6:7	Κυριου	האלהים

2 Samuel	𝕲	𝔐
6:12	Θεου + Κυριου	האלהים (2 times)
6:13	lacking	יהוה
6:16	lacking	יהוה
7:11	Κυριος (1 time)	יהוה (2 times)
7:18, 19, & 20	Κυριε μου Κυριε	אדני יהוה
7:22	Κυριε	יהוה אלהים
7:23	lacking	ואלהיו
7:25	Κυριε	יהוה אלהים
7:28	Κυριε μου Κυριε	אדני יהוה
7:29	Κυριε μου Κυριε	אדני יהוה
12:20	Θεου	יהוה
15:24	Κυριου	האלהים
15:31	Κυριε ο Θεος	יהוה
16:12	Κυριος (1 time)	יהוה (2 times)
22:8	Κυριος	lacking
22:31	lacking	האל
22:33	lacking	האל
22:48	Κυριος	האל
23:1	Κυριος	lacking
23:4	Κυριος	lacking
24:16	Θεου	lacking

Early Essene Eschatology: Judgment and Salvation *according to* Sapiential Work A

TORLEIF ELGVIN

Norwegian Lutheran School of Theology

Sapiential Work A presents us with previously unknown material that enriches our knowledge of the sapiential and apocalyptic traditions of the second century B.C.[1] This paper concentrates on the eschatology of this composition and discusses in detail two eschatological discourses that appear in the book.

I am indebted to the Research Council of Norway for financial support, and to cand. theol. Anders Aschim for valuable feedback. This article is partially paralleled by two other papers: "Wisdom, Revelation, and Eschatology in an Early Essene Writing" in *SBLSP* (1995), 440–63, and "The Mystery to Come: Early Essene Theology of Revelation" in *Qumran between the Old and the New Testament,* ed. Th. L. Thompson and N. P. Lemche (Sheffield University Press, forthcoming).

[1]   For an introduction to *Sap. Work A*, see my paper "Wisdom, Revelation, and Eschatology in an Early Essene Writing," which deals with the book's genre and community of origin as well as its relation to *1 Enoch*. See further Torleif Elgvin, "Admonition Texts from Qumran Cave 4," in *Methods of Investigation of the Dead Sea Scrolls and the Khirbet Qumran Site: Present Realities and Future Prospects*, ed. Michael O. Wise et al. (New York: New York Academy of Sciences, 1994), 179–96; Daniel J. Harrington, "Wisdom at Qumran," in *The Community of the Renewed Covenant: The Notre Dame Symposium on the Dead Sea Scrolls*, ed. Eugene Ulrich and James C. VanderKam (Notre Dame: University of Notre Dame Press, 1994), 137–52.

Sap. Work A is preserved in seven fragmentary copies, one from Cave 1 (*1Q26*) and six from Cave 4 (*4Q415, 416, 417, 418a, 418b, 423*).[2] Six copies display early Herodian script (30–1 B.C.), while one (*4Q423*) represents a late Herodian hand (A.D. 1–50). The large number of copies and the fact that this book was being copied even until a late stage in the history of the Qumran settlement show that it was highly regarded within the Essene Community.[3] Two of the copies (*4Q415* and *4Q416*) were rolled in a less common way with the beginning on the inside of the scroll when they were deposited the last time, a fact that probably indicates that these scrolls were still in active reading use by A.D 68.[4] I have elsewhere calculated the length of the book to be between 26,000 and 31,000 letter spaces and have located most of the major fragments within the original scrolls.[5]

Sap. Work A is a didactic book that provides instruction for man's relation to his fellowman and to God. Most of the book is an address to the wise and understanding individual in second person singular. Large parts of the book consist of wisdom sayings, often in proverbial form, that provide practical admonitions for life in family and society in areas of relations with parents, wife, and children; financial matters (loans and surety); working ethics (relations to superiors and subordinates); agri-

---

[2]   The Hebrew text of the various fragments is available in Ben Zion Wacholder and Martin G. Abegg, *A Preliminary Edition of the Unpublished Dead Sea Scrolls: The Hebrew and Aramaic Texts from Cave Four: Fascicle Two* (Washington: Biblical Archaeological Society, 1992). The *DJD* edition of *Sap. Work A* (by John Strugnell and Daniel Harrington; the present writer is responsible for one of the copies) is in preparation.

[3]   Further, probably only copies of the most important books were hidden in Cave 1. Hartmut Stegemann, *Die Essener, Qumran, Johannes der Täufer und Jesus*, 4th ed. (Freiburg: Herder, 1994), 89–90.

[4]   Torleif Elgvin, "The Reconstruction of Sapiential Work A," forthcoming in *RQ* 16/4 (1995).

[5]   Ibid. The original *4Q417* scroll contained between 17 and 20 columns, each of ca. 28 lines of 50–60 letter spaces. The length of this scroll was ca. 260 cm (± 30 cm).

cultural matters (seasons and festivals, sanctification of the first-born of the livestock), etc. A lengthy section with such material, approximately four consecutive columns, is preserved by the overlapping fragments *4Q417 1/4Q416 2* (this section probably covered columns III–VI in both scrolls).

Further, the book contains discourses which deal with eschatology and the revelation of God's mysteries to the elect. These discourses abound with apocalyptic material. An eschatological discourse on the coming judgment and the lots of the elect and the ungodly occupies two full columns of the book (*4Q416* VI 17–VIII 15 = *4Q416* frgs. 4, 1, 3). Another discourse that elaborates on the future judgment of the wicked and the salvation of the righteous occupies almost a full column (*4Q418* frg. 69). Exhortations which deal with the hope of the righteous are also interspersed with wisdom sayings. A lengthy discourse on the revelation of God's mysteries is followed by a fragmentarily preserved exhortation to praise the God who provides knowledge (*4Q417* frg. 2, probably cols. IX and X out of ca. 18 columns). Biblical verses are either alluded to or freely integrated in the running text of the admonitions, not introduced with quotation formulas.

Community and Milieu of Origin

The admonitions presuppose life in a regular society that also deals with outsiders, although the addressee is related to some kind of community. He has knowledge of the community's interpretation of the scriptures and God's mysteries and is exhorted to continue his meditation and study. The work does not reflect a hierarchically structured community, as the *yaḥad* does. Only two small passages deal with purity matters or priestly traditions.

The author/redactor seems to be a lay teacher who addresses "the enlightened," the members of his community. His advice is related to the everyday life situations of his readers—to the challenges posed by family life, business matters, finances, and job relations. At the same time he is occupied by eschatological issues: the hope of the righteous and his knowledge of the secrets of God shall provide perspective for his everyday situation, and he needs to be reminded of this. Although *Sap. Work A* is a literary product, the book reflects the experience of a teacher relating to a specific audience. The active use of a wide range of literary traditions points to scribal circles as the milieu of origin.

The idea of the remnant community as the true Israel is prominent.[6] The members are the elect ones, those who already enjoy God's pardon and favor; they are אנשי רצון (*4Q418* 81 10; cf. *1QS* VIII בחירי רצון, *1QHᵃ* IV 32–33, XI 9 בני רצונכה/רצונו, *4Q298* [*4QcrA Words of Sage to Sons of Dawn*] I 3–4 וי[ד]עים דר[ש]ו] א[לה והשיב[ו] א[נשי רצו[נו [לדרך] חיים, Luke 2:14 ἐν

---

[6] Cf. especially *4Q418* 81 1–14: [1]Open your lips as a fountain to bless the holy ones. And you, as an eternal fountain praise [ ]. He separated you from all [2]the spirit of flesh. <Hence> you shall separate from everyone He hates and keeps apart from all abominations of the spirit. [Fo]r He made everyone [3]and bequeathed them, each man his inheritance, and He is your portion and your inheritance among the sons of men. [In] His [inhe]ritance He gave you authority. And you, [4]honour Him for that when you sanctify yourself to Him. As He set you to sanctify the holy ones for all [ ], and among all[ ] [5]He cast your lot and greatly increased your glory, and set you as His firstborn in[His council (?). Did He]n[ot say to you (?)] [6]"My favour I will give you"? Is not His goodness yours? <So> walk always in His faithfulness[. . .] [7]your deeds. And you, seek His judgments. From the hands of all your opponents (?)[. . . He shows favour toward all who] [8]love Him and mercy and kindness toward all who keep His word and ob[serve His commandments. . . .] [9]He opened for you insig[ht], gave you authority over His storehouse and determined the accurate ephah [for you . . .] [10]they are with you. It is in your hands to turn aside wrath from the men of <His> favour and appoint[. . .] [11]with you. Before you take your portion from His hand, honour His holy ones, and be[fore you . . .] [12]He opened[a foun]tain <for> all the ho[ly] ones, all who by His name are called holy o[nes, . . . they will be] [13]for all the eras the splendours of His sprout, as an [ete]rnal planting [ ] [14]. . . will walk all those who will inherit the land, for by [His] name[are they called." For a closer discussion of this passage, see my paper "The Mystery to Come: Early Essene Theology of Revelation."

ἀνθρώποις εὐδοκίας). Similar to the Enochic books, *Sap. Work A* does not ascribe to the remnant community a clearly defined role in history as do later sectarian writings, although the designation מטעת עולם *eternal planting* (*4Q418* 81 13, *4Q423* 1–2 7; cf. Isaiah 60:21, 61:3) indicates that the community is the nucleus of the future restored Israel. In sectarian parlance the "planting," a tiny plant that will grow into a large tree that will cover the earth (Isaiah 60:21, Ezekiel 31), refers to the group of the elect, now few but destined to rule the world in the future.[7] The community behind *Sap. Work A* sees itself as the remnant and nucleus of Israel that represents a fulfillment of the prophecies in Isaiah 59–61.[8] Similar to *4QpPs^a* it draws upon Psalm 37, Proverbs 2:21–22, and passages from Trito-Isaiah

---

[7] *1QS* VIII 5–6, XI 8; *CD* I 7; *1QH^a* VI 15, VIII 4–26, cf. *1 Enoch* 10:16, 84:6, 93:5, 10; *Jubilees* 1:16, 36:6. On the imagery of the eternal plant in *QL* and rabbinic tradition, see Jaacov Licht, "The Plant Eternal and the People of Divine Deliverance" (in Hebrew), in *Essays on the Dead Sea Scrolls in Memory of E. L. Sukenik*, ed. Chaim Rabin and Yigael Yadin (Jerusalem: Hekhal ha–Sefer, 1961), 1–27; David Flusser, "He has planted it [i.e., the Law] as eternal life in our midst" (in Hebrew), *Tarbiz* 58 (1988–89): 147–53; Devorah Dimant, "Qumran Sectarian Literature," in *Jewish Writings of the Second Temple Period: Apocrypha, Pseudepigrapha, Qumran Sectarian Writings, Philo, Josephus*, ed. Michael E. Stone (Assen: Van Gorcum, 1984), 539.

[8] *4Q417* 1 i 10–11 rephrases Isaiah 61:3 and borrows שמחת עולם from Isaiah 61:7: "Gaze upon the mystery to come, understand the birth-times of salvation and know who will inherit glory and corruption. Will not[garland be given for their ashes] and eternal joy for their sorrow?" A similar use of this biblical verse is found in *1QH^a* XVIII 15. Isaiah 59–61 played an important role for the sectarians, and the same is reflected in *Sap. Work A*. The sectarians saw themselves as מטעת עולם "the eternal plant" of 60:21; 61:3 (*1QS* XI 8, *1QH^a* VI 15). They are the שבי פשע "the penitents" of 59:20 (cf. *CD* II 5) who long to see "the coming of the redeemer to Zion." They are the ענוים "the poor ones" of 61:1 that mourned for Zion and have a glorious future (ענו and אביון are common self-designations of the sectarians, *Sap. Work A* prefers אביון). The importance of Isaiah 61 is reflected in *11QMelch* and *4Q521* (*4QMessianic Apocalypse*). Cf. Naphtali Wieder, *The Judean Scrolls and Karaism* (London: East and West Library, 1962), 125–26.

for its teaching on the end-time; the ungodly will be annihilated, and the pious will inherit the land.[9]

The community is not described as a spiritual temple, and we do not encounter a hierarchically structured community. The remnant community is not connected to "the renewed covenant" or to a specific historical situation as in *CD*. There are no indications that the community or the individual is connected to a specific charismatic leader.

A number of phrases and motifs from the Hebrew sections of Daniel recur in *Sap. Work A,* especially those related to wisdom, revelation, and the elect.[10] As there is no clear literal dependence between Daniel and *Sap. Work A*, it seems probable that both are dependent on a common tradition. The circles behind *Sap. Work A* might be related to the *maskilim* of the book of Daniel,[11] although our book must be dated well after the persecution of Antiochus, as there are no references to any persecution of righteous Jews. Both books reflect scribal activity and a quest for divine communication; neither is concerned with the sacrificial cult of the temple.[12] In its eschatology *Sap. Work A* is apocalyptic, not restorative, which indicates a distance from the Maccabean/Hasmonean establishment.

---

[9]   Cf. Diethelm Michel, "Weisheit und Apokalyptik," in *The Book of Daniel in the Light of New Findings*, ed. Adam S. van der Woude (Leuven: Peeters, 1993), 413–34.

[10]   The most important are רז, יודע/דעת, להבין/מבין, השכיל/משכיל/שכל, גלה, קודש/קדוש/קדושים/קודשים, חרפה, חיי עולם, and קץ. It should be noted that *Sap. Work A* understands the word קץ as "period" like the sectarians, not as "end" like Daniel 8–12; see n. 62.

[11]   Cf. John J. Collins, "Was the Dead Sea Sect an Apocalyptic Movement?," in *Archaeology and History in the Dead Sea Scrolls: The New York University Conference in Memory of Yigael Yadin*, ed. Lawrence H. Schiffman (Sheffield: Sheffield Academic Press, 1990), 28–29.

[12]   Cf. Philip R. Davies, "Reading Daniel Sociologically," in *The Book of Daniel in the Light of New Findings*, 345–61.

The terminology of *Sap. Work A* is closely related to the *Rule of Discipline*, the *Damascus Document*, and the *Hôdāyôt*.[13] Terminological similarities can be observed also with the *Book of Mysteries* (*1Q27, 4Q299/300/301*). One sentence from *1QHᵃ* X 27–28 also occurs in *Sap. Work A*: לפי דעתם יכבדו איש מרעהו "according to their knowledge they shall be honoured, each one by his neighbour" (*4Q418* 55 10). As my tentative conclusion is to date *Sap. Work A* before the *Hodayot*, either this *hodayah* quotes from *Sap. Work A* or both depend upon a common tradition.

Apart from early sectarian writings, the books of Enoch seem to be most closely related to *Sap. Work A*. The greatest number of parallels are found in the *Book of Watchers* and the *Epistle of Enoch*. Our wisdom composition shares with *1 Enoch* the themes of the final judgment of the wicked and the glorious hope of the righteous. In both books divine wisdom is given the elect of the remnant community only through revelation. Terminological similarities indicate some kind of dependence between these writings. Both works foresee that the elect shall "inherit the earth" (*1 Enoch* 5:7; *4Q418* 81 14; cf. Matthew 5:4) and use the phrase *eternal planting* for the elect community (*1 Enoch* 10:16; 84:6; 93:5, 10; *4Q418* 81 13; *4Q423* 1–2 7). These phrases recur in sectarian writings (*CD* I 7–8, VIII 14–15; *1QS* VIII 5–6, XI 8; *1QHᵃ* VI 15, VIII 6, 10, 20; *4QpPsᵃ* II 2–11). The phrase *they shall walk in eternal light* occurs in both compositions.[14] The eschatological understanding of history and its

---

[13]   The theological discourses have more "sectarian terminology" than the sections with wisdom sayings. The wisdom sayings might reflect an older tradition, to which a writer close to the early Essene community added discourses of his own, especially dealing with revelation and eschatology. On sectarian terminology in *Sap. Work A*, see Elgvin, "Admonition Writings," 184–86.

[14]   *1 Enoch* 92:4 and *4Q418* 69 14 (this text is presented below). In the same line of this passage on the eschatological lot of the elect, we find the triad רוב הדר . . . כ[בו]ד . . . אור עולם "eternal light—glory—abundant honour." The same triad is found in the description of the bliss of the righteous in *1QS* IV 7–8 וכליל כבוד עם מדת הדר באור עולמים "a crown of glory

periods, which are among the mysteries of God revealed to the elect, unites *Sap. Work A* with both *1 Enoch* and sectarian literature.[15] Some important Enochic themes are not mentioned in *Sap Work A*: the fall of the angels, the interest in cosmology, the spatial dualism between heaven and earth, and the ontological dualism between humans and the world of the spirits.

In contrast to *1 Enoch* 91:13; *Jubilees* 1:17, 29; *11QT^a* XXIX 8–10; and *4QFlor* I 2–5, but similar to *1QS* there is no mention of the new temple of the last days. The developed angelology of *1 Enoch* and many Qumran writings is not reflected (in *4Q418* frg. 81 the phrase *the holy ones* is used in referring to the angels and probably also to the elect; in *4Q417* 2 i 17 it refers to the elect).

The differences between *Sap. Work A* and the literature of the *yaḥad* probably indicate that our composition predates the *yaḥad* as an established community. In its terminology, however, *Sap. Work A* is closer to the writings of the *yaḥad* than to the Enoch literature.

The presupposition of the remnant community could point to a situation between *MMT* (160–152 B.C.) and *1QS/CD* (last decades of second century B.C.), before sectarian theology had crystallized, for the origin of *Sap. Work A*. In this case, *Sap. Work A* should be seen as a representative of the wider Essene movement, not of the *yaḥad*.

---

and a garment of honour in eternal light," and in *1QH^a* XII 15 about the lot of the elect עו]לם לאור כבודכה הדר "the honour of Your glory in eternal light."

[15]   See especially *4Q417* 1 i 10–12, *4Q416* frg. 1, *4Q417* 2 i 12–14, *4Q418* frg. 69, *4Q418* 123 ii 2–5. Cf. Dimant's characteristic of Qumran eschatology: "the sequence of periods is enigmatic and mysterious, and therefore is designated by the term 'the mysteries of God' (רזי אל). Only the knowledge of these mysteries enables a true understanding of the historical process, its direction and its approaching End." Dimant, "Qumran Sectarian Literature," 536. See further Shemaryahu Talmon, "Waiting for the Messiah—The Conceptual Universe of the Qumran Covenanters," in *The World of Qumran from Within* (Jerusalem: Magnes, 1989), 273–300, esp. 294–97.

The other option is to ascribe *Sap. Work A* to the preteacher community mentioned in *CD* I. If so, *Sap. Work A* would have its origins in one of the groups that provided the background for the Essene movement and that used the Enoch literature and possibly authored parts of it.[16] Tentatively I would date the composition of *Sap. Work A* to somewhere between 160 and 130 B.C. *Sap. Work A* testifies to the intensive contact between scribal and apocalyptic circles in the third and second centuries B.C.[17]

Wisdom and Revelation

The enlightened reader, to whom the end-time mysteries of God have been revealed, is repeatedly admonished to continue to reflect on these mysteries and his eschatological hope. The text achieves its persuasiveness by referring to the spiritual inheritance of the elect (through the community he has experienced God's blessings) and to the *raz nihyeh* (the mystery which is coming into being, the unfolding mystery), God's mysterious plan for creation and history, for mankind and redemption of the elect.[18] The author does not present his own

---

[16]   George W. E. Nickelsburg has proposed that the *Epistle of Enoch* derives from circles ancestral to the Essenes, "The Epistle of Enoch and the Qumran Literature," *JJS* 33 (1982): 333–48. *Sap. Work A* is closer to the sectarian thinking than is the *Epistle*.

[17]   Cf. George W. E. Nickelsburg, "Wisdom and Apocalypticism in Early Judaism: Some Points for Discussion," in *SBLSP* (1994), 715–32.

[18]   On *raz nihyeh* see Elgvin, "Admonition Texts" 189–91; Harrington, "Wisdom at Qumran"; Lawrence H. Schiffman "4QMysteries[a]: A Preliminary Edition and Translation," in *Solving Riddles and Untying Knots: Biblical, Epigraphic, and Semitic Studies in Honor of Jonas C. Greenfield*, ed. Ziony Zevit, Seymour Gitin, and Michael Sokoloff (Winona Lake: Eisenbrauns, 1995), 207–60, esp. 210–11 n. 11; Armin Lange, *Weisheit und Prädestination: Weisheitliche Urordnung und Prädestination in der Textfunden von Qumran* (Leiden: Brill, 1995), ch. 2; Dr. Lange kindly made available to me two chapters of this dissertation. נהיה is probably a *Nip'al* participle of *haya*, see *4Q418* 123 ii 3–4, where כול הנהיה (participle

instruction as inspired;[19] *raz nihyeh* and the *Book of Hagi*,[20] however, have a divine origin. The addressee is exhorted to meditate on *raz nihyeh*, which must be a well-known concept for him. This meditation is presumably connected to the study of both biblical and sectarian books.

Sap. Work A lacks a number of the central characteristics of apocalyptic literature[21] and should not be counted as an apoca-

---

of *haya*) occurs in line 3 and רז נהיה in line 4 (for a translation of this fragment, see n. 38).

[19] Compare *CD* I and *1QS* VIII, which attribute revelation to the community, but do not claim themselves to be pieces of such revelation, George W. E. Nickelsburg, "*1 Enoch* and Qumran Origins: The State of the Question and Some Prospects for Answers," *SBLSP* (1986): 341–60, esp. 342–43.

[20] According to *4Q417* 2 i 11–18 the *Book of Hagi* is revealed to the elect community: "and in a proper understanding he will kn[ow the hid]den things of His thought when he walks in [p]urit[y in all]his d[ee]ds. Seek them always, and look [at al]l their outcome. Then you will have knowledge of [eterna]l glory [wi]th the mysteries of His wonder and His mighty deeds. And you, understand the poverty of your deed when you remember the ti[me. For] the engraved law has come, deciding every commandment, for engraved is the law <= the Law of Moses> by God for all iniquity of the sons of perdition (בני שית). And the Book of Memory was written before Him for those who keep His word. It is the Vision of Hagi and a Book of Memory. He gave it as inheritance (וינחילה) to man (לאנוש) with a spiritual people (עם רוח), for He fashioned it as a model for the holy ones. He had not yet given the Hagi to the spirit of flesh, for he could not discern between [goo]d and evil with the judgment of his [sp]irit." This passage is discussed in my paper "The Mystery to Come: Early Essene Theology of Revelation."

[21] Stegemann characterizes apocalypses as literary works which claim to be divine revelations. He adds the following criteria: (1) the main theological *locus* of the work is presented as divinely revealed; (2) the problem of authority is solved by immediate access to the will of heaven; (3) the book is usually ascribed to a sage from Israel's history; (4) the contact between man and heaven is attained by vision, audition, or an ascent to heaven; (5) the right understanding of what is seen or heard is provided by a heavenly mediator; (6) the heavenly knowledge is characterized as "hidden" or "secrets"; (7) innovative teachings deal with doctrine (calendar, dualism, determinism), the meaning of history, cosmology, angelology, or future

lyptic book per se. The wisdom of this book is not revealed through angels or a sage from Israel's early history (see below, however, on the reference to Noah in *4Q418* 201; further, לאנוש in *4Q417* 2 i 16 can be interpreted both as "to mankind" and "to Enosh"). The revelations are not transmitted within a narrative framework. Visions, auditions, or heavenly journeys are probably not a central feature in the revelation of divine wisdom.[22] Different from Daniel, dreams and their interpretation are not mentioned at all. Past history is not reviewed in any form.

Apocalyptic motifs, however, are to be found in *Sap. Work A,* as in Qumran sectarian writings. Similar to the main sectarian writings, we find an eschatological understanding of history and its periods (but not a detailed apocalyptic view of history). The theme of esoteric divine wisdom revealed to the elect is central. The word pair *raz* and *galah,* appearing frequently in Daniel, indicates some kind of esoteric knowledge that cannot be attained by Israelites in general.[23] A heavenly book written in

---

salvation; (8) revelations are transmitted within a narrative framework; (9) the apocalypses reflect specific educational levels (priests, teachers) and (10) a situation of religious crisis (11) and aim at bringing divine order into a disordered world; (12) the authors viewed writing of apocalypses as the best way of achieving their aim; Hartmut Stegemann, "Die Bedeutung der Qumranfunde für die Erforschung der Apokalyptik," in *Apocalypticism in the Mediterranean World and the Near East*, ed. David Hellholm (Tübingen: Mohr, 1983) 495–530, esp. 526–28. On the characteristics of apocalypses, see also John J. Collins, "Introduction: Towards the Morphology of a Genre," *Semeia* 14 (1979): 1–20.

[22] Cf., however, the designation of the *Book of Hagi* as הזון ההגי, *4Q417* 1 i 16. Some lines below (on line 22) we find the admonition כול הזון דע, but it is not clear to what kind of visions this line refers.

[23] Also Sirach asserts that wisdom is a gift bestowed by God only on those who love him (1:10, 39:1–8); cf. Alexander A. Di Lella, "The Meaning of Wisdom in Ben Sira," in *In Search of Wisdom*, ed. Leo G. Perdue, Bernard B. Scott, William J. Wiseman (Louisville: Knox, 1993), 133–48. The apocalyptic motifs of *Sap. Work A*, however, set it apart from Sirach. In its thinking of wisdom and revelation Sap. Sol. occupies a position between traditional wisdom and the apocalyptic writings, Nickelsburg, "Wisdom and Apocalypticism," 723.

God's presence is essential for obtaining wisdom and for the right understanding of history. The book has a hortatory character and a clear interest in the afterlife.

Wisdom is not only transcendent, but it is also attainable on earth. Divine wisdom has been revealed to the elect of the remnant community. According to *4Q417* 2 i 11–12 the secrets of God are revealed to the elect: ובכושר מבינות נוד[ע נס]תרי מחשבתו "in a proper understanding he will know the hid]den things of His plan." For the sectarians נסתרות are the hidden secrets of God which he reveals to the elect community; cf. *CD* III 13–14, *1QS* V 11, and *5Q13 (5QSectarian Rule)* 1 11. In the sectarian view the Bible contained both "clear laws" (נגלות) and "hidden laws" (נסתרות). The latter could be discovered through the covenanters' careful searching in the scriptures. הבין נסתרות (cf. the word מבינות above) means to understand God's secrets through study of scripture[24] and sectarian books. The verb גלה is used to represent the community's understanding of the Bible and specifically on the meaning of history. This passage in *Sap. Work A* reflects this same sectarian way of thinking.

We encounter a "realized eschatology" that perceives the enlightened, to whom God's mysteries have been revealed, as partakers of God's knowledge. The enlightened community shares the glory of Adam and the wisdom of Solomon. Similar to *1 Enoch*, the reception of wisdom is constitutive of salvation and life eternal. *Royal wisdom* might be a key phrase in *Sap. Work A*'s interpretation of biblical traditions that are currently related to the individual: the royal categories in which Adam is described (Genesis 1–2, Psalm 8),[25] the wisdom of David

---

[24] Elisha Qimron and John Strugnell, "Some Principles of MMT's Halakha and Their Consequences," in *Qumran Cave 4: Miqṣat Maʿaśe ha-Torah, DJD* 10:132.

[25] In the ancient Near East the king's wisdom corresponds to the wisdom of Primeval Man. Helmer Ringgren, *Word and Wisdom: Studies in the Hypostatization of Divine Qualities and Functions of the Ancient Near East* (Lund: Ohlssons: 1947), 143; Geo Widengren, "Det sakrala kungadömet bland öst– och västsemiter," *Religion och Bibel* 2 (1943): 49–75, esp. 74.

(2 Samuel 14:17, 20) and Solomon (1 Kings 3–4),[26] the divine sonship of the Davidic king (2 Samuel 7, Psalm 2),[27] wisdom as a messianic quality (Isaiah 11:2, Jeremiah 23:5), wisdom regarded as royal (Proverbs 8:23),[28] and wisdom bestowing upon her disciple a beautiful crown (Proverbs 4:9).[29] *Sap. Work A* addresses the elect who has received royal wisdom from God and therefore is called a firstborn son of God.[30] It is possibly not incidental that no saying about a future messianic ruler is preserved from *Sap. Work A*: it would be difficult to find a place for such a figure in this democratized messianism. In traditional ancient Near Eastern wisdom the figure of the sacred king empowered with divine wisdom played a central role. The Israelite adaptation of this motif is reshaped in *Sap. Work A*. Further, the promise to Aaron, "I will be your share and your

---

[26] On the 'Solomonic' phrases in *4Q418* frg. 81 (cf. n. 6 above), see my forthcoming paper, "The Mystery to Come: Early Essene Theology of Revelation."

[27] The individual elect is thrice called a firstborn son of God; see n. 70.

[28] Cf. Ringgren's translation: "I was installed from everlasting, From the beginning, at the origin of the earth," *Word and Wisdom,* 99–102, 141–43.

[29] Also Ezekiel 28, Proverbs 8:14–16, and Sap. Sol. 6:20–21 testify to a persistent Israelite belief in the connection between wisdom and royalty. Cf. Norman W. Porteous, "Royal Wisdom," in *Wisdom in Israel and in the Ancient Near East,* ed. Martin Noth and D. Winton Thomas (Leiden: Brill, 1969), 247–61; Ringgren, *Word and Wisdom,* 141–43; Ivan Engnell, *Studies in Divine Kingship in the Ancient Near East* (Uppsala: Almqwist & Wiksell, 1943), 25–31. The comment of Jonathan Z. Smith, "Wisdom and Apocalyptic," in Smith, *Map Is Not Territory: Studies in the History of Religions* (Leiden: Brill, 1978), 86, is fitting: "Apocalypticism is Wisdom lacking a royal court and patron and therefore it surfaces during the period of Late Antiquity not as a response to religious persecution but as an expression of the trauma of the cessation of native kingship."

[30] Similar traditions are found in Sirach and Sap. Sol.—while Sirach attributes royal categories to the Torah (24:4, 11–12), he also portrays Wisdom bestowing royal ornaments upon her disciple (6:29–31; 15:5–6). According to Sap. Sol. 5:16 the righteous shall receive the kingship and the crown from the hand of the Lord; cf. also James 1:12, Revelation 3:21.

inheritance among the Israelites" (Numbers 18:20), is reinterpreted as a promise to the individual (*1Q26* 1 7, *4Q418* 81 3),
and the saying of Exodus 20:6, "I show kindness to thousands
of those who love me and keep my commandments," is reinterpreted for the elect of the new community only (*4Q418* 81 7–8;
cf. n. 6 above).

Nickelsburg has noted the number of apocalyptic terms in
1QS XI 3–9: "revelation in the form of enlightening and seeing;
the mystery to come; the fount of righteousness, knowledge
hidden from humans; the dwelling place of glory; standing in the
presence of the holy ones; the sons of heaven."[31] All these concepts seem to be inherited from *Sap. Work A,* which molds traditional wisdom within a framework of apocalyptic concepts.[32]
In its understanding of world and man, *Sap. Work A* is influenced more by apocalypticism than by traditional wisdom.

Eschatology

Sap. Work A does not reflect the developed philosophical
dualism of the Two-Spirit Treatise in *1QS* III–IV and the *War
Scroll*. Dualistic concepts, however, do appear (more in the discourses than in the sections with practical admonition, cf. especially *4Q416* frg. 1 [see below], *4Q418* frg. 81 [see n. 6
above]): God has separated the elect from "the spirit of all flesh"
and given him his spiritual inheritance. Hence he shall separate
from all (or, from everyone) hated by God, *4Q418* 81 1–3, *4Q423*
5 7 קוד[שים? הפץ עדת? ה]בדל מכ[ל] בעל אולת ה[בדל את שכל א]יש ואתה
"You are a m]an of understanding, k[eep] the foolish man [apart
from al]l[the property of the community (?) of the ho]ly ones"
(cf. *1QS* I 3–11, IX 16–23). This ethical dualism is reflected in
the pairs *truth* and *evil, wisdom* and *folly*: when he meditates on
the mystery to be, the elect "will know truth and evil, wisdom
[and fol]ly," *4Q417* 2 i 6–7. The eschatological discourse of

---

[31]   Nickelsburg, "Wisdom and Apocalypticism," 724.
[32]   Cf. Michel, "Weisheit und Apokalyptik," 432–34.

4Q416 frg. 1 distinguishes "the sons of evil" from "the sons of truth." There comes a day of judgment on all iniquity, and the period of truth shall be completed. God will overcome the evil powers opposing him. The extant fragments do not mention any demonic prince that rules the spirits of men, an idea that we encounter for the first time in *Jubilees*[33] and that recurs in the sectarian writings (cf. *1QS* I 18, 23–24, II 19 and the Two-Spirit Treatise, *CD* V 18, XIX 14, *1QHᵃ* III 28–29, *1QM* XIII 4, 11–12, XVIII 1).[34]

In its discourses on the coming judgment and salvation, *Sap. Work A* draws upon various passages from biblical prophets and psalms.[35] In its eschatology it is a close relative of *1 Enoch*, *Jubilees*, and the main sectarian writings, and it differs from a more biblically oriented restoration eschatology as represented by the *Words of the Luminaries*.[36] *Sap. Work A* shares with *1 Enoch* (cf. especially the *Apocalypse of Weeks* and the *Animal Apocalypse*) and sectarian writings an eschatological understanding of history and its periods.[37] In the present period God has chosen to reveal the mysteries of history and the

---

[33]   *Jubilees* 1:20 (Belial), 48:2–49:2 (Mastema).

[34]   Cf. Collins, "Was the Dead Sea Sect an Apocalyptic Movement?," 42–43; Dimant, "Qumran Sectarian Literature," 493. If מֹמְשֶׁלֶת רשעה is correctly reconstructed in *4Q418* 212 1/*4Q416* 1 10, a full-fledged cosmic dualism with a supernatural power of evil opposed to God is evident. The *Book of Mysteries*, which is related to *Sap. Work A*, refers to such powers: "and all the adherents of the mysteries of transgression are to be no more," *1Q27* 1 i 7.

[35]   E.g., Isaiah 61 in *4Q417* 1 i 11–12; Nahum 1:6 in *4Q417* 1 i 15–16; Psalm 77:17 in *4Q416* 1 12.

[36]   Cf. Collins, "Was the Dead Sea Sect an Apocalyptic Movement?," 44.

[37]   The idea that all history is divided into a set number of periods is found both in Jewish and non-Jewish sources in the Hellenistic period and is probably influenced by Persian millennial speculation; see David Flusser, "The Four Empires in the Fourth Sibyl and in the Book of Daniel," *Israel Oriental Studies* 2 (1972): 148–75.

eschaton to the elect.[38] God's judgment will put an end to רשעה
קץ "the period of evil." While the term קץ רשעה (*4Q416* 1 11–
12) is frequent in sectarian teachings of the periods,
קץ אמֹת "the period of truth" (*4Q416* 1 14) does not occur in the
main sectarian writings. This might indicate that *Sap. Work A*
derives from a time before sectarian theology was fully developed. It is not explicitly stated that the present time of the community is קץ רשעה or that the author's time is marked by vio-
lence and deceit, as is presupposed by the *Epistle of Enoch*,
1 Enoch 93:9.

None of the eschatological passages of *Sap. Work A* mentions any restoration of Zion or the people of the twelve tribes, a
Davidic king, or any other eschatological figure.[39] There is no
eschatological war between the sons of light and the sons of
darkness, as in the *War Scroll*, *4QPseudo-Daniel*, and *4QNew
Jerusalem*.[40] As in the main sectarian writings, the eschatology
of *Sap. Work A* is not centered around a messianic figure, but
around an eschatological community—it displays a "collective
messianism."[41] Based on the Bible and contemporary writings,
it would be strange if *Sap. Work A* did not share the expectation

---

[38] Cf. *4Q418* 123 ii 2–6: "at the coming of the years and the going
of the periods [. . .] everything that is in it with what came into being and
what will be [. . .] its period, as God opened the ear of those who understand
for the mystery to come[. . . and] you that understand when you meditate
upon all these things [. . . , in] her [ha]nd are balanced your deeds with
[their] times[."

[39] A similar eschatology can be found, for example, in *1 Enoch*,
Sap. Sol., and *Assumption of Moses* 10. The related *Book of Mysteries* is
more national and less sectarian than *Sap. Work A*, as it refers both to a
king and to the people of Israel, *4Q299* 10 1–3, 50 12, 62 3, 64 1–2.

[40] Émile Puech, "Messianism, Resurrection, and Eschatology at
Qumran and in the New Testament," in *The Community of the Renewed
Covenant*, 247.

[41] A phrase coined by André Caquot, "Le messianisme qumrânien," in
Qumrân: Sa piété, sa théologie et son milieu, ed. Mathias Delcor (Leuven:
Leuven University Press, 1978), 231; cf. Dimant, "Qumran Sectarian Lit-
erature," 538.

of a messianic ruler, but this figure did not occupy a crucial role
in the eschatological drama.

The detailed eschatology of the midrashim and pesharim is
not found in our composition. The phrase אחרית הימים *the end
of days* does not occur.[42] Similarly, the phrase דור אחרון *the last
generation*, which is used by the pesharim about the generation
of their time, does not occur. It seems that *Sap. Work A* testifies
to an earlier period of the movement that later produced works
such as *4QMidrEschat* and *11QMelch*.[43]

Sap. Work A has a clear conviction of the coming judgment
and salvation, but there are no clear signs of a tense *Naherwar-
tung*.[44] Similar to sectarian writings, *Sap. Work A* describes the
end-time judgment of the cosmos with separation between the
righteous and the evil ones. The eschatological discourses in
4Q416 frg. 1 and *4Q418* frg. 69 have close parallels in *1QS* IV

---

[42] In *QL* אחרית הימים is a central sectarian phrase for "the last period
of time," which primarily belongs to the pesharim and midrashim. The earliest sectarian references are in *4QMMT* C 14, 16, 21, *1QSa* I 1. Cf.
Annette Steudel, "אחרית הימים in the Texts from Qumran," *RQ* 16 (1993):
225–46. The only occurrence in a nonsectarian Qumran text is *4QDibHam*[a]
1–2 iii 13. I concur with Steudel and Chazon in their classification of the
Words of the Luminaries as a presectarian composition, contra Puech
(Steudel, ibid. 227; Esther G. Chazon, "Is *Divrei ha-me'orot* a Sectarian
Prayer?" in *The Dead Sea Scrolls: Forty Years of Research,* ed. Devorah
Dimant and Uriel Rappaport [Leiden: Brill, 1992], 3–17; Puech,
"Messianism, Resurrection, and Eschatology," 248).

[43] According to Steudel, "אחרית הימים in the Texts from Qumran,"
233–42, the detailed scheme for the last days was developed by the sectarians towards the end of the life of the Teacher (end of first century B.C.) with
4QMidrEschat and *11QMelch* as primary examples.

[44] The earliest Enoch literature, the *Book of Watchers* and the *Astronomical Book* as well as *Jubilees* are more concerned with the inevitability
of the judgment than its proximity, while the *Epistle of Enoch* expects an
imminent judgment. Cf. Collins, "Was the Dead Sea Sect an Apocalyptic
Movement?" 33; George W. E. Nickelsburg, "The Apocalyptic Construc-
tion of Reality of *1 Enoch*," in *Mysteries and Revelations: Apocalyptic
Studies since the Uppsala Colloquium,* ed. John J. Collins and James H.
Charlesworth (Sheffield: Sheffield Academic Press, 1991), 54.

6–14, *CD* II 5–10, *1QH^a* III 29–36, *4QAmram^f ar* 1–2 ii 4–10[45]
and fit Hippolytus's description of the eschatological teachings
of the Essenes.[46]

There is a clear hope for an afterlife: "If <God> commits
<you> to die in your poverty, entrust yourself to Him and do
not rebel against Him in your spirit. Then you will rest with the
truth, and in your death your remembrance will blosso[m for
eve]r, and in the end you will inherit joy" (*4Q416* 2 iii 6–8);
"know who will inherit glory and who corruption. Will not[
garland be given for their ashes] and eternal joy for their sorrow?" (*4Q417* 1 i 11–12); "you [will inherit g]lory and abundant
honour" (*4Q418* 69 14). Although the texts do not speak clearly
on this point, the connections with Danielic and Enochic traditions (cf. Daniel 12:2, *1 Enoch* 91:10) indicate that this hope
included a resurrection of the righteous. The statement "the
seekers of truth will wake up to the judgment[of God (?)"

---

[45]   This eschatological passage from *4QAmram^f ar* (*4Q548* frg. 1) displays "sectarian terminology" (*sons of truth, sons of light, sons of darkness*). Puech, "Messianism, Resurrection, and Eschatology," 247 n. 33,
who dates the *Visions of Amram* to ca. 200 B.C., remarks, "the attribution
of this manuscript to Visions of Amram is not certain, only probable." If it
does belong to *Visions of Amram*, this manuscript could have been
reworked by a sectarian writer. Dating this manuscript around 200 B.C. does
not seem probable based on its sectarian vocabulary. The only option would
be to ascribe to this manuscript the invention of the terms *sons of light* and
sons of darkness, and postulate a later adoption of these terms from
4QAmram^f ar by the sectarians.

[46]   *Refutatio* XXII: "They acknowledge both that the flesh will rise
again, and that it will be immortal, in the same manner as the soul is
already imperishable. And they maintain that the soul, when separated in the
present life, (departs) into one place, which is well ventilated and lightsome,
where, they say, it rests until judgment. . . . Now they affirm that there
will be both a judgment and a conflagration of the universe, and that the
wicked will be eternally punished." Morton Smith noted that on this point
Hippolytus's description is more "Jewish" and probably more reliable than
the parallel account in Josephus, *Bellum* II, 154–58; Morton Smith, "The
Description of the Essenes in Josephus and the Philosophumena," *HUCA*
29 (1958): 285.

(*4Q418* 69 7) is most easily interpreted as a rephrasing of
1 Enoch 91:10 "then the righteous one shall arise from his
sleep."

Realized Eschatology

Our text displays a *realized eschatology*: the hope for the
eschaton is combined with the knowledge that salvation is a present reality, as is fellowship with God and participation in His
mysteries:

ובכושר מבינות נוד[ע נס[תרי מחשבתו עם התהלכו[ן ת[מ]י[ם
בכול מ[ע]שיו אלה שחר תמיד והתבונן [בכו[ל תוצאותמה
ואז תדע בכבוד ע[ו]לם ע[ם רזי פלאו וגבורות מעשיו

and in a proper understanding he will kn[ow the hid]den
things of His thought when he walks in [p]erfecti[on in
all]his d[ee]ds. Seek them always, and look [at al]l their
outcome. Then you will have knowledge of [eterna]l
glory [wi]th the mysteries of His wonder and His
mighty deeds. (*4Q417* 2 i 11–13)

The elect has access to the hidden mysteries of God: when he
meditates on the deeds of God and their consequences and when
he understands the times, he will have knowledge of eternal
glory and God's wondrous mysteries.[47] Salvation is present,
already the elect has knowledge of eternal glory, כבוד עולם.[48]
The same consciousness of partaking of the eschatological salvation is known from major sectarian documents.[49]

---

[47] The phrase רזי פלא recurs in the sectarians writings; *CD* III 18,
1QS IX 18, *1QH^a* II 13, IV 27–28.

[48] Cf. *1QH^a* XIII 5–6: God has bestowed כבוד עולם and ש[מחת עד
upon the elect.

[49] Cf. Heinz-Wolfgang Kuhn's characterization of the Hôdāyôt with
the words "Enderwartung und gegenwärtiges Heil," in *Enderwartung und
gegenwärtiges Heil: Untersuchungen zu den Gemeindeliedern von Qumran
mit einem Anhang über Eschatologie und Gegenwart in der Verkündigung
Jesu* (Göttingen: Vandenhoeck und Ruprecht, 1966), and Carol Ann

In *4Q417* 1 i 10–12 we find the exhortation:

הבט ברז נהיה וקח מולדי ישע [50] ודע מי נוֹחל כבֹוד
וע[ו]ל הלוֹא[ינתן פאר לאפריהמה] ולאבליהמה שמחת עולם

Gaze upon the mystery to come, understand the birth-times of salvation and know who will inherit glory and corruption. Will not[garland be given for their ashes] and eternal joy for their sorrow?

The message is clear: when you study God's mysterious plan of redemption, you will understand the pangs of salvation—the secrets about the end time—and thereby you will know who will inherit glory (namely, the elect) and who corruption (namely, the sons of the pit).[51] Similar passages that urge the man of understanding to meditate upon God's mysteries and thereby gain knowledge are found in *4Q417* 2 i 2–8 and *4Q416* 2 iii 12–15.

In the following section, I will discuss the main sections of the two eschatological discourses contained in *Sap. Work A* in greater detail. Special attention will be paid to the similarities with *1 Enoch* and the writings of the *yaḥad*.

Newsom's comment on *1QS:* "the separation and purification characteristic of the eschatological age are already embodied in the language of the community's discourse. To speak such a language is an implicit claim to participate already in eschatological reality," in "Apocalyptic and the Discourse of the Qumran Community," *JNES* 49 (1990): 141.

[50] The sentence וקח מולדי ישע is parallel to הבט ברז נהיה. מולדי ישע can be interpreted as "birth-times/birth-pangs/origins of salvation"; cf. *1QHᵃ* XII 7–8 where מולדי עת carries the meaning "beginnings of the set times."

[51] It is tempting to connect this passage (and the concept of רז נהיה) with the role of the Teacher of Righteousness who revealed the hidden eschatological meaning of the scriptures to the sect, cf. *1QpHab* VII 1–14 (esp. lines 12–14: כיא כול קצי אל יבואו לתכונם כאשר חקק להֹ[ם] ברזי ערמתו "for all the periods of God will come in their order, as He ordained for them in the mysteries of His wisdom"). If *Sap. Work A* predates the Teacher, he must have inherited the basics of his eschatological hermeneutics from Enoch traditions and *Sap. Work A*, and only systematized them for his followers.

The Cosmic Judgment, *4Q416* col. VII

This text is part of an eschatological discourse which covered two columns of text (*4Q416* frg. 4 = last three lines of *4Q416* col. VI, *4Q416* frg. 1 = col. VII, *4Q416* frg. 3 = col. VIII 9–15). [52]

2	<u>כֹּל רוֹֹח</u> [בשר [
3	ולתכן **חפצו** [<u>על כל עולה וסוף?</u> {ל}<u>נהיה הודיע אל נח</u> [
4	**מועד במועד** ° <u>ויסגר **בעד כול בני עולה**]</u>
5	לפי צבאם למ[שׁ]<u>ור **במשורה ולדור** ודור לעיר ועיר?לממלכה]</u>
6	וממלכה למד]ינה **ומדינה לאיש ואישׁ** [
7	לפי מחסור צבאם [**ומשפט כולם לי**°° [
8	וצבא השמים הכין מ[קדם ויתן כוכבים?[53] **ומאורות**]
9	למופתיהמה ואתות מו[עדיהמה כל אחד בסדרו]?[54]
10	**זה לזה** וכל פקודתמה ו[מועדיהמה [ספרו] לו [
11	**בשׁמים ישפוט על** עבודת רשעה **וכל בני אמת** ירצו ל[מועד?]
12	קצה **ויפחדו ויריעו כל אשר התגללו**
	<u>בה כי שמים יר[ו]נׄ]ׄן</u> <u>תרעש מ[מ]שׁלת רשעה</u>?[55]
13	מים **ותהמות פחדו ויתערערו** כל רוח בשר <u>ובני השמי]ם יגילו ביום]</u>
14	[מש]פׄטׄ ה **וכל עולה** תחם **עד ישׁלם** קץ האמ]ת וישלוט?]
15	ב**כל קצי עד כי אל אמת הוא** ומקדם שני]ו ויופיע? אל]
16	**להכין צדק**° **בין טוב ל**ר[ע] לה[כי]ר

---

[52] Underlining or bold typeface in transcription or translation indicates parallel text in other fragments. *4Q416* frg. 1 is here reconstructed with fragments from *4Q418a* (4Q418 frgs. 73, 201, 213, 212, underlined) and *4Q418b* (4Q418 frgs. 286, 1, 2, bold). Far more text is presented in this reconstruction than in the version of Wacholder/Abegg.

[53] For the reconstruction, cf. *1QH^a* I 11–12[כב]הׄם כוכבים לתיבותׄ֯ם מאורות לדׄ֯יהם.

[54] For the reconstruction, cf. *1QS* X 3–4, which also deals with the order of the heavenly host and the set times עם מסרותם זה לזה.

[55] For the proposed reconstruction, cf. *1QM* XVII 5–6 שר מנשלת רשעה.

כל משפֿ]טי אל ויבין כל יצור? כיא[

[17 י]צר בשר הואה ומבינו]תٝו

[18 בֿראתיו בֿי הֿ]

[19 ו]יٝדעٝ]

bottom margin

Translation

2. all the spirit [of flesh
3. and establish His <u>will</u> [<u>over all evil. He made known to
   Noah</u> the end (?) <u>which is to come</u>   ]
4. <u>set time upon</u> set time [<u>He will close behind all
   the sons of evil</u>]
5. according to their hosts, h[<u>in upon hin,</u> generation upon
   generation, city upon city (?), kingdom]
6. upon kingdom, provi[nce upon <u>province, man upon man</u>
                 ]
7. according to the needs of <u>their</u> host [<u>and the judgment upon
   all, to . .</u>   ]
8. and the host of heaven He established from[the beginning,
   He set stars (?) <u>and luminaries</u>]
9. as their signs and as symbols of [their] set [times   each
   one in <u>its</u> order (?)]
10. <u>each one in relation to</u> the other, and all their order and[set
    times]were counted[before Him
11. In <u>heaven</u> He will jud<u>ge</u> the work of iniqui<u>ty, and all</u> the
    sons of truth will be pleased by[the appointed time (?)]
12. of its period, and all those who have defiled themselves in it
    will fear and wail, for the heaven will shou[t, the kingdom
    of iniquity (?) will tremble,]

---

[56] *4Q418* frg. 2 reads להבין צדיק בין טוב לֿרٝע "that the righteous shall
discern between good and evil." The version of *4Q416* should be preferred in
this context of eschatological judgment.

13. the water and the depths will fear, all the spirit of flesh will be stripped naked and the sons of heave[n will rejoice on the day]

14. of its [jud]gment. And all iniquity shall be consummated when the period of tru[th] is completed[and He will reign (?)]

15. in all the ages of eternity, for a God of truth is He and [His] years from the days of old [God will appear (?)]

16. to establish righteousness between good and evi[l,] so that everyone should k[no]w the judg[ments of God, and every creature will understand (?) that]

17. it is a creature of flesh,[57] and [his] understandi[ng

18. when he sees that . .[

19. and he shall know[

This text which describes God's end-time judgment at the culmination of the periods of history demonstrates close similarities to sectarian descriptions of the end-time judgment. The preserved text was probably preceded by a passage similar to *1 Enoch* 1:9: "Behold He comes with the myriads of His holy ones, to execute judgment on all, and to destroy all the godless, and to convict all flesh (cf. כל רוח בשר in line 2) for all the deeds of their godlessness which they have done."

Line 3. The discourse portrays Noah as receiver of divine revelation about the coming judgment: "He made known to Noah [the end][58] which is to come" (*4Q416* 1 3, reconstructed

---

[57]   The reconstruction of line 16 and the interpretation of the phrase כיא [י]צר בשר הואה in lines 16–17 as "that it is a creature of flesh" and not "for it is the inclination of flesh" are suggested by the following parallel in the Rosh Hashanah liturgy: וידע כל פעול כי אתה פעלתו, ויבן כל יצור כי אתה יצרתו "every creature will know that you made him, and every being understand that you formed him," *Machzor Rabba*, Ashkenazi Version, *Rosh Hashana* (Jerusalem: Eshkol, n.d.), 177.

[58]   The word סוף "end" is reconstructed based on the occurrence of this word in *1 Enoch* 10:2 and the Rosh Hashanah liturgy as well as *4Q418* 211 4] להשמ[י]ד? עולה כיא יבוא סוף "to extermin]ate (?) evil, for an end will

with *4Q418* 201), a saying which rephrases *1 Enoch* 10:1–2 "Go to Noah and tell him in my name, 'Hide yourself,' and reveal to him the end which is coming, for the earth and everything will be destroyed."[59] The Rosh Hashanah liturgy mentions both "the end" and Noah in a similar way: צופה ומביט עד סוף כל־הדורות "You look and see unto the end of all generations," "and You remembered Noah in love and endowed him with the word of salvation and mercy." Noah is a popular figure in the second century B.C. Both biographical material about Noah's birth and life as well as the *Words of Noah* were circulating. Parts of these Noah traditions are preserved in the *Genesis Apocryphon*, *1 Enoch*, *Jubilees*, and *4QMess ar.*[60] *1 Enoch* 10 and 60:1–6, 25 represent the same tradition as our text: To Noah are revealed the secrets about the end-time.

Line 4. The word מועד is used in sectarian literature on the appointed times within the periods of history; compare *1QHᵃ* I לכול קצי נצח ותקופות מספר שני עולם בכול מועדיהם 24 "for everlasting ages, and for the numbered cycles of the eternal years in all their seasons." The sentence יסגור בעד כל בני עולה "He will close behind all the sons of evil" has a close parallel in *1QHᵃ* III 18 עול הרית בעד שחת דלתי ויסגרו "the gates of the pit will be closed behind her who is pregnant with wickedness." The

---

come," a passage which should be located somewhere in this eschatological discourse.

[59] Cf. Nickelsburg's characterization of *1 Enoch* 10: "The biblical description of the postdiluvian restoration of the earth (Genesis 9) is rewritten as a scenario of eschatological recreation," in "Enoch, First Book of," in *Anchor Bible Dictionary* 2:510.

[60] See recently Florentino García Martínez, *Qumran and the Apocalyptic: Studies on the Aramaic Texts from Qumran* (Leiden: Brill, 1992), 1–44; Richard C. Steiner, "The Heading of the *Book of the Words of Noah* on a Fragment of the Genesis Apocryphon: New Light on a 'Lost' Work," *DSD* 2 (1995): 66–71. Cf. the preface of *Sefer ha-Razim*, which presents itself as a book of mysteries revealed to Noah by an angelic mediator and later disclosed to Solomon.

phrase בני עולה "the sons of evil" belongs to sectarian vocabulary, *1QHª* V 8, compare *1QS* X 20 אנשי עולה "the men of evil."

Lines 5–6. God will judge everything created; "hin upon hin, g[eneration upon generation, city upon city (?), kingdom] upon kingdom, province upon province, man upon man." The phrase מדינה ומדינה occurs nine times in Esther at 1:22; 3:12(2x), 14; 4:3; 8:9, 13, 17; 9:28; compare especially 9:28 בכל־דור ודור משפחה ומשפחה מדינה ומדינה ועיר ועיר. The fact that the same stereotype listing appears in lines 5–6 of our text indicates some kind of relation between our text and the book of Esther: our text knows either Esther or a related tradition.[61]

Lines 8–10 describe how God established the heavenly hosts and the luminaries. The same theme is found in *1 Enoch* 2 and 72–82 (the Astronomical Book). *1 Enoch* compares the order of the heavenly realms with the sin and disorder which characterizes the world of men. Although our text is fragmentarily preserved, it probably carried the same thought. For the idea that the set times and festivals are decided by the signs of the luminaries, compare Genesis 1:14, *1QS* X 1–3, *1QHª* XII 4–6, *4Q299 (4QMystª)* 5 1–4, *4Q381 (4QNoncanonical Psalms B)* 1 8.

Lines 11–15 describe the end-time judgment in heaven and on earth. The passage draws on biblical theophanies (Isaiah 24:18, Psalm 77:17) and shows similarities with *1 Enoch* 1 and 100:10–102:3. In the latter section of *1 Enoch*, the luminaries are called to testify against the ungodly, and heaven and earth will quake and tremble when God appears at the judgment. Compare also *Assumption of Moses* 10:4 "And the earth will tremble, even to its ends shall it be shaken. And the high mountains will be made low," *Sibylline Oracles* 3:675–82 "And earth, the universal mother, shall shake in those days at the hand of the Eternal . . . and all souls of men and every sea shall shudder at

---

[61]   *4Q550 (4QProto-Esther Aramaic)* has demonstrated that stories related to the biblical Esther were known in Qumran. Jozef T. Milik, "Les modèles araméens du livre d'Ésther dans la grotte 4 de Qumran," *RQ* 15 (1992): 321–406.

the presence of the Eternal and there shall be panic. And the towering mountain peaks and the hills of the giants He shall rend, and the murky abyss shall be visible to all."

We note the use of the term בני אמת "sons of truth" for the elect in line 11 (not "sons of light" as in *1QM* and *1QS* I). For בני אמת compare *1QS* IV 5–6 (the Two-Spirit Treatise), *4QD^b* 18 v 7. See also *1QH^a* VI 29, VII 30, IX 35, X 27, XI 11 בני אמתכה/אמתו "sons of Your/His truth," *1QpHab* VII 10, *4Q298* III 6–7 אנשי האמת, *4Q548* (*4QAmram^f ar*) 1 8 בני ק[שוט.

In lines 12, 14, and 15 we encounter the word קץ "period of history." The suffix of קצה in line 12 refers to רשעה in the pre-ceding line. The phrase קץ רשעה/רשע occurs in *CD* VI 10, 14; XII 23; XV 7, 10; *1QpHab* V 7–8, *4Q301* (*4QMyst^c*) 3 8. The phrase כול קצי עד of line 15 is found in *4QSb* V 18; compare *11QMelch* II 20 לכול קצי עולם, *4Q417* 2 i 7 בכול קצי הע[ולם, *1QM* I 8–9 [עולמים] לכול קצי, X 15–16 ותקופות שנים וקצי עד, *1QH^a* I 24 לכול קצי נצח. Aramaic works from Qumran use the parallel phrase כול דרי עלמין/עלמא, *4Q213* (*4QAramaic Levi^a ar*) 2 7, *4Q542* (*4QTQahat ar*) 1 ii 4, *4Q545* (*4QAmram^c*) 2 4, *4Q547* (*4QAmram^e ar*) 2 7. Our text seems to share the sectarian historiography, which divides history into successive periods, קצים.[62] It describes the time of judgment (קץ משפט; cf. *1QH^a* VI 29) that comes after קץ רשעה, the present age of wickedness. Within the Enoch corpus the closest parallel to these lines can be found in the *Apocalypse of Weeks*.

According to line 12 those who have defiled themselves by iniquity, (התגללו בה) (ברשעה), will tremble at the judgment. Also this phrase belongs to sectarian parlance; *1QS* IV 19 התגוללה בדרכי רשע "it has been defiled on the ways of wicked-ness" *1QH^a* VI 22 מחשבת רשעה יתגללו באשמה] "in accordance with] their wicked plans they defile themselves in sin," *CD* III

---

[62] Talmon, "Waiting for the Messiah," 294–97; cf., for example, *4Q180* 1 1 פשר על הקצים אשר עשה אל "Pesher on the periods which God ordained." In contrast, Daniel 8–12 (8:17; 9:26; 11:27, 35, 40; 12:4, 9, 13) frequently use קץ in a stereotypical way with the meaning "end" as in the Bible (cf. Amos 8:2; Ezekiel 7:2–3).

והתגוללו בפשע אנוש ובדרכי נדה 17 "they defiled themselves in the sin of man, on ways of uncleanness."

In line 13 we encounter בני שמי[ם "the sons of heaven." In *1 Enoch* 6:2, 14:3 "the sons of heaven" are the fallen angels (cf. Genesis 6:2 בני-האלהים). In our text as well as frg. 69 (see below) "the sons of heaven" are the angels, as in *1QS* IV 22, XI 8; *1QHᵃ* III 22, frg. 2 10.

"The day of its judgment" (ב]יום משפטה) appears in lines 13–14. For this phrase compare *1 Enoch* 104:4 "the day of the great judgment," 10:6 "the great day of judgment" (of Azazel). The suffix of משפטה refers to רשעה (lines 11–12) or ממש[לת רשעה (line 12). In *1 Enoch* 10 Azazel is the head of the forces of evil, this chapter from the *Book of Watchers* thus represents a clear parallel to the judgment upon evil in our text.

The hope that "all evil shall be consummated" (וכל עולה תתם, line 14) is a central feature in apocalyptic thinking (cf. *1 Enoch* 1:9, 10:13–22, 91:8–9, 107:1) and belongs to the conceptual world of the Qumran covenanters; compare *1QHᵃ* VI 30 וכול בני אשמה לא יהיו עוד "and all the sons of iniquity shall be no more," XI 22 עד כלות עולה "until iniquity is consumed," XIV 15–16 וכול עולה [ור]שע תשמיד לעד "You will blot out all wickedness [and s]in for ever," *1QS* IV 20 להתם כול רוח עולה "rooting out all spirit of falsehood," *1Q27* (*1QMyst*) 1 i 5–7 כן יתם הרשע לעד "so shall wickedness cease for ever," *4Q301* (*4QMystᶜ*) 3 8 בכלו[ת [קץ רשעה "at the consummation of the period of evil." Compare further *Jubilees* 23:29 "there shall be no Satan nor any evil destroyer," *Assumption of Moses* 10:1 "then the devil will have an end; Yea, sorrow will be led away with him," Rosh Hashanah liturgy והרשעה כולה כעשן תכלה "and all evil will disappear like smoke."[63]

According to line 14 "the period of truth will be completed." For a similar terminology compare the Two-Spirit Treatise, *1QS* IV 19 ואז תצא לנצח אמת תבל "and then truth shall arise in the world for ever." An Aramaic equivalent to קץ האמת, שביע קשוט,

---

[63] The prayer *Ten Pachdeka* of Rosh Hashana, *Machzor Rabba*, 174.

is found in the *Apocalypse of Weeks, 1 Enoch* 91:12, (*4QEn⁸ ar* 1 iv 15).

The statement אל אמת הוא has close parallels in *1QS* XI 4 כיא אמת אל היאה סלע פעמי "for the rock of my steps is the truth of God," *1QHᵃ* XV 25 אל אמת אתה "You are a God of truth." The phrase "the God of truth" is also found in *Apocalypse of Adam* 1:9: "After those days the eternal knowledge of the God of truth withdrew from me and your mother Eve."[64]

Essene Apocalyptic and Synagogue Liturgy

There are significant parallels between this text, an eschatological passage in the *Book of Mysteries*,[65] and the Amidah prayers of Rosh Hashanah.[66]

---

[64] The early gnostic *Apocalypse of Adam* is influenced by Jewish apocalyptic traditions. See, for example, George W. E. Nickelsburg, "Some Related Traditions in the Apocalypse of Adam, the Books of Adam and Eve, and 1 Enoch," in *The Rediscovery of Gnosticism,* ed. Bentley Layton (Leiden: Brill, 1981), 515–39.

[65] *1Q27* 1 i 5–7: "And this shall be the sign to you that it is taking place: When the origins of unrighteousness are delivered up, and wickedness is removed from before righteousness, as darkness is removed from before light. Then, just as smoke wholly ceases and is no more, so shall wickedness cease forever, and righteousness shall be revealed as the sun establishes itself to the world. And all the adherents of the mysteries of transgression are to be no more. But knowledge shall fill the world, nor shall folly evermore be there."

[66] I am indebted to Moshe Weinfeld for the initial observation of the parallels between this passage and the liturgy. The parallels between *Sap. Work A* and the Rosh Hashanah liturgy are discussed more elaborately in Torleif Elgvin and Moshe Weinfeld, "Qumran Apocalyptic and the Rosh Hashanah Liturgy" (forthcoming). Cf. David Flusser, " 'The Book of Mysteries' and a Synagogal Prayer" (in Hebrew), in *Knesset Ezra: Literature and Life in the Synagogue: Studies Presented to Ezra Fleischer*, ed. Shulamit Elizur, Moshe D. Herr, Gershon Shaked, Avigdor Shinan (Jerusalem: Ben-Zvi Institute, 1994), 3–20. Already Joshua Bloch noted the apocalyptic character of these Rosh Hashanah prayers in *On the Apocalyptic in Judaism* (Philadelphia: Dropsie College, 1952), 62–65.

Line 2 deals with God's judgment on all flesh. According to lines 16–19 everyone will know his judgments and understand that man is only flesh before the divine judge. In the liturgy we meet the same themes:

וידע כל פעול כי אתה פעלתו, ויבין כל יצור כי אתה יצרתו

"every creature will know that You made him, and every being understand that You formed him."

The stereotypical listing of the objects of God's judging activity in lines 5–6; "h[in upon hin, generation upon genera-tion, city upon city (?), kingdom] upon kingdom, provi[nce upon province, man upon man" is paralleled in the liturgy:

ועל המדינות בו יאמר, איזו לחרב ואיזו לשלום, איזו לרעב ואיזו לשבע

"and on the provinces <sentences> will be pronounced, which one to the sword and which to peace, which one to famine and which to abundance."

According to lines 8–10 God has measured out and estab-lished the heavenly host; the luminaries give signs for the times and festivals on earth. It is this God of heaven who will set through his judgment (line 11)—themes which recur also in the liturgy. The statement כי אל אמת הוא "for a God of truth is He" (line 15) is paralleled by the liturgy's כי אתה אלהים אמת.

The usurpant/evil kingdom which recurs in Birkat Haminim appears in the Musaf prayers: כי תעביר ממשלת זדון מן הארץ "for You will remove the usurpant kingdom from the earth." The evil kingdom was probably also mentioned in our text (according to the reconstruction מֶמְשֶׁלֶת רשעה in line 12): כי שמים ירֹ[י]עֹו] תרעש מֶמְשֶׁלֶת רשעה?] מים ותהמות פחדו "for the heaven will shou[t, the kingdom of iniquity (?) will tremble,] the water and the depths will fear." The "kingdom of iniquity" is here (as in the Musaf prayer) clearly connected to cataclysmic cosmic events at the end of days. Flusser is therefore correct when he asserts that the origin of the phrase ממשלת זדון should be sought in dualistic apocalyptic thinking about the evil powers opposed to God, not in skepticism against the Roman empire based on the fourth kingdom in Daniel 7.[67]

It seems that the Rosh Hashanah prayers, *Sap. Work A*, and the *Book of Mysteries* all reflect a common eschatological tradition in the second century B.C., and that the nucleus of the Rosh Hashanah prayers was formed in this time. I would like to propose that eschatological texts from *1 Enoch* are the primary sources of inspiration for the eschatological discourses in *1QMyst and Sap. Work A*. These discourses (whether they existed separately before the composition of *1Q/4QMyst* and *Sap. Work A* or not) not only influenced the eschatological thinking and terminology of the *yaḥad*, but also the phrasing of prayers for Rosh Hashanah (the biblical day of blowing the shofar, Leviticus 23:24–25; Numbers 29:1–6). The liturgies of Rosh Hashanah deal with the fate of men and countries, both for the year to come and eternally. Apocalyptic motifs fit well into this context.

J. Bloch has argued that the apocalyptic stream in early Judaism was less "sectarian" than usually acknowledged, and that apocalyptic thoughts belonged to mainstream Judaism from the second century B.C. onwards.[68] When the apocalyptic *writings* were censored from mainstream Judaism after the fall of the temple the Rabbis could not ignore the popularity of apocalyptic *teaching*. Thus these motifs found their way into rabbinical literature and the liturgy of the synagogue. Enochic traditions exercised considerable influence both on talmudic and medieval literature.[69]

---

[67]   Flusser, " 'The Book of Mysteries' and a Synagogal Prayer," 16–17. Only in the tannaitic period was ממשל זדון identified with מלכות העליזה, i.e., Rome.

[68]   Bloch, *On the Apocalyptic in Judaism*; cf. Alexander J. Saldarini, "Apocalyptic and Rabbinic Literature," *CBQ* 37 (1975): 348–58; Alexander J. Saldarini, "Apocalypses and 'Apocalyptic' in Rabbinic Literature and Mysticism," *Semeia* 14 (1979); 187–205.

[69]   This is especially evident in *3 Enoch* and *Hekalot Rabbati*. Cf. Bloch, *On the Apocalyptic in Judaism*, 79–85; Hugo Odeberg, *3 Enoch or The Hebrew Book of Enoch*, 2nd ed. (New York: Ktav, 1973), 38–51.

On the Ultimate Fate of the Ungodly and the Righteous, *4Q418* 69 4–15

ועתה אוולי לב מה טוב ללוא	*vacat*	4
[נעשה? ומה]השקט ללוא היה ומה משפט ללוא		5
נוסד ומה יאנחו מתים על מ[שפט]ם		
אתם [ל[ש[א]ו]ל נוצרתם ולשחת עולם תשובתכם		6
כי תקן] °[ל°[ ]חْتْאْכמהْ[		
מחשכים̊ יצרחו על רובכם וכול נהיה עולם דורשי		7
אמת יעורו למשפתן] אל?[		
ישמדו כול אוולי לב ובני עולה לוא ימצאו		8
עוד] וכ]ול מחזיקי רשעה יבש[ו]		
במשפטכם יריעו מוסדי הֿרקיע וירעמו כול צ]באות		9
א]ל] ויגילו כו]ל̊ אהבי̊] צדק]		
ואתם בחירי אמת ורודפי] צדק	*vacat*	10
ב]משפֿ]ֿט אל]? [שֿוקֿל̇]ים]		
על כול דעה איכֿה תאמרו יגענו בבינה ושקדנו לרדוף		11
דעת צ̊]דיק? הוא]ה̊ בכול מ̊]עשיו ?[		
ולא עיף בכול {נ}שני עולם הלוא באמת ישעשע		12
לעד ודעה] ובינה]תשרתנו וב̊]נ̊י]		
שמים אשר חיים עולם נחלתם האמור		13
יאמרו יגענו בפעלות אמת ויעפ]נו]		
בכול קצים הלוא באור עולם יתהֿל]כו	תנחלו	14
כ]בֿוד ורוב הדר אתם] וירעד?[		
ברקיע] קודש י]סוד אולים כול]	]margin	15
ואתה בן]]ֿבכור[70]	[vac	
[bottom]		

---

70   I have juxtaposed here a small fragment of four letters, not registered in the *PC*, inv. no. 495, which preserves the left and possibly bottom margin of a column: בכור°[. This reconstruction which yields the text בן]]ֿבכור and ואתה is highly probable within the framework of *Sap. Work A*, cf. *4Q418* 81 5 וישימכה לו בכור and *1Q26* 3 2 where the reading should be corrected from יْחיד לבן לי אתה כי to בֿ]כור לבן לו אתה כי.

Translation

4. And now, you foolish of heart, how can there be goodness which was not

5. [demonstrated (?), and how can there be] peacefulness which never existed, and how can there be righteousness if it was not established, and how will the dead groan because of their j[udgmen]t?

6. [For Sheo]l you were formed, and your return will be eternal damnation, for . . . [ ]your sins[ ]

7. the dark places will shine on your multitude and all that ever came into being. The seekers of truth will wake up to the judgments[of God (?)[71]]

8. All the foolish of heart will be destroyed and the sons of iniquity will not be found any more, [and a]ll those who support evil will be asham[ed]

9. at your judgment. The foundations of the firmament will shout, and all the h[osts of God]will thunder, [and al]l who love[righteousness will rejoice.]

10. But you are the elect of truth, those who pursue[righteousness according to the j]udgment of God (?) [w]atchful

11. according to all knowledge. How can you say "We have toiled for understanding and we have been awake to pursue knowledge." R[ighteous (?) is H]e in all [His work]s (?)

12. and He has not tired during all the years of eternity. Does He not delight in truth forever? Knowledge[and Understanding]will minister to Him. And even the s[ons

13. of heaven, whose inheritance is eternal life, will they <not> say "We have toiled in the deeds of truth, and have ti[red]

14. during all the ages"?—will they not wal[k] in eternal light? [ ] also you [will inherit g]lory and abundant honour,[and tremble (?) will]

15. in the [holy]firmaments[the foun]dation of beginnings,[72] all [ ] And you are a firstborn son

---

[71] Or למשפ[ט כ]ם "to the judgment upon y[ou."

Three *vacats* introduce new paragraphs: line 4 opens an address to the ungodly, line 10 an address to the elect, line 15 a proclamation to the elect of his God-given status. Lines 4–10 contain two parallel addresses in second person plural, the first to the ungodly, the second to the righteous. The addresses to the ungodly and the elect are closely related to (and probably inspired by) *1 Enoch* 103:1–104:6. The second person plural form, which is unique within the framework of *Sap. Work A,* is likely inherited from this section of the *Epistle of Enoch.* The address to the ungodly, lines 4–9, opens with four rhetorical questions which relate the pain of the unrighteous after death to their ungodly lives. Lines 6–7 describe a woe directed to the ungodly (although the word "woe" is lacking), like *1 Enoch* 103:5–8. Line 6 elaborates their fate: Sheol and eternal damnation. Lines 7–9 (and 14–15) describe the final judgment. The righteous will wake up and witness the judgment, the evil ones will be destroyed forever, the universe and the righteous will shout and rejoice.

Lines 10–15 exhort the elect to see their life in the right perspective vis-à-vis God and the sons of heaven (the angels). The elect will inherit eternal glory. The last words of line 15 introduce a new paragraph on the status of the elect, which continued on the following (missing) column. The fact that this discourse draws upon the *Epistle of Enoch* supports a date for the origin of the Epistle in the first half of the second century B.C. rather than in the second half.[73]

---

[72]   Or סוד אולים "the secret of beginnings."

[73]   Cf. Nickelsburg, "Enoch, First Book of," in *Anchor Bible Dictionary* 2:512. The Epistle was probably composed in pre-Essene circles slightly before the middle of the century. Thus Nickelsburg, "Epistle of Enoch"; and Nickelsburg, *1 Enoch* and Qumran Origins"; James C. VanderKam, *Enoch and the Growth of an Apocalyptical Tradition* (Washington: Catholic Biblical Association of America, 1984), 142–49; John J. Collins, *The Apocalyptic Imagination: An Introduction to the Jewish Matrix of Christianity* (New York: Crossroad, 1984), 52–53; John J. Collins, "Wisdom, Apocalypticism, and Generic Compatibility," in *In Search of Wisdom,* 165–85. A later dating (the time of Hyrcanus) of the

This eschatological passage has another emphasis than the one in *4Q416* col. VII, which concentrates on God's acts and the universal aspects of the judgment. Our text contains an elaborate eschatological doctrine on the fate of men: Sheol is the place of the damned between death and the day of judgment and is a place of toil and affliction. The affliction the foolish of heart experience in Sheol is related to the unrighteousness they have shown in their lives. Although "eternal damnation" is their end, the unrighteous will be ultimately destroyed at the day of judgment. The fate of the damned is preordained by God.

In contrast to the foolish of heart are portrayed the elect, the seekers of truth. They suffer hardships now, but will inherit glory and honor in fellowship with the angels. According to line 7 the righteous who are dead will wake up at the day of judgment to witness God's judgment and then inherit eternal bliss. The contrast between the present burdensome situation of the elect and the expected afterlife is a common apocalyptic theme, which is found also in the New Testament and rabbinic literature.[74]

Lines 4–5 contain four rhetorical questions styled in a 3+1 pattern. They ask the foolish of heart about the affliction they will meet after death: The first three ask the foolish how they can expect goodness, peacefulness, and righteousness in the afterlife when they did not demonstrate these virtues during their lives. These questions lead up to the fourth, which emphasizes the painful affliction of the dead until the day of judgment (meaning only the unrighteous, as the righteous will only experience glory and honor; see line 14).

Epistle of Enoch is still held by Klaus Koch, "Sabbatstruktur der Geschichte: Die sogenannte Zehn-Wochen-Apokalypse (1 Hen 93, 1–10 91, 11–17) und das Ringen um die alttestamentlichen Chronologien im späten Israelitentum," *ZAW* 95 (1983): 420.

[74]   Cf. 2 Maccabees 7, Syr. Bar. 15:7–8, Herman L. Strack and Paul Billerbeck, *Kommentar zum Neuen Testament aus Talmud und Midrasch*, 5 vols. in 6 parts (München: Beck, 1922–56) to Luke 13:2; 24:26; Romans 8:18.

Line 6. The reconstruction with the word Sheol yields a synthetic parallelism which describes the fate of the damned: Sheol and eternal damnation. Their way to perdition is pre-ordained by God, another example of the Qumran view of pre-destination. As in *1 Enoch* 103:7, Sheol is probably the place of the damned only after death, not of the righteous. Compare the description in *CD* II 5–6 of the fate of those departing from the way: "power, might and great flaming wrath by the hand of all the angels of destruction towards those who depart from the way and abhor the precept." For a contrasting use of the terms שחת and שאול, compare *1QH^a* III 19 כי פדיתה נפשי משחת ומשאול אבדון העליתני לרום עולם "for You have redeemed my soul from the pit, and from the hell of Abaddon You have raised me up to everlasting height." The phrase שחת עולם is found in the section on the judgment on the ungodly in *1QS* IV 12, and in *1 Enoch* 5:5–6. The word תשובתכם is related to death; *1QH^a* XI 20 and XII 26 uses תשובה about man's return to dust in his death.

Line 7. The first part of line 7 is difficult to interpret. I choose to understand רובכם as "your multitudes": the dark places of the universe, including Sheol, will illuminate the damned multitude and all that existed and was done in history: the life and deeds of all men will be illuminated before God; compare Hebrews 4:12–13: "Nothing in all creation is hidden from God's sight. Everything is uncovered and laid bare before the eyes of him to whom we must give account." מחשכים are the "dark places" of Sheol, as in *1QS* IV 13. *1 Enoch* 88:1 describes the abyss where the fallen stars are thrown, as deep, empty, and dark. *1 Enoch* 103:8 mentions darkness as one of the characteristics of Sheol. וכול נהיה עולם means "all that was done and happened in history"; compare *1QS* III 15 מאל הדעת כול הווה ונהיה and XI 3–4 ואורת לבבי ברז נהיה והווא עולם משען ימיני. The statement דורשי אמת יעורו למשפתי אל? "the seekers of truth will wake up to the judgments[of God (?)" is probably a rephrasing of *1 Enoch* 91:10 "then the righteous one shall arise from his sleep": the righteous among the dead will wake up to God's judgment. Compare 1 Thessalonians 4:15–16: "those who have fallen asleep . . . and the dead in Christ will rise first."

Line 8. Three parallel sentences express that the unrighteous will be ultimately destroyed. In the three statements, the unrighteous are called *foolish of heart, sons of iniquity*, and *those who support evil*. Their end is described with the phrases *will be destroyed, will not be found any more*, and *will be ashamed*. In spite of the phrase *eternal damnation* in line 6, the phrases *will be destroyed, will not be found any more* indicate an eschatology in which the unrighteous will perish at the day of judgment and not experience eternal pain. The same teaching is found in the Two-Spirit Treatise, *1QS* IV 12–14, in which the punishing angels pester the unrighteous until they perish in the fire of the dark places. *4Q548* (*4QAmram^f ar*) frg. 1, a sectarian (?) text on the day of judgment, likewise foresees destruction and annihilation for the sons of darkness. Also *1 Enoch* contains the teaching that the unrighteous will perish, 1:1 "the day of tribulation at the removal of all the ungodly ones," 97:1 "the sinner[s] are due for a shame, they shall perish on the day of oppression." Chapter 22 of *1 Enoch*, in contrast, foresees eternal pain for the sinners, as is probably also the case in Daniel 12:2: ואלה לחרפות לדראון עולם.

Line 9. Three parallel sentences describe the threefold audience that will witness God's judgment and rejoice: the foundations of heaven, the angelic hosts of God, and those who love righteousness (the elect).

Lines 10–15 contain the exhortation addressed to the elect: they should not lose courage if they tire—even the angels tire in their work. Only God is the one who never tires. Like the angels, the elect can look forward to eternal bliss. Their God-given election is affirmed in the first sentence, "But you are the elect of truth, those who pursue[righteousness." In line 11 the speaker quotes the complaint of his supposed audience, who have toiled and tired in their struggle for the right knowledge.

In lines 11–14 the discourse changes from addressing the elect in second person plural to a reference to God and his characteristics and then to "the sons of heaven" in third person plural. The tiresome situation of the elect is compared with God, who never tires—he that always rejoices when truth is performed on earth—and with the lot of the angels. Their glorious lot will also be the inheritance of the elect.

Line 12. Not only Truth, but also Knowledge and Understanding are his company. Knowledge and Understanding are described in a personified way, almost as angelic beings ministering before God. A close parallel is *CD* II 4:

.חכמה ותושייה הציב לפניו ערמה ודעת הם ישרתוהו

Both these texts draw inspiration from biblical texts in which divine characteristics are portrayed as hypostases or distinct entities in God's presence; compare חכמה in Proverbs 1–9, Job 28, and משפט, חסד, and אמת in Psalm 89:14:

צדק ומשפט מכון כסאך חסד ואמת יקדמו פניך.[75]

Lines 12–14. The angels are brought into the exhortation. Also they have struggled and tired in their work for truth. As their lot is eternal light, so will be that of the elect. The angels tell about their unceasing ministry for God through all the period of history (בכול קצים).

Lines 13–14 have close parallels in the description of the bliss of the righteous in *1QS* IV 7–8:

עם כול ברכות עד ושמחת עולמים בחיי
נצח וכליל כבוד עם מדת הדר באור עולמים

"with every everlasting blessing and eternal joy in life without end, a crown of glory and a garment of majesty in unending light." For the phrase חיים עולם, compare Daniel 12:2 חיי עולם, *1QS* IV 7 שמחת עולמים בחיי נצח "eternal joy with life everlasting," *CD* III 20 לחיי נצח וכל כבוד אדם "for eternal life and all the glory of Adam." The term "eternal life" becomes central in the New Testament, especially in the Johannine literature, and occurs also in rabbinical literature as a term for the inheritance in

[75] Ringgren, *Word and Wisdom*, 89–106, 156. Cf. the description of the angels serving in God's heavenly presence in *Testament of Levi* 3.

the world to come.[76] נחלתם denotes the spiritual-eschatological inheritance of the elect.[77]

The statement יגענו בפעלות אמת ויעפ[נו] בכול קצים "We have toiled in the deeds of truth, and have ti[red] during all the ages," which is put in the mouth of the angels, as well as יגענו בבינה (line 11), is probably inspired by *1 Enoch* 103:9, 11: "Those who were righteous and kind during their lifetime, will they not say:[78] 'In the days of our toil, we have surely suffered hardships and have experienced every trouble . . . we toiled and laboured.' "

The phrases אור עולם . . . כ[בו]ד . . . רוב הדר (line 14) are found in *1QS* IV 7–8 וכליל כבוד עם מדת הדר באור עולמים "a crown of glory and a garment of majesty in unending light," and in *1QHᵃ* XII 15 about the lot of the elect הדר כבודכה לאור ע[ולם. "the splendour of Your glory to eternal light." The sentence באור עולם יתה̇ל[כו seems to be quoted from *1 Enoch* 92:4 "they shall walk in eternal light."

Lines 14–15. The eschatological discourse ends with the reaction of the foundations of heaven to the judgment and the eternal glory. The same thought is found in *1QHᵃ* III 35. In *1 Enoch* 94:10 it is God the Creator who rejoices over the judgment on the evil ones. For וירעד[? ברקיעי] קודש י[סוד אולים compare *1QHᵃ* III 30–31:

באושי חמר תאוכל וברקוע יבשה יסודי הרים לשרפה

---

[76] Cf. Mark 10:17–22 (par Matthew 19:16–17), which connects "eternal life" with keeping the commandments. According to Tosefta *Suta* 7:11 words of Torah bring life to the world (חיין בעולם) and convey life eternally (חיין לעולם). Cf. also the blessing after the reading of the Torah, which may have originally contained the phrase אשר נתן לנו תורת אמת, חיי עולם נטעה בתוכנ. Cf. Flusser, "He has planted it." Rabbinic literature uses both the Danielic form חיי עולם and חיים/חיין עולם, which is used in our text.

[77] Cf. Moshe Weinfeld, "The Heavenly Praise in Unison," מקור חיים: *Festschrift für Georg Molin an seinem 75. Geburtstag,* ed. Irmtraut Seybold (Graz: Akademische Druck- u. Verlagsanstalt, 1983), 430–32.

[78] "Will they not say" instead of the usual translation from the Ethiopic "do not say." I suppose the Semitic original had הלא יאמרו. The Greek text has μὴ γὰρ εἴπητε οἱ δίκαιοι.

"It consumes the foundations of the earth and the expanse of dry land, the bases of the mountains shall blaze," III 35:

יתמוגגו וירעדו אושי עולם

"the foundations of the world shall stagger and sway."

A new paragraph starts after the *vacat*. After the elaboration of the hope of the righteous and the judgment of the universe, the text continues to describe the sonship of the elect under God, ואתה בן[]ב[כור.

Concluding Remarks

Sap. Work A seems to have considerably influenced the framing of sectarian thought and terminology, especially with regard to Essene theology relating to creation order, dualism, eschatology, the remnant community, and revelation of God's wisdom to the elect. *Sap. Work A* represents a bridge between the apocalyptic Enoch literature and the clearly defined sectarian community. If this preliminary conclusion is correct, Stegemann's assertion that in the early Essene community eschatology was of secondary importance compared with Torah observance, can hardly be sustained.[79] The evidence of *Sap. Work A* rather supports the positions held by Licht, Cross, and Hengel that the Dead Sea Community developed from the apocalyptic streams in second-century B.C. Judaism.[80]

The lack of connections between *Sap. Work A* on the one hand, and *MMT* and priestly sectarian traditions on the other,

---

[79]   Stegemann, "Die Bedeutung der Qumranfunde," 523. The same would be true of Philip R. Davies's assertion that cosmic dualism was a secondary development of the sect well after the time of the Teacher, "Eschatology at Qumran," *JBL* 104 (1985): 50–52.

[80]   Licht, "The Plant Eternal"; Frank Moore Cross, *The Ancient Library of Qumran and Modern Biblical Studies*, 3rd ed. (Minneapolis: Fortress, 1995), 89–93, 143–70; Frank Moore Cross, "New Directions in the Study of Apocalyptic," *Apocalypticism, Journal for Theology and the Church* 6 (1969): 157–65; Martin Hengel, *Judaism and Hellenism* (Philadelphia: Fortress, 1974), 1:218.

does indicate that the sectarian movement represents a merger between two different streams: a lay community which fostered the apocalyptic and dualistic traditions of *1 Enoch* and *Sap. Work A,* and a priestly group which brought with it Zadokite temple traditions and the wish to structure hierarchically the new community.

The Book of Numbers at Qumran: Texts and Context

DANA M. PIKE

Brigham Young University

In this paper I examine the significance of the book of Numbers for the covenant community at Qumran. By way of background, I will relate the reason I chose this topic.

My assignment as an editor of fragments for *DJD* is to prepare about sixty plates of miscellaneous and mainly unidentified fragments from Cave 4 at Qumran for publication. While some of these fragments have been identified and have been or will be published by others, I have well over 1,000 fragments with which to work. Most are quite small. Andrew Skinner, a colleague of mine at Brigham Young University, has recently joined me in this task.

I appreciate the opportunity extended to me by FARMS to participate in this conference and the support of the Department of Ancient Scripture at Brigham Young University. I thank Professor Emanuel Tov for the opportunity to prepare some of the material from Qumran Cave 4, previously a portion of John Strugnell's allotment, for publication in *DJD* 32.

Please note that all passages quoted from the Bible follow the NRSV, and that English translations of Qumran texts follow Geza Vermes, *The Dead Sea Scrolls in English*, 4th ed. (New York: Penguin, 1995), unless otherwise indicated. My alterings of Vermes's use of "Thee, Thine," etc., are enclosed in stylized brackets { } so as to be distinguishable from his textual restorations in square brackets [ ].

While reviewing these plates I noticed a fragment assemblage on PAM 43.679 that contained the first few verses of Numbers 4, but I could find no previous mention of a fragment of Numbers on this plate. It did not take long to discover that this fragment was a portion of *4QLev-Num^a* that has recently been published by Professor Eugene Ulrich in *DJD* 12, in which it is designated as fragment 35.[1] Neither Ulrich nor anyone else seems to have been aware that this fragment, along with an additional small piece that was not published in *DJD* 12, was on PAM 43.679, a photo that was taken later than the plates cited for this fragment in *DJD* 12. This small fragment contains the lower 90 percent of the letters of two words, the tops of which are preserved on the fragment to which it joins.[2] Ulrich was happy to learn that he had restored the text correctly at this point! These fragments are no longer physically located on PAM 43.679, but fragment 35, along with this additional small piece, are found on PAM 43.035 (Mus Inv #419).[3] I mention this experience to update the information on *4QLev-Num^a* in *DJD* 12 and to highlight the excitement and the frustration involved in trying to track fragments through multiple arrangements on many plates.

Even though I have no new fragment of Numbers on which to report, I was motivated to determine, at least in a preliminary fashion, the significance of Numbers for the community at Qumran. To accomplish this purpose I will first review the number and nature of the textual witnesses of Numbers found at Qumran. This analysis will be followed in the second portion of the paper by a survey of the passages from Numbers as they are

---

[1]   Eugene Ulrich, ed., "4QLev-Num^a," in *Qumran Cave 4, VII: Genesis to Numbers*, ed. Eugene Ulrich et al., *DJD* 12 (Oxford: Clarendon, 1994), 165, pl. 27.

[2]   The fragment contains the major portion of the letters לה ועד בן, and corresponds to Ulrich's reading ומע] לה וֹעֹד בֹן on line 8 in *DJD* 12:126, "Frgs. 32 col. ii, 34 col. i-43" (Numbers 3:51–4:12).

[3]   I thank Andrew Skinner for confirming the location of these fragments in the Rockefeller Museum.

used in the principal sectarian documents of the community at Qumran.

I. The Text of Numbers at Qumran

It is common practice to judge the significance of a biblical book at Qumran by the number of copies of that book that have been discovered there. While this approach has inherent draw-backs, such as the random nature of preservation, it is clear that there is merit, at least in *relative* terms, in relating the number of preserved copies of a book to the community's perception of the value of that book. On this basis it has been observed that the portions of the thirty-six copies of Psalms, the portions of the twenty-nine copies of Deuteronomy, and the portions of the twenty-one copies of Isaiah (one nearly complete) that have been discovered in the caves around Qumran indicate the popularity and significance of these books in the Qumran community.[4] Following these books in number of attested copies are three of the books of the Torah—portions of seventeen copies of Exo-dus, portions of fifteen copies of Genesis, and portions of thir-teen copies of Leviticus are preserved. Although portions of eight copies of Numbers are cited as being preserved, I prefer to count only seven, for reasons discussed below.[5] This smaller

---

[4]   These figures are given by James C. VanderKam, *The Dead Sea Scrolls Today* (Grand Rapids, Mich.: Eerdmans, 1994), 30–31. The most convenient way to compute the number of copies of biblical books discovered at Qumran is to use Stephen Reed, comp., with Marilyn J. Lundberg, ed., *The Dead Sea Scrolls Catalogue* (Atlanta: Scholars Press, 1994). How-ever, the way some fragments are counted and the confidence given to some identifications will obviously result in different figures. See, for example, the generally higher calculations cited by Lawrence H. Schiffman, *Reclaim-ing the Dead Sea Scrolls* (Philadelphia: Jewish Publication Society, 1994), 163. Neither VanderKam nor Schiffman cite a source for their figures. See also Emanuel Tov, *Textual Criticism of the Hebrew Bible* (Minneapolis, Minn.: Fortress, 1992), 104–5.

[5]   It is not clear to me how Schiffman, *Reclaiming the Dead Sea Scrolls*, 163, arrived at twelve "Qumran manuscripts" of Numbers.

quantity in comparison with the other books of the Torah is not too surprising. Genesis and Exodus contain many foundational episodes of significance to Israelites. The emphasis placed on the Law by Jews of the Second Temple period, as found in Exodus and especially in Leviticus and Deuteronomy, would account, at least in part, for the relative frequency of attestation of these books at Qumran. The relationship of the contents of Numbers to the interests of the community will be discussed in the next section of this paper. I here emphasize that while more copies of Numbers are preserved at Qumran than copies of the so-called historical books and some of the prophetic books, Numbers is by far the *least* well attested, and thus seemingly the least significant, of any of the books of the Torah for the Qumran community.[6]

With this perspective in mind, I will now review the textual nature of the copies of Numbers that have been discovered and then note how this data correlates with the general picture of biblical texts preserved at Qumran.[7] The following texts of Numbers have been found in Caves 1 and 2.

---

[6]   Note that fragments of Numbers have been discovered elsewhere in the Judean desert: there is evidence of two copies from Nahal Ḥever and one from Wadi Murabbaʿāt; Reed and Lundberg, *The Dead Sea Scrolls Catalogue*, 227, 263. However, these manuscripts are not included in this survey of Numbers at Qumran.

[7]   For a recent review of the evidence of the copies of Deuteronomy from the Judean desert, similar to my approach in the first portion of this paper, see Florentino García Martínez, "Les manuscrits du désert de juda et le Deutéronome," in *Studies in Deuteronomy*, ed. Florentino García Martínez et al. (New York: Brill, 1994), 63–82. I thank Professor García Martínez for sharing a copy of this article with me.

1Q3, referred to variously as *1QpaleoLeviticus*, *1QpaleoLeviticus(+Numbers)* and *1QpaleoNumbers*(?)[8]

Originally published by editor D. Barthélemy with the view that these several, small pieces of a paleo-Numbers text might have been on the same scroll as a paleo-Leviticus text,[9] these fragments are now thought to have comprised a separate manuscript.[10] Only two of the fragments, numbers 8 and 9, preserve text of any consequence, and fragment 9 has full orthography, against the MT, in one of the two words preserved. Given the orthography and the paleo-Hebrew script, one might be tempted to associate this text with the pre-Samaritan witnesses, but the minimal evidence does not make it possible to determine which textual witness these fragments of Numbers represent. This is the only copy of Numbers preserved in paleo-Hebrew at Qumran.[11]

2Q6, or *2QNumbersᵃ*[12]

Two small fragments exist that appear to represent the tradition of the MT, as noted by editor M. Baillet,[13] but they are not much to work with.

---

[8] Dominique Barthélemy, "Lévitique et autres fragments en écriture 'phénicienne,'" in *Qumran Cave 1, DJD* 1, ed. Dominique Barthélemy and Josef T. Milik (Oxford: Clarendon, 1955), 53, pl. 9; preserves portions of Numbers 1 and 36.

[9] See *DJD* 1:51–53. These fragments of Numbers are listed under *1Q3*, "paleoLev," in Reed and Lundberg, *The Dead Sea Scrolls Catalogue*, 15.

[10] See Mark D. McLean, "The Use and Development of Palaeo-Hebrew in the Hellenistic and Roman Periods" (Ph.D. diss., Harvard University, 1982), 42, 60; and Tov, *Textual Criticism*, 105 n. 79.

[11] It is interesting to note in passing that all five books of the Torah are represented at Qumran by at least one paleo-Hebrew text.

[12] Maurice Baillet, "Nombres (premier exemplaire)," in *Les 'petites grottes' de Qumran, DJD* 3, ed. Maurice Baillet, Josef T. Milik, and Roland De Vaux (Oxford: Clarendon, 1962), 57–58, pl. 12; preserves portions of Numbers 3:38–41 and 3:51–4:3.

2Q7, or 2QNumbers^b[14]

One small fragment with examples of full orthography and two attestations of the plural pronominal suffix -מה, against the MT, suggested to Baillet a possible association with the tradition of the Samaritan Pentateuch.[15] Emanuel Tov tentatively classified *2QNum^b* as a text that exhibits evidence of the Qumran scribal practice, but found "insufficient evidence" to be certain.[16]

2Q8, or 2QNumbers^c[17]

One small fragment has three and a half words preserved on two lines. These words occur only once in the Bible in the combination found on the fragment, making the identification fairly certain; however, not much evidence exists for determining which textual witness is represented.

2Q9, or 2QNumbers^d[18]

The few partial words preserved on this small fragment do not allow any conclusions. Note, however, that one word is written *plene*, against the MT. Baillet remarked that "l'identification est conjecturale," suggesting that this may be a fragment of *2QNum^b*, and others have reiterated his reservations.[19] I mention this fragment here, but do not include it for purposes of computing the number of copies of Numbers found at Qumran.

---

[13]   *DJD* 3:57.

[14]   *DJD* 3:58–59, pl. 12; preserves portions of Numbers 33:47–53.

[15]   *DJD* 3:58.

[16]   Emanuel Tov, "The Orthography and Language of the Hebrew Scrolls Found at Qumran and the Origin of These Scrolls," *Textus* 13 (1986): 54; see also Tov, "Hebrew Biblical Manuscripts from the Judaean Desert: Their Contribution to Textual Criticism," *JJS* 39 (1988): 15 n. 39.

[17]   *DJD* 3:59, pl. 12; preserves a portion of Numbers 7:88.

[18]   *DJD* 3:59–60, pl. 12; perhaps preserves a portion of Numbers 18:8–9.

[19]   Baillet, "Nombres (quatrième exemplaire?)," in *DJD* 3:59. See also, for example, Reed and Lundberg, *The Dead Sea Scrolls Catalogue*, 34.

Obviously, all the fragments of Numbers from Caves 1 and 2 are quite small. They do not generally constitute sufficient evidence for determining the nature of their textual witness, nor is it possible to assert with confidence that they all represent individual copies of Numbers, as opposed to quotations or excerpts from Numbers in some other text. A number of texts from Cave 4 also exist.

4Q23, or *4QLeviticus-Numbers*[a][20]

Editor Eugene Ulrich notes that "the manuscript is carefully and clearly inscribed in an early Hasmonaean formal script, dating from approximately the middle or latter half of the second century BCE." He further notes that "the orthography is generally similar to that of 𝔐 and 𝔰𝔪," although some inconsistency is found in each of the witnesses.[21] The text, especially those portions preserving Numbers, basically reflects that of the MT and can thus be described as proto-Masoretic.

4Q27, or *4QNumbers*[b][22]

According to Nathan Jastram, who edited this text, "the orthography of 4QNum[b] is very full." Jastram cites Cross's analysis of the script of *4QNum[b]* as "Early Herodian semiformal"; this manuscript thus dates from between 30 B.C.E. and C.E. 20, although Jastram and Cross favor "the earlier portion of that range." Concerning the character of the text, Jastram states that "the array of readings in 4QNum[b] sets up a remarkable pattern of correlation with the other textual witnesses of the book of Numbers," including the LXX and especially the SP. Furthermore, *4QNum[b]* "has a significant number of unique readings."[23]

---

[20]   *DJD* 12:153–76, pl. 23–30; preserves portions of Numbers 1–4; 8–13; 22; 26; 30–35.

[21]   Ulrich, "4QLev-Num[a]," in *DJD* 12:154.

[22]   *DJD* 12:205–67, pl. 38–49; preserves portions of most of the chapters of Numbers 11–36.

[23]   Nathan Jastram, "4QNum[b]," in *DJD* 12:211–15.

4QNum^b is classified as "pre-Samaritan," and Tov has described this text as an example of the so-called Qumran scribal practice.[24]

4Q121, or *4QLXXNumbers*[25]

Noting a "few possible minor orthographic or phonological differences between 4QLXXNum and [the LXX]," editor Ulrich describes this text as a "superior witness to the Old Greek translation." He suggests that the paleography dates this text "from around the late first century B.C.E. or the early first century C.E."[26]

The remains of the three copies of Numbers found in Cave 4—*4QLev-Num^a*, *4QNum^b*, and *4QLXXNum*—have close affinities with what have become known as the MT, the SP, and the LXX, respectively, although *4QNum^b* does go its own way occasionally. Again, this latter text has been categorized by Tov as representing the Qumran scribal practice. Since the remains of copies of Numbers from Caves 1 and 2 are scanty, the most that can be said with any degree of confidence is that one text, *2Q6*, or *2QNum^a*, is most likely proto-Masoretic, while another, *2Q7*, or *2QNum^b*, may be pre-Samaritan or represent the Qumran scribal practice.

This survey reveals that of the seven likely copies of the text of Numbers preserved in the Qumran caves (discounting *2Q9*), only five of them—*2QNum^a* and *2QNum^b*, *4QLev-Num^a*, *4QNum^b*, and *4QLXXNum*—can be employed with relative confidence as witnesses of the text of this biblical book. Of

---

[24] Tov, *Textual Criticism*, 99, 109, 115; see also Emanuel Tov, "Groups of Biblical Texts Found at Qumran," in *Time to Prepare the Way in the Wilderness*, ed. Devorah Dimant and Lawrence H. Schiffman (Leiden: Brill, 1995), 97.

[25] Eugene Ulrich, "4QLXXNumbers," in *Qumran Cave 4, IV: Palaeo-Hebrew and Greek Biblical Manuscripts*, DJD 9, ed. Patrick W. Skehan, Eugene Ulrich, and Judith E. Sanderson (Oxford: Clarendon, 1992), 187–94, pl. 42–43; preserves portions of Numbers 3–4.

[26] *DJD* 9:188–89.

these five, two, or 40 percent, are proto-Masoretic texts; one, or 20 percent, is LXX; and two, or 40 percent, may be pre-Samaritan or exhibit the Qumran scribal practice. Note that this breakdown is not consistent with the approximate figures computed by Tov concerning the types of biblical texts at Qumran:

Proto-Masoretic Texts	60%
Texts in the Qumran Style	20%
Nonaligned Texts	10%
Pre-Samaritan Texts	5%
Texts associated with the LXX	5%[27]

Thus the evidence that has been preserved suggests greater diversity in the texts of Numbers that were included in the community's library, most of which appear to have been brought to Qumran, than is found in the overall picture suggested by Tov's calculations. Unfortunately, this observation is of little value in our efforts to understand the community's view of the text of Numbers, since this breakdown itself does not tell us in what regard the Qumran people held these various textual witnesses of Numbers nor to what use they put them. Furthermore, our sample of texts is so *relatively* small that it is not possible to tell if it is statistically valid. This situation does serve to remind us, however, that while the proto-Masoretic text was on average the more frequently attested text in the community's archives, this may not have been the case for every book that eventually found its place in the biblical canon, including Numbers.

---

[27] See Tov, *Textual Criticism*, 115–17. This must be the source for the figures cited by Schiffman, *Reclaiming the Dead Sea Scrolls*, 171–72. Tov's earlier, preliminary figures, apparently employed by VanderKam in *The Dead Sea Scrolls Today*, 134, for example, were published in "Groups of Biblical Texts Found at Qumran," 101. Note that the work of all the contributors to Dimant and Schiffman, eds., *Time to Prepare the Way in the Wilderness*, including this article by Tov, was completed by 1990, even though the publication date is 1995.

II. The Book of Numbers in Context at Qumran

Besides quantifying evidence of preserved manuscripts, another means of evaluating the significance of Numbers or any book at Qumran is to evaluate the impact of the book on the community's own literature by evaluating the use made of the book's contents (themes or significant passages) in the sectarian documents. I am not talking here about portions of Numbers that appear in works such as *4QR[eworked]P[entateuch]* or *Jubilees*, but in the principal works of the community. Although some studies have focused on the biblical materials in a particular sectarian document,[28] the approach taken here is basically different, i.e., to examine evidences of the influence of one biblical book in the context of the sectarian documents.

Such an approach necessitates defining the sectarian corpus of the community, and on this scholars exhibit relative unanimity. Examples of attempts to define, to one degree or another, the principal corpus of the Qumran group include those of (1) Dimant, who distinguishes between texts exhibiting what she terms "community terminology" and those that do not;[29] (2) Talmon, who refers to "foundation documents";[30] and (3) Tov, who categorizes texts according to evidence of the Qumran

---

[28] See, for example, P. Wernberg-Møller, "The Contribution of the *Hodayot* to Biblical Textual Criticism," *Textus* 4 (1964): 133–75; and Jean Carmignac, "Les citations de l'Ancien Testament dans 'La Guerre des Fils de Lumière contre les Fils de Ténèbres,' " *RB* 63 (1956): 375–90. Other studies have overviewed the situation, citing many biblical passages as attested in many Qumran documents. See, for example, Andrew Chester, "Citing the Old Testament," in *It Is Written: Scripture Citing Scripture*, ed. D. A. Carson and H. G. M. Williamson (Cambridge: Cambridge University Press, 1988), 141–50.

[29] Devorah Dimant, "The Qumran Manuscripts: Contents and Significance," in *Time to Prepare the Way in the Wilderness*, 31–33.

[30] Shemaryahu Talmon, "The Community of the Renewed Covenant: Between Judaism and Christianity," in *The Community of the Renewed Covenant: The Notre Dame Symposium on the Dead Sea Scrolls*, ed. Eugene Ulrich and James VanderKam (Notre Dame: University of Notre Dame Press, 1994), 11.

scribal practice or the lack thereof.[31] Their views on what texts constitute the principal corpus of the community's own works are summarized in the following chart:

Dimant	Talmon	Tov
1QS: Rule of the Community	*1QS*	*1QS*
1QSa: Rule of the Congregation	*1QSa*	
1QSb: Rule of the Blessings		
1QM: War Scroll	*1QM*	*1QM*
1QH: Hodayot	*1QH* ("to some extent")	*1QH*
CD: Damascus Document	*CD*	
Songs of the Sabbath Sacrifice ("partly")		*4Q511, Shir[b]*
pesherim (including biblical pesherim, *Melchizedeq, Florilegium*, etc.)	*1QpHab*	*1QpHab*, and other pesherim, and *Florilegium* and *Testamonia*
Mysteries		*1Q27: Book of Mysteries*
Rule of the Farmer		
4QMMT: Miqṣat Maʿaśe Ha-Torah		
Sapiential texts		
Prayers for Festivals		
	Temple Scroll[32]	*Temple Scroll*

---

[31] Tov, "The Orthography and Language of the Hebrew Scrolls," and Tov, "Hebrew Biblical Manuscripts from the Judaean Desert," 10–16.

[32] Interestingly, Dimant lists the *Temple Scroll* as a text that does *not* exhibit "community terminology," while Talmon, "The Community of the Renewed Covenant," 11, specifically states that it is a "foundation document" of the covenant community. Dimant is not alone in postulating that the *Temple Scroll* is not a document that originated with the community; see also, for example, Lawrence H. Schiffman, *Sectarian Law in the Dead Sea Scrolls* (Chico, Cal.: Scholars Press, 1983), 14. However, those

Since disagreement exists among scholars concerning which documents qualify as "foundation documents" or as texts containing "community terminology," I have elected to work with those documents found on at least two of the above three lists, reviewing them for quotations or other evidence of influence from Numbers. The following discussion deals with the relevant connections in a topical fashion. All these connections have been observed before, but to my knowledge they have never been collected for the purpose of the evaluation undertaken here.

1. Ages for various types of service

There are several correlations between the age requirements prescribed in the Bible for levitical service and the age requirements for the activity of males in the Qumran community. For example, Numbers 8:24 declares that "from twenty-five years old and upward [the Levites] shall begin to do duty in the service of the tent of the meeting." This may be compared with the *Rule of the Congregation*, *1QSa*, I 12–13, which declares that "at the age of twenty-five years he may take his place among the foundations (i.e., the officials) of the holy congregation to work in the service of the congregation." Since admittance into the covenant community could take place at a minimum of twenty years of age (*1QSa* I 9–11; *CD* XV 5–6), it appears that twenty-five years is the minimum age restriction regarding "service" involving officiating.[33] Thus, according to *CD* X 4–10, twenty-five was the minimum age for a man to be a judge in the congregation. This minimum age benchmark is associated with a dif-

---

who share Talmon's opinion include Vermes, *The Dead Sea Scrolls in English*, 152, and Yigael Yadin, ed., *The Temple Scroll*, 3 vols. (Jerusalem: Israel Exploration Society et al., 1983), 1:390–99. Although a valid case can be made for suggesting that the *Temple Scroll* did not originate at Qumran, I have decided to treat it as one of the community's principal documents in this discussion.

[33] For a convenient discussion of this see Lawrence H. Schiffman, *The Eschatological Community of the Dead Sea Scrolls: A Study of the Rule of the Congregation* (Atlanta: Scholars Press, 1989), 20.

ferent function in the *War Scroll, 1QM*, VII 2–3, which records
that "the despoilers of the slain, the plunderers of booty, the
cleansers of the land, the keepers of the baggage, and those who
furnish the provisions shall be from twenty-five to thirty years
old."[34] While no specific mention is made in these Qumran texts
of the passage in Numbers 8 about the initial age for levitical
service, the fact that the age for significant types of service at
Qumran matches the minimum age for levitical service is certainly suggestive of conscious patterning or reliance. This reliance probably has more to do with actual practice in Jewish
society, based on the tradition of Numbers 8, than on mere literary influence.

Similarly, a correlation seems to exist between other age
requirements in principal sectarian documents from Qumran and
Numbers 4. In this biblical passage YHWH instructed Moses
and Aaron to take a census of the Levites who were thirty to
fifty years of age, by their clans. After they had fulfilled this
command, we read: "all those who were enrolled of the Levites,
whom Moses and Aaron and the leaders of Israel enrolled, by
their clans and their ancestral houses, from thirty years old up to
fifty years old, everyone who qualified to do the work of service
and the work of bearing burdens relating to the tent of meeting,
their enrollment was eight thousand five hundred eighty"
(Numbers 4:46–48). These verses strongly suggest that active
levitical service began at a minimum age of thirty years, a
seeming contradiction to the prescription just mentioned in
Numbers 8, which defines twenty-five years of age as the
minimum. Among the various attempts to reconcile this apparent
discrepancy is the rabbinic suggestion that a twenty-five year old
Levite was in training for a period of five years, becoming an

---

[34]   Again, discussed by Schiffman, *The Eschatological Community*,
22, who relies on Yigael Yadin, *The Scroll of the War of the Sons of Light
against the Sons of Darkness*, trans. by B. Rabin and Chaim Rabin (Oxford:
Oxford University Press, 1962), 76–79.

active participant at the age of thirty.[35] Several passages in the community's principal documents mention a minimum age of thirty for certain activities. The *Damascus Document* records that "the Priest who enrolls the Congregation shall be from thirty to sixty years old" (XIV 6–7). The next few lines of the *Damascus Document* stipulate that "the Guardian of all the camps shall be from thirty years to fifty years old" (XIV 8–9).[36] Thirty is also the minimum age requirement for official responsibilities in the eschatological Qumran community, as outlined in *1QSa* I 14–18: "at the age of thirty years he may approach to participate in lawsuits and judgments, and may take his place among the chiefs of the Thousands of Israel, the chiefs of the Hundreds, Fifties, and Tens, the Judges and the officers of their tribes, in all their families, [under the authority] of the sons of [Aar]on the Priests." Likewise, the *War Scroll* VI 12–13 cites thirty as the minimum age for cavalrymen in the great eschatological battle: "their riders shall be gallant fighting men and skilled horsemen, and their age shall be from thirty to forty-five years."[37] The explanation that young Levites spent five years in preparatory service, from age twenty-five to thirty, helps clarify the requirements for military service in the Qumran sectarian documents: while service of a training and background nature began at twenty-five, active duty did not begin until thirty.

It should be mentioned here that not only age requirements, but also matters of general organization in the community seem to be modeled after patterns found in Numbers 1–10.[38] Regard-

---

[35] Discussed by Schiffman, *The Eschatological Community*, 22, who cites, in n. 64, *Sifre Be-Midbar* 62, *Numbers Rabba* 4:12, and so on.

[36] Note that this age span is *incorrectly* rendered as "between thirty and sixty [*sic*] years of age," in Florentino García Martínez, *The Dead Sea Scrolls Translated: The Qumran Texts in English*, trans. Wilfred G. E. Watson (Leiden: Brill, 1994), 44.

[37] Again, this is discussed by Schiffman, *The Eschatological Community*, 21–22, with references to Yadin and others.

[38] See, for example, the comments of Yadin, *The Scroll of the War*, 38–64, and Philip R. Davies, *1QM, the War Scroll from Qumran: Its Structure and History* (Rome: Biblical Institute Press, 1977), 28–35.

ing this, Schiffman has observed that "the system of authority and communal structure envisaged for the end of days was a reflection of that practiced by the sect in their attempt to live the eschatological life in this world. . . . Here again we see the nexus of the desert heritage with the eschatological future. The very same communal and military organization which cemented the desert community of Israel was put into practice to the greatest extent possible by the sect."[39] Note again that no passage from Numbers is directly quoted or referred to, but the awareness of and reliance on these passages from Numbers by the community at Qumran cannot be missed.

2. The Priestly Blessing

Given the significance of the Aaronic priestly blessing (Numbers 6:22–28) in the Bible and in Second Temple period Judaism, and the emphasis on a righteous priestly leader at Qumran, it would be a surprise not to find any attestation of this blessing in the principal sectarian documents of the Qumran community.

> The LORD spoke to Moses, saying:
> Speak to Aaron and his sons, saying,
> Thus you shall bless the Israelites: You shall say to them,
>
> The LORD bless you and keep you;
>
> יברכך יהוה וישמרך
>
> the LORD make his face to shine upon you, and be gracious to you;
>
> יאר יהוה פניו אליך ויחנך
>
> the LORD lift up his countenance upon you, and give you peace.
>
> ישא יהוה פניו אליך וישם לך שלום

---

[39] Schiffman, *The Eschatological Community*, 23.

So they shall put my name on the Israelites, and I will bless
them.

(Numbers 6:22–27)

Although the passage is not quoted intact in any of the community's surviving documents, it has long been recognized that an
expanded form of the priestly blessing does occur in the *Rule of
the Community, 1QS*, and that several phrases of the blessing
occur in the *Rule of the Blessings, 1QSb (1Q28b)*. Consider
these lines from *1QS* II 2–4, in which the additions to the biblical text are italicized:

> May He bless you *with every good* and keep you *from every
> evil*;
> May He enlighten *your heart with immortal wisdom* and
> favor you *with eternal knowledge*;
> May He lift up his *merciful* countenance upon you for *eter-
> nal* peace.[40]

Bilhah Nitzan has commented on "the addition of a concise
homily connected to each verb of the priestly blessing recited in
the biblical form."[41]

While phrases and words of the priestly blessing are evident
in *1QSb*, they are used in a more random or varied way, in
contrast to *1QS*. Note that key words and phrases from the
priestly blessing are attested in I 3 (יברככה א[דני]) and 5
(יחו[נכה]); II 22–27 (ו[י]חונכה] occurs in each of these lines; and
III 1 (ישא אדוני פניו אליכה), 3 (ישא . . . פניו), 4 ([א]ישא), 21
(שלומכה), and 25 (יברככה אדני). This led Schiffman to conclude
that "most of the text may be regarded as an expansion upon the

---

[40] Translation by Bilhah Nitzan, *Qumran Prayer and Religious Poetry*
(Leiden: Brill, 1994), 148.

[41] Ibid. See George J. Brooke's discussion of this passage in *Exegesis
at Qumran* (Sheffield: JSOT, 1985), 295–301, in which he comments on
the "expansions of the benediction of Num 6:24–26 [as] a clear example of
the exegetical technique of *ʾasmaktâ*, the use of biblical citations and allusions to support a biblical quotation" (pp. 298–99).

priestly blessing,"[42] while Nitzan has commented on "the free poetic use of selected verbs from the blessing."[43] It seems clear that these passages in *1QSb* exhibit conscious literary dependence on the priestly blessing in Numbers 6.

3. Balaam's Prophecy

Of the four passages from Numbers that are quoted and interpreted in the *Damascus Covenant* or *Document* (*CD*), Numbers 24:17 is the most significant. This is the passage in which Balaam prophesies about a star and scepter:

> I see him, but not now;
> I behold him, but not near—
> a star shall come out of Jacob,
> and a scepter shall rise out of Israel;
> it shall crush the borderlands of Moab,
> and the territory of all the Shethites.
>
> (Numbers 24:17)

A portion of Balaam's statement is quoted and interpreted in *CD* VII 19–21; however, it is preceded by quotations from, and interpretations of, phrases from Amos 9:11 and Amos 5:27:

> When the two houses of Israel were divided, Ephraim departed from Judah. And all the apostates were given up to the sword, but those who held fast escaped to the land of the north; as God said: *I will exile the tabernacle of your king and the bases of your statues from my tent to Damascus* (Amos v, 26–7).
>
> The Books of the Law are the *tabernacle* of the king; as God said, *I will raise up the tabernacle of David which is fallen* (Amos ix, 11). The *king* is the congrega-

---

[42]   Schiffman, *The Eschatological Community*, 74, in which he also outlines the key words and phrases as listed here.

[43]   Nitzan, *Qumran Prayer*, 148.

tion; and the *bases of the statues* are the Books of the Prophets whose sayings Israel despised. The *star* is the Interpreter of the Law who shall come to Damascus; as it is written, *A star shall come forth out of Jacob and a sceptre shall rise out of Israel* (Num. xxiv, 17). The *sceptre* is the Prince of the whole congregation, and when he comes *he shall smite all the children of Seth* (Num. xxiv, 17). (*CD* VII 12–21)

The star is equated with the "Interpreter of the Law," דורש תורה, who is best understood as the great priestly figure of the future, referred to elsewhere as "Messiah," משיח, and "Chief Priest," כוהן הראש.[44] The equation of the scepter with the "prince of the congregation," נשיא (כל) העדה, correlates with other passages that refer to this "prince" as the great messianic military leader.[45] This passage in Numbers 24:17 was thus seen by those in the community at Qumran as referring to the two eschatological messiahs, the priestly ("star") and the davidic ("scepter"). While it is true that a messianic interpretation of this passage is not unique to Qumran, the way it is woven with commentary into the *Damascus Document* indicates that the Qumran community had made it their own.[46]

---

[44] See, conveniently, the recent summary of messianic related titles by James VanderKam, "Messianism in the Scrolls," in *Community of the Renewed Covenant*, 220–34.

[45] See ibid., 212–19, especially 218–19, in which VanderKam discusses passages from *1QSb*, *1QM*, *4QpIsaᵃ*, and *4Q285*, concluding that the "Prince of the [whole] congregation" is one of the "three principal messianic titles for the davidic messiah [the others being 'Messiah' and 'Branch of David'], and as noted earlier, the three are equated with one another" (ibid., 219). See also John J. Collins, *The Scepter and the Star: The Messiahs of the Dead Sea Scrolls and Other Ancient Literature* (New York: Doubleday, 1995), 63–64; pages 80–82 contain Collins's summary discussion and evaluation of the "Amos-Numbers midrash."

[46] For a convenient survey of non-Qumran documents in which Numbers 24:17 is viewed messianically (Philo, Aqiba, and so on), see Collins, *The Scepter and the Star*, 63–64.

It is also important to note that Numbers 24:17 is quoted in two other texts attributed to the Qumran community, *1QM* and *4QTest* (*4Q175*). In neither case does explicit interpretation accompany the quotation, but the context in both instances is eschatological. The passage in *1QM* contains praises of God's power and means of deliverance:

> Truly the battle is {Yours} and the power from {You}! It is not ours. Our strength and the power of our hands accomplish no mighty deeds except by {Your} power and by the might of {Your} great valour. This {You have} taught us from ancient times, saying, *A star shall come out of Jacob, and a sceptre shall rise out of Israel. He shall smite the temples of Moab and destroy all the children of Sheth. He shall rule out of Jacob and shall cause the survivors of the city to perish. The enemy shall be his possession and Israel shall accomplish mighty deeds* (Num. xxiv, 17–19). (*1QM* XI 5–7)[47]

Balaam's prophecy of a star and scepter, included in *4QTest*, lines 9–13, is placed in the context of four other biblical passages, including Deuteronomy 18:18–19 ("I will raise up for them a prophet like you"), which immediately precedes the quotation of Numbers 24:15–17. The perception at Qumran of the messianic nature of such passages reminds us again that Numbers 24:17 was understood and employed as a significant messianic prophecy at Qumran.[48]

Also deserving of mention in this regard is the blessing on the "prince of the congregation," found in *1QSb* V 27, in which it is said of the prince that "God raised you up as a scepter/rod

---

[47] Note Collins's disagreement with Fitzmyer that this context (*1QM*) precludes the fulfillment of this prophecy by a messianic figure; Collins, *The Scepter and the Star*, 65.

[48] See Brooke, *Exegesis at Qumran*, 311–19, for interesting comments on the relationship between the structure and content of *4QTest*.

(שבט)," again suggesting a link between the content of Numbers 24:17 and the future messiah of the Qumran community.[49]

4. The "Song of the Well"

Numbers 21 contains the story of the Israelites' trek around Edom as they headed north for the Arnon and Moab. The episode of Moses making the bronze serpent is related in Numbers 21:4–9, followed by an account of several of the places the Israelites stopped on their journey. Then we read,

> From there they continued to Beer; that is the well of which the LORD said to Moses, "Gather the people together, and I will give them water." Then Israel sang this song:
>
> "Spring up, O well!—Sing to it!—
> the well that the leaders [שׂרים] sank,
> that the nobles of the people dug,
> with the scepter, with the staff."
>
> (Numbers 21:16–18)

The majority of this "song" is quoted in *CD* VI 3–4. After hearing that Israel had strayed from their covenants with the Lord, we read that

> God remembered the Covenant with the forefathers, and he raised from Aaron men of discernment and from Israel men of wisdom, and He caused them to hear. And they dug the Well: *the well which the princes [שׂרים] dug, which the nobles of the people delved with the stave* (Num. xxi, 18). The *Well* is the Law, and those who dug it were the converts of Israel who went out of the land of Judah to sojourn in the land of Damascus. God called them all *princes* because they sought Him, and

---

[49]   As noted by James H. Charlesworth, "Blessings (1QSb)," in *The Dead Sea Scrolls, 1: Rule of the Community and Related Documents*, ed. James H. Charlesworth (Tübingen: Mohr, 1994), 121.

their renown was disputed by no man. The *Stave* is the Interpreter of the Law of whom Isaiah said . . . [Isa. liv, 16]. . . . And the *nobles of the people* are those who come to dig the *Well* with the staves with which the *Stave* ordained that they should walk in all the age of wickedness—and without them they shall find nothing—until he comes who shall teach righteousness at the end of days. (*CD* VI 2–11)

Again we meet the דורש תורה, or "Interpreter of the Law." In this case, however, this title appears to be used not in reference to the future priestly figure mentioned above, who is also referred to as כוהן הראש, but in reference to the historical Teacher of Righteousness. As Collins has recently observed, the collective evidence "suggests that such titles as Interpreter of the Law and Teacher of Righteousness could be variously used to refer to figures past or future, and that they are interchangeable."[50] My purpose is met in indicating that this passage from Numbers 21 is quoted and interpreted in connection with a significant community leader.

5. The *Temple Scroll*

Even though the contents of the *Temple Scroll*, designated *11QTemple^a* or *11Q19*, deal with the ideal temple and the cultic activities associated with it, and draw heavily on Deuteronomy, Exodus, and Leviticus, it is not surprising that it also quotes or alludes to passages and phrases from Numbers. This is especially true of passages that deal with the purity of the Israelite camp/temple and with festivals and vows. The disagreement over the origins and status of the *Temple Scroll* at Qumran was noted above, and I realize that in many ways this text is a reworking of Torah material. This latter point raises questions of

---

    50   John J. Collins, "Teacher and Messiah? The One Who Will Teach Righteousness at the End of Days," in *The Community of the Renewed Covenant*, 194; cf. 193–95. See also Collins, *The Scepter and the Star*, 102–4.

classification in many cases (e.g., is a given passage a "mod-
ified" quotation or does it merely show a great deal of literary
dependence?). Furthermore, the inclusion of the *Temple Scroll*
in this study tends to skew the picture of the use of passages
from Numbers in principal sectarian documents since it draws
upon large amounts of Torah material in a way that is quite different from most of the other principal documents. I have, therefore, as a means of illustration, limited my comments to one
passage, in which it is possible to ascertain the use of Numbers
in this text.

After various strictures regarding sacrifices, columns LIII 14
through LIV 5 of *11QTemple*[a] contain instructions from YHWH
concerning the making of and release from vows. The contents
of LIII 14–21 follow Numbers 30:3–6 quite closely, although
YHWH's decrees are presented in the first person, as is the style
in this scroll. As expected, the orthography is full; some readings are similar to the SP and occasionally to the LXX, against
the MT.

YHWH's instructions concerning vows continue into column LIV 1–5, and are based on Numbers 30:6–16, but "with
certain modifications."[51] For example, lines 4–5 concern a vow
made by a widow or divorcee:

4   וכול נדר אלמנה וגרושה כול אשר אסרה על נפשה

5   יקומו עליה ככול אשר יצא מפיה

As noted by Yadin, (1) this passage comes at the end of the section on vows in *11QTemple*[a], after the instructions regarding a
vow made by a wife, but it is located in Numbers 30:10, in the
middle of the instructions on vows, before the instructions
regarding a vow made by a wife; (2) the phrase ככול אשר יצא מפיה
in line 5 is not in Numbers 30:10, but derives from 30:3, in
which it is used in reference to a vow made by a man; and (3)
the first word in line 5, יקומו, follows the LXX, against יקום in

---

51   Yadin, *The Temple Scroll*, 2:241. Yadin's comments on this passage are found in 2:237–43.

the MT. Even freer use of Numbers 30:13–16 appears to be exhibited in column LIV 1–3.[52]

Other examples of material from Numbers can be seen in *11QTemple*[a] columns XVII, XV, XVII–XVIII, XLIX, and so on.[53] The varied and often free use of material from Numbers— the quotations and paraphrases that agree with different witnesses of the biblical text and the reordering of passages—illustrates again both a great familiarity with the text of Numbers and the apparent lack of any concern for a received text on the part of the author. It is not exactly clear what this indicates about the community at Qumran, but suggests that they had no standard biblical text of Numbers, although some texts were similar to the so-called proto-Masoretic tradition and had no single "approved" way to incorporate biblical material into their own documents.[54]

6. Varia

A number of other passages from the Qumran sectarian literature that quote or might relate to Numbers are collected here.

---

[52]   Ibid., 2:242–43.

[53]   The index of biblical passages in Yadin's *The Temple Scroll* is convenient for locating many such passages. I have found the notations by Joseph A. Fitzmyer, *The Dead Sea Scrolls: Major Publications and Tools for Study*, rev. ed. (Atlanta: Scholars Press, 1990), 211–12, concerning passages of Numbers that are included in the *Temple Scroll* to be misleading; some that could be included are not and some that seem less than significant are included. Note that neither Vermes nor García Martínez attempted to provide citations for any biblical passages in their English translations of *11QTemple*[a].

[54]   See, similarly, the comments of Wernberg-Møller, "The Contribution of the *Hodayot*," 136–37, concerning the biblical quotes and paraphrases in *1QH*, especially this statement: "We have in 1QH an apparently bewildering number of cases where the form in which a Biblical tag is quoted agrees now with this, and now with that Version, against MT. It is difficult to imagine that the author(s) composed these Hymns with a variety of recensions of the Biblical texts before them, dipping now into this, and now into that recension." Regarding *1QH*, he concluded that the "Biblical text" employed "exhibited these variants" (p. 137).

They generally exhibit less impact or influence than those passages already reviewed. Little if any comment is made about each of these passages, since there is not sufficient space to deal extensively with any of them.

 a. Other quotations from Numbers. In addition to Numbers 21:17–18, quoted in *CD* VI, and Numbers 24:17, quoted in *CD* VII, *1QM* XI, and *4QTest,* there are three other quotations from Numbers included in the community's own documents (not including the *Temple Scroll*).

 The first of these is Numbers 10:9, which appears in *1QM* X 5–8 as part of the officers' instructions to their men who are participating in the great eschatological battle:

> Our officers shall speak to all those prepared for battle. They shall strengthen by the power of God the freely devoted heart, and shall make all the fearful of heart withdraw; they shall fortify all the mighty men of war. They shall recount that which {You} [said] through Moses: 'When you go to war in your land against the oppressor who oppresses you, [you] shall blow the trumpets, and you shall be remembered before your God and shall be saved from your enemies' (Num. x, 9).

While Numbers 10:1–10 contains YHWH's instructions to Moses regarding the manufacture and use, both military and nonmilitary, of two silver trumpets, the emphasis in *1QM* X is God's ability to preserve the righteous forces in battle.[55]

 Second, after it is stated in *CD* XVI 8–9 that vows to keep the Law should never be broken, "even at the price of death," and that vows that involve breaking the Law should never be fulfilled, we read concerning vows made by women:

> Inasmuch as He said, *It is for her husband to cancel her oath* (Num. xxx, 9), no husband shall cancel an oath

---

[55] See Brooke, *Exegesis at Qumran,* 294, for some thoughts on the relationship between this quotation from Numbers and the quotation from Deuteronomy 20 that precedes it in *1QM* X.

without knowing whether it should be kept or not. Should it be such as to lead to transgression of the Covenant, he shall cancel it and shall not let it be kept. The rule for her father is likewise.(*CD* XVI 10–12)

Third, another passage from the same chapter of Numbers, which contains instructions from YHWH to Moses concerning vows, is quoted elsewhere in the *Damascus Document*:

And if they live in camps according to the rule of the Land, . . . marrying . . . and begetting children, they shall walk according to the Law . . . which says, *Between a man and his wife and between a father and his son* (Num. xxx, 17). And all those who despise . . . shall be rewarded with the retribution of the wicked when God shall visit the Land. (*CD* VII 6–9)

These three passages from Numbers (10:9, 30:9 and 17) quoted in *1QM* and *CD* remind us again of the covenant community's familiarity with biblical material and its ability and willingness to use it in idealized patterns of community life.

b. Possible allusions to passages in Numbers. The following remarks provide three examples of suggestions that have been made by scholars concerning passages in the community's principal documents that may either allude to or be based upon passages in Numbers but do not quote directly from it. These examples are meant to be representative, not comprehensive.

First, while the Teacher of Righteousness is never termed a "prophet" in the community's writings, it has been noted that the passage in the community's commentary on Habakkuk, *1QpHab* II 1–3, "those who were unfaithful together with the Liar, in that they [did] not [listen to the word received by] the Teacher of Righteousness from the mouth of God," is "reminiscent" of the passage in Numbers 12:8 in which YHWH declared that he spoke with Moses "mouth to mouth" (פֶּה אֶל־פֶּה; = "face to face" in NRSV).[56]

---

[56]   Collins, *The Scepter and the Star*, 112.

Second, according to *CD* XV 5–7:

> And when the children [better as "sons"; בניהם] of all
> those who have entered [הבא] the Covenant, granted to
> all Israel for ever, reach the age of enrollment, they shall
> swear with the oath of the Covenant. And thus shall it be
> during all the age of wickedness for every man who
> repents of his corrupted way.

A relationship has been proposed between the biblical concept of
תרומה, in which the priest's household shared with him in the
offerings he received by virtue of his service, as prescribed in
Numbers 18:11–14, 25–32, and the implication inherent in this
statute in *CD* XV, that while men explicitly covenanted to
become a member of the covenant community, "wives and
daughters were members of the sect by virtue of the status of
their male relatives."[57]

Third, it has been suggested that the content of Numbers
15:31 and 19:20 *might* be alluded to in quotations and interpretations contained in *CD* VII and *4QFlor (4Q174)* I, respectively.[58] Although space does not allow evaluation of these suggestions, the very tentative nature of the suggestion regarding
Numbers 15:31 and 19:20 serves to illustrate the subjective
nature of attempting to posit possible allusions for specific biblical passages.[59]

---

[57] Schiffman, *The Eschatological Community*, 17.

[58] Brooke, *Exegesis at Qumran*, 307 (see 343 n. 144), and 136, 166,
respectively.

[59] Other suggested allusions to passages in Numbers can be found in
Wernberg-Møller, "The Contribution of the *Hodayot*," 145, who cites one
allusion (to Numbers 5:14) in the *Hodayot*; and Carmignac, "Les citations
de l'Ancien Testament," 385, who cites at least ten possible allusions to
Numbers in *1QM*.

Summary and Conclusion

The latter portion of this study, which has surveyed the use of passages from Numbers in the Qumran sectarian documents in an effort to understand the community's regard for Numbers, can only be viewed as preliminary for two reasons. The effort and space needed to catalogue and evaluate the influence of suggested allusions to passages from Numbers in the sectarian documents would have to be far more extensive than is possible here. Furthermore, any conclusions regarding the impact of the content of Numbers on the content of the community's principal documents can only be fully evaluated and appreciated in the context of similar studies involving the other four books of the Torah, something that has not yet been undertaken.

However, this survey has revealed an interesting cross section of the *kind* of uses made of this biblical material in the principal documents of the community at Qumran: (1) direct quotation, often with an accompanying interpretation based on the community's world view, as in the use of passages from Numbers 10, 21, 24, and 30 (not counting material in the *Temple Scroll*); (2) the employment of dominant phrases and words woven into the community's own works, indicating literary dependence, examples of which include the use of words and phrases from the priestly blessing of Numbers 6 in *1QS* and *1QSb*, and possibly the use of 30:6–16 in the *Temple Scroll* (LIV 1–5); and (3) evidence of patterns of activity at Qumran that rely on but do not specifically cite the practices and prescriptions of the biblical text of Numbers, as was suggested, for example, regarding the ages for various types of service (based on Numbers 4 and 8).

My impression is that the contents of Deuteronomy and Leviticus, and probably Exodus, provide the basis for more patterns and prescriptions in the community's principal documents than is the case with Numbers. I am not sure, however, about Genesis in this regard. Discounting the *Temple Scroll*, relatively few passages from the Torah are actually quoted in the community's documents. The most significant passage from Numbers is the prophecy of "the star and the scepter," which is quoted in three different texts and probably alluded to in a fourth.[60] Concerning the impact of Numbers on the life of the community, the correlation of certain age requirements for levitical service with age requirements for some types of service in the community and the general pattern of organization of the community are the most obvious and probably the most significant. Thus the contents of Numbers seem to have had only a moderate impact on the principal sectarian documents from Qumran. The impact may well have been greater on the lives of those who studied and accepted these documents.

Numbers was important to the Qumran community because it was part of the Torah and because of a few key passages and patterns of organization, but it was one of the *less* significant of those five books in the writings of the "community of the new covenant." This evaluation correlates with and reinforces the results of the quantification of textual remains discussed in the first portion of this study, in which it was noted that of all the books of the Torah, Numbers is the least represented at Qumran.

---

[60]   A survey of the quotations from the Torah (phrases to multiple verses) noted by Vermes in his English translations of *1QS*, *1QSa*, *1QSb*, *1QM*, *4QTest*, and *4QFlor* provides the following: two from Genesis, four from Exodus, four from Leviticus, seven from Numbers, and fourteen from Deuteronomy. Vermes does not include biblical citations in *11QTemple*ᵃ or *1QH*.

The Barki Nafshi *Texts* (4Q434–439)

DAVID ROLPH SEELY

Brigham Young University

Although the scrolls from Qumran were discovered nearly fifty years ago, some very important texts still remain to be "rediscovered" in the Qumran corpus. Among the relatively unknown texts from Cave 4 are a series of six scrolls referred to as the *Barki Nafshi* texts, numbered *4Q434* through *4Q439*, which are named after the opening line of *4Q434*, which reads ברכי נפשי את אדוני "Bless, O my soul, the Lord." These texts were originally assigned to John Strugnell, who then reassigned them to Moshe Weinfeld for official publication in the *DJD* series. Since then, I have been invited to work with Professor Weinfeld on these texts. We are at various stages in our work for each of the texts, and much of the following discussion is of a preliminary nature. Strugnell has done some significant work on the texts and has sent us some of his notes. At several points I am indebted to his work as indicated in the text and footnotes.

The *Barki Nafshi* texts consist of six sets of fragments, apparently sorted according to the scribal hand, and in some cases according to the similarities of the leather upon which they are written. Several of these texts have been published recently: a set of fragments, referred to as *4Q434a*, has been published by Professor Weinfeld, who identified the fragments as an early form of the Grace after Meals for Mourners.[1] Three of the texts, *4Q434, 434a,* and *436,* have been published by Eisenman and Wise;[2] more recently translations of all three of these texts have been published by García Martínez;[3] and Vermes, in the fourth edition of his collection of Dead Sea Scroll texts, has included a translation of *4Q434.*[4] Furthermore, in the last several years allusions to these texts have been made in various books and articles dealing with the Qumran texts.

Many of the recent statements that have appeared in print about these texts need to be clarified. For example, some texts have been categorized as blessings or prayers; others have been described as hymns of praise or thanksgiving; and one text published by Weinfeld, *4Q434a,* has been labeled a liturgical text. Eisenman and Wise call these texts "Hymns of the Poor" and argue that the words of the poor found in them should be understood as terms of self-designation by the Qumran community, which they believe was the forerunner of the early Christian sect of the Ebionites.[5] Scholars have suggested that these texts represent a *Barki Nafshi* genre of texts. Some scholars have seen them as various copies of the same hymn, and others have described them as "copies of a collection of hymns."[6] Likewise, *4Q439,* which appears to be different from the other texts, is

---

[1] Moshe Weinfeld, "Grace after Meals in Qumran," *JBL* 111 (1992): 427–40.

[2] Robert Eisenman and Michael Wise, *The Dead Sea Scrolls Uncovered* (London: Penguin, 1992), 238–41. Eisenman and Wise identify *4Q436* as "Fragment 1," *4Q434* as "Fragment 2," and *4Q434a* as "Fragment 3."

[3] Florentino García Martínez, *The Dead Sea Scrolls Translated,* trans. Wilfred G. E. Watson (Leiden: Brill, 1994), 436–37, 439.

[4] Geza Vermes, *The Dead Sea Scrolls in English,* 4th ed. (London: Penguin, 1994), 280–81.

[5] Eisenman and Wise, *The Dead Sea Scrolls Uncovered,* 233–41.

[6] Eileen M. Schuller, "Prayer, Hymnic, and Liturgical Texts," in *The Community of the Renewed Covenant: The Notre Dame Symposium on the Dead Sea Scrolls,* ed. Eugene Ulrich and James VanderKam (Notre Dame, Ind.: University of Notre Dame Press, 1994), 158.

counted as one of the *Barki Nafshi* texts by some and is described by others as "a work similar to *Barki Nafshi*."[7]

There is an old parable about five blind men who all go to examine an elephant. They approach the elephant together, but then separate as one of them goes to examine the trunk, one to the foot, one to the tail, one to the stomach, and one to the ears. Each develops his own individual impression of the elephant, which is quite different from that of his companions, and which does not represent the nature of the whole elephant. When they get together to discuss their encounter with the elephant, they cannot agree on what they have experienced. Since each has in his mind an incomplete impression of the elephant, those individual impressions are not accurate.

Because five of our six sets of fragments are almost certainly from the same text or collection of texts, in this paper I would like to compare the *Barki Nafshi* texts to the elephant, and rather than looking at just one part of the elephant, or one particular text, I would like to look at the whole elephant, represented by all the texts. By looking at the whole elephant, I hope to clarify some of the aforementioned issues: the nature of these texts, the number of texts represented in this collection, the relationship of the texts to each other, and the possible relationship of these texts to the other texts at Qumran.

This study then will consist of three parts. First, I will give a brief overview of the six collections of fragments that have been entitled *Barki Nafshi*, dealing first with the contents and condition of each set of fragments. Second, I will attempt to demonstrate our current understanding of the relationship of these sets of fragments to each other—an important issue in the interpretation of the texts. And third, I will discuss briefly how these texts appear to fit into the corpus of texts found at Qumran.

---

[7]   For example, García Martínez refers to *4Q434* as a "first copy of a composition with hymns of praise which usually begin with the sentence: Bless, Oh my soul" and *4Q439* as "three tiny fragments of a composition similar to the preceding." Martínez, *The Dead Sea Scrolls in English*, 501.

Description of the Texts

4Q434 (PAM 43.513, 43.523)

4Q434 consists of approximately fifteen fragments and contains the largest segment of text in our collection. The largest fragment (*4Q434.1*) contains large portions of sixteen lines in the first column and portions of five lines in the second column. This text begins with the phrase ברכי נפשי את אדוני "Bless, O my soul, the Lord," a phrase known from Psalms 103 and 104— both of which begin and end with this phrase (Psalms 103:1–2, 22; 104:1, 35). It is likely that the opening of this text is a deliberate attempt to follow the biblical model, suggesting, perhaps, a genre of *Barki Nafshi* texts, but I do not know of any other texts from Qumran that contain this phrase. The contents of *4Q434* are perhaps best described as a hymn of praise and thanksgiving, praising the Lord for his power and expressing gratitude that he has delivered his people from distress and destruction.

In this text the author makes repeated reference to the Lord in the third person. A few short samples will illustrate the nature of this text:

(1) ברכי נפשי את אדוני
על כול נפלאותיו עד עולם
וברוך שמו
כי הציל נפש אביון
ואת (2) ענו לא בזא
ולא שכח צרת דלים
פקח עיניו אל דל
ושועת יתומים שמע
(3) {ש} זע<ק>תם ויט אוזניו אל

(1) Bless, O my soul, the Lord,
for all his wonders forever,
and blessed be his name.
For he has delivered the soul of the poor,
and the (2) humble he has not despised,
and he has not forgotten the distress of the helpless.

He has opened his eyes to the helpless,
and the cry of the orphans he has heard,
and he has turned his ears to (3) their cry.

(4Q434.1.i, lines 1–3)*

The group the Lord has delivered is identified in the opening
lines of this text as the אביון "poor," ענו "humble," and the דלים
"helpless." These terms are familiar biblical vocabulary
and are also well attested at Qumran. For example, the particular
phrase in line 3, כי הציל נפש אביון "for he has delivered the
soul of the poor," is found in Jeremiah 20:13. Similar phrases
are found in the *Hôdāyôt*. *1QH^a* V, 13 preserves the phrase,
ותצל נפש עני "you have delivered the soul of the humble," and
1QH^a V, 18 the phrase, ונפש אביון פלטתה "you have saved the
soul of the poor."

Naturally, one of the questions we ask of such a text is
whether this language of the poor is meant to be a self-designation by the community of Qumran. The answer is not a simple
one. Many passages in texts from Qumran, as in the Bible, use
this language in a general sense, referring simply to a socio-
economic category of people who are helpless in society because
they have little in terms of material possessions. Leander Keck,
in 1966, surveyed the uses of terms for poverty in the sectarian
texts from Qumran, looking for examples in which they might
be used as terms of self-designation by the community at
Qumran. He concluded: "Designations using *'ebyōn* or *'anaw*. .
. are infrequent. The sectarians apparently preferred terms with
clear theological significance in place of terms which called
attention to their circumstances, such as the oppressed, the per-
secuted or the poor. Nevertheless, among the many secondary
phrases of self-descriptions, 'the Poor' is included."[8] Keck has
collected several of the passages from the sectarian texts that
might be construed as self-designation by the Qumran commu-

---

[8]   Leander E. Keck, "The Poor among the Saints in Jewish Christianity and Qumran," *Zeitschrift für die neutestamentliche Wissenschaft* 57
(1966): 68.

nity. One of the most convincing of these passages is found in
4QpesherPsalms^a (*4Q171*), which interprets Psalm 37:11,
וענוים ירשו ארץ והתענגו על רב שלום "And the poor shall inherit the
land and delight themselves in abundant prosperity." The *pesher*
says,

פשרו על עדת האביונים אשר יקבלו את מועד התענית
ונצלו מכול פחי בליעל

"Its interpretation concerns the congregation of the poor who
will tolerate the period of affliction and will be delivered from all
the snares of Belial," a phrase that sounds very much like a reference to the Qumran community. The same phrase, האביונים
עדת "congregation of the poor," is found later in the *pesher* in
the portion in which Psalm 37:22 is interpreted.

Several other references to the "poor" are found in our texts.
While the vocabulary of the poor does not pervade these texts,
certainly the group designated at the beginning as being delivered by the Lord is characterized as such. I believe the study of
the language of the poor at Qumran will be enhanced by the
publication and study of our texts about this group. *4Q434.1.i*
goes on to say:

(3) ברוב רחמיו חנן ענוים
ויפקח עיניהם לראות את דרכיו
ואזנ[י]הם לשמוע (4) למודו
וימול עורלות לבם
ויצילם למען חסדו
ויכן לדרך רגלם . . . .
(7) שפטם ברוב רחמו . . .
(9) ויתן לפניהם מחשכים לאור
ומעקשים למישור

(3) In the abundance of his mercy he was gracious to the needy
and he has opened their eyes to see his ways
and their ears to hear (4) his teaching.
And he has circumcised the foreskins of their heart,
and he has delivered them because of his grace
and he set their feet to the way. . . .

(7) He has judged them in the abundance of his mercy . . .
(9) and he made the dark places light before them,
and the crooked places straight.

(*4Q434.1.i,* lines 3–4, 7, 9)

At this point the text becomes quite fragmentary, but line 10 preserves the phrase כְּלֵב אֱחֵ]ר נתן להם "He gave them another heart," a theme found elsewhere in our texts.[9]

The other large section of text is found in two fragments containing sections of thirteen lines of text, which were recently published by Weinfeld as a Grace after Meals text.[10] Weinfeld refers to this text as *4Q434.2,* but in recent lists of texts this one is almost always referred to as *4Q434a.* For convenience we will refer to it as *4Q434a* in this discussion. In his article Weinfeld argues convincingly that the fragments should be read together and should be entitled "Grace after Meals for Mourners" since they preserve all the elements of the grace after meals common in rabbinic Pharisaic Judaism. Weinfeld believes this text to be a liturgical one not necessarily related to the rest of the *Barki Nafshi* hymns. The contents of the text do seem to be distinct from the hymn in *4Q434.1*; however, the text on these fragments also begins with an allusion to the poor— להנחם על אבלה עניה "to be comforted for the poor in mourning" (*4Q434a,* line 1)—and continues to refer to God in the third person. Furthermore, in line 11 of *4Q434a* there appears to be the word ברכי, all of which evidence suggests the possibility of a relationship between the two texts.

The rest of the fragments do not preserve much text except for *4Q434.7,* which contains parts of two lines and which mentions Moab and Edom.

4Q435 (PAM 43.523)

4Q435 consists of five small fragments, the biggest fragment containing three or four words from each of the ends of

---

[9] See page 210, below.
[10] Weinfeld, "Grace after Meals in Qumran," 427–40.

five lines and the first few letters of five lines from an adjacent column. The content of the text of these fragments is insignificant in itself since almost all the text is attested more completely in the other *Barki Nafshi* fragments (*4Q434*, *436*, and *437*). But these fragments are invaluable in that they have preserved important clues about the relationship of four of the *Barki Nafshi* texts, suggesting that each represents portions of a single text or collection of hymns. We will discuss this evidence in some detail below when we examine the relationship between the texts.

4Q436 (PAM 43.528)

4Q436 consists of four fragments. The two largest fragments fit together and preserve most of the text in a column of ten lines (*4Q436.1*). God is addressed throughout in the second person, rather than in the third person as in *4Q434* and *4Q434a*. In addition, in this text the author refers to himself several times. The opening of this text is, however, reminiscent of *4Q434* in referring to the power of the Lord in regard to the poor. The first line reads, לנחם דלים בעת צרתמה וידי נופלי[ם] לקומם "to comfort the helpless in their time of trouble; to raise up the hands of those who fall" (*4Q436.1*, lines 1–2).

The theme of this text, rather than thanksgiving for deliverance as in *4Q434* and *4Q437*, is the power of God to give understanding and knowledge to those whom the Lord has delivered. In fact, if someone were to read this text out of context of the other *Barki Nafshi* hymns, one might classify it as a wisdom text. These fragments contain the terms בינה "insight," דעה "knowledge," חכמים "the wise," and שכל "understanding." Consider the following from lines 2–4 referring to God's power:

(2) לעשות כלי דעת
לתת לחכמים דעה
וישרים יוסיפו לקח
(3) להתבונן בעלילותיכה אשר עשיתה

בשני קדם שני דור ודור
שכל עולם
אשׁר] (4) [שמת]ה לפני
ותנצור תורתכה לפני
ובריתכה אמנתה לי

(2) To make (them) vessels of knowledge
to give knowledge to the wise,
and that the upright may gain more learning;
to meditate (3) on your deeds which you have done
in former years, the years of generation after generation;
(to meditate) on the eternal understanding
which (4) you have set before me,
and how you have kept your law before me,
and have confirmed your covenant for me.[11]

(4Q436.1, lines 2–4)

In regard to the wisdom language in this text, many have
noted that such vocabulary is found elsewhere in the sectarian
texts from Qumran that are not necessarily "wisdom texts."
Recently Daniel Harrington has reviewed this material and concluded, "Many published Qumran texts of the clearly sectarian
type have Wisdom elements."[12] He cites as evidence examples
from the *Community Rule*, the *Damascus Document*, and the
Hôdāyôt. I believe our text here is best described as a "sectarian
text with wisdom elements" rather than as a "wisdom text."

The text in *4Q436.1* ends with the description of the power
of God that changed the author's heart: ותשם לב טהור תחתיו "and
you have placed a pure heart in its stead" (*4Q436.1,* line 10).
Once again there are links with the text in *4Q434.1.i* in terms of
the poor and of the change in heart that the Lord made possible
for the author of the text.

---

[11] Following Strugnell's translation.
[12] Daniel J. Harrington, "Wisdom at Qumran," in *The Community of
the Renewed Covenant,* 138.

4Q437 (PAM 44.104; 43.528)

4Q437 consists of many fragments, large and small. One of the fragments, *4Q437.1*, contains portions of the exact text found in *4Q434.1.i.* Many of the other fragments have been assembled together to form what we will call *4Q437.2*—a text that preserves large portions of sixteen lines of one column and parts of six lines in an adjacent column. Unfortunately, the beginning and ending of most of the lines are missing, as well as large portions of the middle of many of the lines, making this a very difficult text to read. Nevertheless, much is comprehensible.

As in *4Q436* God is addressed in the second person, but the theme of this text is much more like *4Q434* than *4Q436*. It seems to be a hymn of praise and thanksgiving for deliverance. A small sample will give us an idea of the nature of this text:

אברך שמך בחיי (4)
אשר הצלתני מקוש גוי[ם . . .
וחסדיך לי צנה סביב (5)
ותשמור נפשי בגוים . . .
בצר לי שמעתה קולי (8)
באשפתיך הס[ת]רתני . . .
ומשאול העלות נפ[ש]י (11)
חיים נתתה]

(4) I will bless your name while I live
who has delivered me from the snare of the nations. . . .
(5) And your grace is for me a surrounding shield,
and you have protected my soul amidst the nations . . .
(8) In my distress you have heard my voice
In your quiver you have hidden me . . .
(11) and from the place of the dead you have brought up my soul,
life you have given (me).[13]

(*4Q437.2*, lines 4, 5, 8, 11)

---

[13] Following Strugnell's translation.

Notice that this text has the same themes of deliverance and
protection from the גוים "nations" alluded to in *4Q434* and that it
speaks on several occasions about the נפש "soul." Like *4Q436*,
but unlike *4Q434*, this poem is a personal one in which the
author refers to himself rather than to his people.

4Q438 (PAM 43.529)

4Q438 consists of thirteen fragments. The text is so fragmentary it is difficult to say much about it. Several passages
preserve text that appears to match words and phrases in the
fragments in *4Q437*, but most of these passages are only three
or four consecutive letters and are problematic. Several other
fragments contain passages with vocabulary from texts found in
4Q437 but with different grammatical configurations, suggesting that if *4Q438* is to be considered a part of the *Barki Nafshi*
texts, and I believe it is, then it is probably most accurate to
argue that it preserves a variant text.

Considering the fact that *4Q438* has the earliest paleography,
late Hasmonean or early Herodian according to Strugnell, some
might even argue that it represents the earliest form of the *Barki
Nafshi* collection of texts. Because the evidence is so fragmentary we have much work to do before we can arrive at any conclusion on these matters.

4Q439 (PAM 43.529)

4Q439 is perhaps the least complicated of the texts we have
to work with, and we will soon have a preliminary edition of
this text ready for publication. It consists of a small fragment of
a text with portions of eight lines extant in one column and the
first word or two of three lines from a second column. Another
fragment preserving one word and a large margin can be logically linked with several different lines of the eight preserved in
the main fragment.

From the few surviving lines this text is probably best characterized as a lament. The author says in line 3, על כן עתי מקר מדם

"therefore my eyes are a fountain of water." The fragment preserved of this text is tantalizing, especially in respect to the identity of the author. Through various allusions the author clearly identifies himself as a leader of a group lamenting the wickedness of his people. Consider the following statements in which the author describes what he is lamenting: In line 5 he laments the demise of his city—כול עירי נהפכה לסירים "all my city is turned into crackling thorns"—and in line 6 he laments the corruption of his judges—כול שופטי נמצאו אוֹיֹלֹ[ים "all my judges have been found to be fools."[14]

Elsewhere in the text, and also related to the issue of the identity of the author, he uses the phrase, בברית אנשי סודי "into the covenant the men of my council" (line 2). Based on other Qumran texts, Strugnell would restore ולהעבי]ר בברית אנשי סודי "[*to make pass over*] into the covenant the men of my council." The phrase אנשי סודי "men of my council" is also found in *1QH*[a] XIV, 18: וכן הוגשתי ביחד כול אנשי סודי "In this way I force all the men of my council into the community." It is tempting to see such allusions to a governing figure like the Teacher of Righteousness, but further work is needed before we can come to any conclusions.

No compelling reason leads one to believe that this particular text is part of the *Barki Nafshi* texts; it is unclear why it was originally included with the other sets of fragments in *4Q434–438*. It would seem that it is part of a different elephant altogether, and at least for now we will not consider it part of the *Barki Nafshi* texts. Because it was originally categorized with the other sets of *Barki Nafshi* fragments, this text has usually been referred to as a "work similar to *Barki Nafshi*." Many other smaller texts at Qumran that lack unique or distinctive features are referred to as "*Hôdāyôt*-like texts" or "works similar to *Hôdāyôt*." These terms are convenient but not very precise. Since the *Hôdāyôt* collection is so large and varied, much of the poetry at Qumran could be called "*Hôdāyôt*-like texts." Because

---

[14] Following Strugnell.

it has more similarities with the *Hôdāyôt* than with the *Barki Nafshi* texts, *4Q439* is probably more accurately referred to as a "*Hôdāyôt*-like text" rather than a "work similar to *Barki Nafshi*." Perhaps with the publication of many of the texts from Cave 4 this text can be more precisely categorized and given a more distinguishing title.

Relationship between the Texts

This overview completed, let us now turn our attention to the relationship of these texts to each other. Concrete evidence exists that the texts *4Q434–437*, and probably *4Q438*, are closely related. In fact, the evidence suggests that the texts found in *4Q434–438* are actually different portions of the same text, and that the sections of text represented in each number approximate the sequence of the complete text. Strugnell has noted most of the evidence presented below in his notes, and this evidence was likely the reason for the original sequential numbering.

Let us quickly review this evidence. The key is found in the small fragments of *4Q435*. *4Q435.1* only has fragments of seven words in a column, sewn to the *page de garde*, but these words match the beginning of the text in *4Q434.1.i*. This confirms that *4Q434.1* is the *incipit* of the text.

The contents of the text in *4Q434a* may be different from *4Q434.1*, but nevertheless, the leather of *4Q434a* matches quite well with *4Q434.1* and is so distinctive that, in my opinion, it must be a part of the same sheet as *4Q434.1*. Visible on the right hand side of the second fragment of *4Q434a* are the holes used in sewing together two sheets of leather. I would argue that *4Q434a* completes the sheet on which *4Q434* is the beginning, perhaps to be continued by the other fragments in the same hand. Fragments *4Q434.7–12* are written in the same hand as *4Q434.1* and *4Q434a*, but are written on different leather, suggesting that they come from a later sheet of leather in the scroll, or possibly even from a different text written by the same scribe.

4Q435.2 preserves text found in *4Q436.1* and *4Q436.2*, leading to the conclusion that *4Q435.2* is from the next column of text. The leather of *4Q435.2* appears to be the same leather as *4Q435.1*, suggesting that the text in *4Q436* follows that in *4Q434*. Likewise, fragments 4 and 5 of *4Q435* appear to be written on the same leather, which is different from *4Q435.1* and *4Q435.2*. *4Q435.5*, although it only contains five words from three lines, matches the same text found in the middle of *4Q437.2*. Thus, the fragments in *4Q435* contain portions of texts from *4Q434, 436,* and *437*. In addition, *4Q437.1* preserves the exact text from the first two lines of *4Q434.1*.

Looked at from another perspective, the fragments of *4Q434* contain text found in *435* and *437*; *4Q435* contains text found in *434, 436,* and *437*; *4Q436* contains text in *435* and *437*; and *4Q437* contains text found in *434* and *435*.

Thus the physical and textual evidence strongly suggests that each of the texts *4Q434, 435, 436, 437,* and perhaps *438,* were originally complete copies of the same text or collection of texts. Whether we call it a single text or a collection of texts probably reflects our own expectation of the nature of an ancient poetic text. It seems likely that *4Q434* represents the beginning of the text, followed by the portion preserved in *4Q436* and then *4Q437*. It is still unclear exactly how *4Q438* fits in.

John Miles, in a New Testament seminar at Harvard in 1968, wrote, "In addition to several large, legible fragments, the *Barki Nafshi* group includes a number of small fragments discovered together as a multi-layered chunk from the scroll. The thickness of this chunk indicates that the *Barki Nafshi* scroll was originally of considerable length."[15] I have not yet been able to ascertain which fragments were stuck together in this multi-layered chunk, but if this statement is true it is possible that much of the *Barki Nafshi* text has disappeared. This would help

---

[15] John A. Miles Jr., "Barki Nafshi: Fragments from a Qumran Hymn Scroll, I," unpublished paper, p. 1, copy in possession of author.

explain why many of the fragments of the various collections do not have counterparts in the other sets of fragments.

It seems clear that the texts in *4Q434–438* all represent different parts of the same text, or elephant. This is an important observation. Without this information we might assume *4Q434* to be a hymn of praise and thanksgiving in which the poet speaks of God in the third person, *4Q436* to be a wisdom hymn, and *4Q437* to be a separate hymn of thanksgiving in which the poet addresses God in the second person. Since we know they are part of the same text or collection of texts, at some point we must attempt to understand the whole elephant— and try to comprehend how these various texts might fit together.

This apparent unity is not without complications. First, a fair amount of diversity exists among these texts. Weinfeld's argument that *4Q434a* is a liturgical text makes it difficult to understand its place in such a collection, and yet the physical evidence strongly suggests it was written on the same sheet of leather as *4Q434.1*. Is it possible that *Barki Nafshi* is a collection of liturgical texts? Is there any evidence that any of the other texts were used as liturgical texts? Likewise, many of the other fragments in the collection do not at first glance fit comfortably into the text. *4Q434.7*, for example, is a fragment preserving two lines that speak of the destruction of Edom and Moab much like a biblical oracle against foreign nations. Of course this fragment was originally put into the collection because the scribal hand matches that of *4Q434* and *434a*, and yet the leather of *4Q434.7–12* is different from *434.1*. Are these pieces of *Barki Nafshi* or are they remnants of another text in the same hand? We have much to do before we understand all the relationships between these fragments.

On the one hand, differences exist between the various preserved portions of these texts that cause us to ask how they fit together. For example, one of the first things we note is that *4Q434* consistently refers to God in the third person, while *4Q436* and *437* refer to him in the second person. Interestingly enough, the biblical models for the beginning of this text in Psalms 103 and 104 follow a similar pattern. Psalm 103 refers consistently to the Lord in the third person and Psalm 104 in the second. Similarly, one could ask why *4Q436* contains "wisdom vocabulary" that is not found in the other texts. A review of other Qumran texts, most notably the *Hôdāyôt*, may demonstrate a similar mixture of such vocabulary.

On the other hand, I believe that a great deal of the continuity between the various portions of this text can be demonstrated by the vocabulary that appears throughout, as well as by certain themes that are repeated in the various fragments.

First, a series of key words is found throughout these texts that serve as leitmotivs.[16] For example, לב "heart" occurs fifteen times in *4Q434, 435, 436,* and *437*; נפש "soul," twelve times in *4Q434, 437,* and *438*; דרך "way," eleven times in all five texts; רוח "spirit" nine times in all five texts; ברך "to bless," nine times in *4Q434, 437,* and *438*; גוים "nations" or "gentiles" eight times in *4Q434, 435,* and *437*; and, the verb נצל "to deliver" occurs seven times in *4Q434* and *437*. Occurrences of the language of the "poor" are not numerous but do appear in three collections of fragments: אביון "poor" only occurs once, in *4Q434*; עני/ענו "humble" appears four times, all in *4Q434*; and דל "helpless" occurs four times in *4Q434, 436,* and *437*. All these, of course, are common words in Hebrew poetry and caution must be exercised in making too much of such evidence, but a certain amount of uniformity in terms of vocabulary is revealed.

In addition, several themes deserving further study, often based on this vocabulary, are found throughout these texts. I will briefly mention three of them. While the vocabulary of the poor is not as prominent as some of the other words, three of the texts do make reference to the power of God to deliver and comfort the poor in the time of their distress (*4Q434, 434a,* and

---

[16]   Many of these terms were noted as leitmotivs by Emanuel Tov in an unpublished paper from 1968, "A Commentary on *4Q437* (Barki Napshi)," 15, copy in possession of the author.

436). Assuming *4Q434* is the *incipit* of the text, the identification of the group as the אביון "poor," ענוים "humble," and the דלים "helpless" at the beginning may be significant. The question must be addressed if this language is meant as a self-designation of the Qumran community, or whether it is simply a metaphor to describe God's power to bless and deliver the disadvantaged in the world.

In three of the texts frequent mention is made of being hidden or delivered from among the nations: ה[ח]ביאם בג̇ם "he hid them among the nations" (*4Q434.1.i*, line 7); הצלתני מ̇ק̇ו̇ש גוי̇ם "you have delivered me from the snare of the nations" (*4Q437.2*, line 4); and הצלתני פן אטבע בו ומשב̇ו̇לת גוים "he delivered me, lest I drown therein and from the river of the nations" (*4Q437.2*, line 10). What do these texts mean by the term גוים "nations" or "gentiles" here? Is this an allusion to a historical event or simply a manner of speaking?

In addition, several references are made throughout these texts to the Lord changing the heart of those he has delivered: וימול עורלות לבם "he circumcised the foreskins of their heart" (*4Q434.1.i*, line 4); ולב א̇[ח]ר̇ נתן להם "he gave them another heart" (*4Q434.1.i*, line 10); ותשם לב טהור תחתיו "and you have placed a pure heart in its stead" (*4Q436.1*, line 10); and, in conjunction with this theme, a statement that God "has set their feet to the way" ויכן לדרך רגלם (*4Q434.1.i*, line 4). All these themes also need to be studied further in the context of biblical and Qumranian texts and language.

The repetition of key words as well as various themes throughout these texts suggest a unity. The next challenge is to investigate the possibility of a logic or rationale to the sequence of these texts that can be better understood from other parallel examples in the biblical or other poetic texts from Qumran. Perhaps further study and comparison with the *Hôdāyôt* and other poetic material from Qumran can help us to better understand how these different texts fit together. It is clear that various issues in the *Barki Nafshi* texts are relevant to the study of many other texts from Qumran.

Barki Nafshi as Sectarian Writings

Most take it for granted that the *Barki Nafshi* texts are of sectarian origin. In fact, until recently most of the nonbiblical texts from Qumran were automatically accepted as sectarian texts. Today some might question the facile way such assignments have been made in the past. As Eileen Schuller says, "the pendulum has swung almost to the point where it is now the sectarian authorship that must be proved, not assumed."[17] While several sets of criteria have been proposed by Esther Chazon, Devorah Dimant,[18] and others, we will briefly survey the *Barki Nafshi* texts in terms of three prominent criteria: (1) paleography, (2) orthography and language, and (3) terminology and ideas.

1. In terms of paleography all our texts fall between the late Hasmonean or early Herodian periods and the end of the Herodian period, making it possible that they were written at Qumran.

2. Emanuel Tov has examined the orthography and language of the three major portions of our text, *4Q434, 436,* and *437,* according to the characteristics of his proposed "system" of a distinct scribal school at Qumran,[19] and has classified *4Q436*

---

[17]   Schuller, "Prayer, Hymnic, and Liturgical Texts," 169.

[18]   Esther G. Chazon, "Is *Divrei Ha-Me'orot* a Sectarian Prayer?" in *The Dead Sea Scrolls: Forty Years of Research,* ed. Devorah Dimant and Uriel Rappaport (Leiden: Brill, 1992), 3–17; Devorah Dimant, "The Qumran Manuscripts: Contents and Significance," in *Time to Prepare the Way in the Wilderness,* ed. Devorah Dimant and Lawrence H. Schiffman (Leiden: Brill, 1995), 23–58.

[19]   See Emanuel Tov, "The Orthography and Language of the Hebrew Scrolls Found at Qumran and the Origin of These Scrolls," *Textus* 13 (1986): 51, 53. Tov has further developed his set of characteristics of the Qumran "scribal school" to include the following five points: (1) a special "system" of orthography and language; (2) the presence of scribal marks; (3) "the use of *initial-medial* letters in final position; (4) the types of materials used; (5) the writing of the divine names in paleo-Hebrew characters; see Emanuel Tov, "Hebrew Biblical Manuscripts from the Judaean Desert: Their Contribution to Textual Criticism," *JJS* 39 (1988): 11–14.

and *437* as fitting clearly in the category of " 'Qumran' Orthography and Language" in the subcategory of " 'Sectarian' and Apocryphal Compositions." *4Q434*, however, falls in the category of "Undecisive Evidence."[20] This is an interesting conclusion, considering that *4Q434* preserves the most text of any of the three. In light of the evidence that all three sets of fragments represent the same text, we might have expected the orthography and language to be more uniform.

3. The third criterion is terminology and ideas. To categorize poetic texts at Qumran according to vocabulary and ideas is a tricky business since much of the language is well known from the Bible and other extrabiblical texts. Only a few terms seem uniquely distinctive to the sectarian texts from Qumran, and the *Barki Nafshi* texts do not mention any of them: יחד "community," סרך "rule," מבקר "overseer," חלקות "smooth things," מורה הצדק "Teacher of Righteousness," and איש/מטיף הכזב "Man/Spouter of Lies."[21]

Chazon suggests, however, that "sectarian writings are clearly distinguished by the constellation of a number of such terms, employed in a sense consistent with sectarian usage and in a particular ideational framework."[22] We have not yet systematically studied all our vocabulary in terms of parallels to sectarian texts, but many of the terms we have looked at today do, in fact, seem to be consistent with those found in other texts considered to be sectarian. For example, the key words we isolated from our *Barki Nafshi* texts—לב "heart," נפש "soul," דרך "way," רוח "spirit," ברך "to bless," גוים "nations," and נצל "to deliver"—as well as the language of the poor are used in ways consistent with other sectarian texts, in particular the *Hôdāyôt*. In addition, *4Q434.1.i*, line 9, has an allusion to "light and darkness" and quotations and paraphrases of Isaiah and the Psalms throughout our texts are consistent with those found in other sectarian texts. It is my preliminary impression that the

---

20   Tov, "Orthography and Language," 51, 53.
21   This list taken from Dimant, "Qumran Manuscripts," 27 n. 11.
22   Chazon, "Is *Divrei Ha-Me'orot* a Sectarian Prayer?" 14.

evidence of paleography, orthography, and language, as well as the constellation of vocabulary and ideas, very strongly argues for a sectarian origin of the *Barki Nafshi* texts.

At the same time we should keep in mind the warning given by Eileen Schuller:

> Although I applaud the attempt to distinguish sectarian and non-sectarian and am confident that we can and will refine our methodology in the coming years, I suspect that this body of texts [prayer, hymnic, and liturgical texts] will remain the most resistant to such a distinction. The very essence of prayer/hymnic discourse, whether sectarian or non-sectarian, is its dependence on a common stock of stereotypical and formulaic, biblically-based phraseology. Those precise features that scholars have singled out as hallmarks in recognizing "sectarian"—whether institutional clues (Teacher of Righteousness, calendar) or theological concepts (predeterminism, dualism)—are least likely to come to expression in a prayer text.[23]

Summary

I have briefly reviewed the contents of the six sets of fragments called *Barki Nafshi*. On the grounds of the textual and physical evidence in these texts I have argued that five of these sets of fragments (*4Q434–438*) represent five different copies of the same text or the same collection of texts. *4Q439* does not appear to be a part of the *Barki Nafshi* text or collection of texts. At a certain level the distinction between the designation "a single text, with various sections" and the designation "a collection of texts" becomes a semantic one. Those who see similarities are often more content with the first, and those who see the differ-

---

[23] This list is taken from Schuller, "Prayer, Hymnic, and Liturgical Texts," 170.

ences are more content with the second. All should consider the basic question of how these various texts are related to each other. We have examined several arguments in terminology and themes for the unity of the various extant portions of the *Barki Nafshi* texts, and have reviewed some of the evidence that these texts are of sectarian origin.

The metaphor of the blind men and the elephant has served us well. In conclusion let us compare the whole corpus of Qumran writings to the elephant and let us compare ourselves to the blind men. Because of our lack of knowledge about many aspects of the ancient world, and the Qumran documents in particular, we must accept the fact that we will always be partially blind. Many of us know much about one part of the elephant and little about other parts. To help resolve this we must continue to speak to each other and to compare our experiences with various parts of the elephant. To make matters worse much of the elephant has disappeared through the years. While, because of the fragmentary nature of the texts, the beast will probably never be completely understood, I am confident that the study of the *Barki Nafshi* texts, along with the study of the many other "rediscovered" treasures from Cave 4, will add much to our understanding of the elephant.

Analysis of Parchment Fragments from the Judean Desert Using DNA Techniques

SCOTT R. WOODWARD
Brigham Young University

GILA KAHILA, PATRICIA SMITH,
CHARLES GREENBLATT
Hebrew University, Jerusalem

JOE ZIAS
Rockefeller Museum, Jerusalem

MAGEN BROSHI
Shrine of the Book, Jerusalem

A number of questions concerning the origin and production of the ancient documents commonly known as the Dead Sea Scrolls may be approached using techniques of DNA analysis. These documents were for the most part written on what is thought to be goat- or sheep-skin parchment and represent a considerable library. Based on radiocarbon and other analyses, these manuscripts date between the mid-second century B.C.E. and the first century C.E.[1] Under most conditions it would be remarkable that intact organic material, like parchment, would be

---

Funding for this research was made available through the Foundation for Ancient Research and Mormon Studies and the Dead Sea Scrolls Foundation.
   [1]   G. Bonani et al., "Radiocarbon Dating of the Dead Sea Scrolls," *Atiqot* 20 (1991): 27–32; G. A. Rodley, "An Assessment of the Radiocarbon Dating of the Dead Sea Scrolls," *Radiocarbon* 35 (1993): 335–38.

present after such a long period of time. However, because of the unique climate and storage conditions, some of the material is remarkably well preserved. Because these parchments were produced from animal skins it is possible that they would contain remnant DNA molecules. Within the last decade new techniques in molecular biology have been developed that have made it possible to recover DNA from ancient sources. The molecular analysis of ancient DNA (aDNA) from the Judean desert parchment fragments would enable us to establish a genetic signature unique for each manuscript. The precision of the DNA analysis will allow us to identify at least three levels of hierarchy: the species, population, and individual animal from which the parchment was produced.

Recovery of DNA from Scroll Fragments

Background

The ability to recover biomolecules in ancient remains, most importantly DNA, has opened a new research area with many implications.[2] Access to aDNA provides the opportunity to study the genetic material of past organisms and identify individual and population histories. Unfortunately, the DNA recovered from archaeological specimens is of such a degraded nature that the usual techniques associated with DNA fingerprinting cannot be used. However, modifications of the traditional procedures by using the polymerase chain reaction (PCR) and short segments of unique DNA from the mitochondria and flanking short simple repeats from nuclear DNA can be used to identify highly polymorphic loci in aDNA and are useful in the precise verification of the origin and identity of biological materials such as preserved skins or parchments.[3]

---

[2]   Bernd Herrmann and Susanne Hummel, "Introduction," in *Ancient DNA*, ed. Bernd Herrmann and Susanne Hummel (New York: Springer, 1994), 1–12.

[3]   Francis X. Villablanca, "Spatial and Temporal Aspects of Populations Revealed by Mitochondrial DNA," in *Ancient DNA*, 31–58.

In 1984 the first reports on the retrieval of informative DNA sequences from an extinct animal appeared[4] and were shortly followed by the cloning of DNA from the skin of an ancient Egyptian mummy dated 2400 before present (BP).[5] The rapid degradation of biomolecules begins immediately following death. Except in unusual circumstances, this process would continue unabated until the molecules would be returned to a native state. DNA, which is found in large quantities of intact molecules in living tissue, degrades rapidly after death, and in most instances only small amounts of short DNA molecules can be recovered from dead tissue. This would normally prevent the ability to recover and analyze DNA sequences from ancient tissue. The advent of PCR[6] in 1985 further opened the possibility of isolating DNA sequences in extracts where the majority of the molecules are damaged and degraded, to an extent that precluded analysis by other molecular techniques. Theoretically, a single intact copy of a target DNA sequence, which only needs to be on the order of 100–200 base pairs in length, is sufficient for PCR, making it an ideal tool for evolutionary biology,[7] forensic sciences,[8] and aDNA studies. PCR products can be sequenced

---

[4]   Russell Higuchi et al., "DNA Sequences from Quagga, an Extinct Member of the Horse Family," *Nature* 312 (1984): 282–84.

[5]   Svante Pääbo, "Molecular Cloning of Ancient Egyptian Mummy DNA," *Nature* 314 (1985): 644–45; Jörg T. Epplen, "Simple Repeat Loci as Tools for Genetic Identification," in *Ancient DNA*, 13–30.

[6]   Randall K. Saiki et al., "Enzymatic Amplification of Beta-globin Genomic Sequences and Restriction Site Analysis for Diagnosis of Sickle Cell Anemia," *Science* 230 (1985): 1350–54.

[7]   Higuchi et al., "DNA Sequences," 282–84; Thomas D. Kocher et al., "Dynamics of Mitochondrial DNA Evolution in Animals: Amplification and Sequencing with Conserved Primers," *Proceedings of the National Academy of Sciences* 86 (1989): 6196–200; Richard H. Thomas et al., "DNA Phylogeny of the Extinct Marsupial Wolf," *Nature* 340 (1989): 465–67.

[8]   Linda Vigilant et al., "Mitochondrial DNA Sequences in Single Hairs from a Southern African Population," *Proceedings of the National Academy of Sciences* 86 (1989): 9350–54; Russell Higuchi et al., "DNA Typing from Single Hairs," *Nature* 332 (1988): 543–46; A. J. Jefferys et

directly (which is preferable) or after cloning in an appropriate vector, making DNA sequence comparisons an extremely useful tool for the study of kinship relationships between individuals and populations. The amplification of mitochrondrial DNA (mtDNA) from ancient bones and teeth dated from 750 to 5450 years BP has been demonstrated recently by a number of investigators.[9] aDNA has also been used in sex identification of skele-

---

al., "Amplification of Minisatellites by the Polymerase Chain Reaction: Towards Fingerprinting of Single Cells," *Nucleic Acids Research* 16 (1988): 10953–71; Erika Hagelberg, I. C. Gray, and A. J. Jefferys, "Identification of the Skeletal Remains of a Murder Victim by DNA Analysis," *Nature* 352 (1991): 427–29; Svante Pääbo, J. A. Gifford, and Allan C. Wilson, "Ancient DNA and the Polymerase Chain Reaction," *Journal of Biological Chemistry* 264 (1989): 9709–12.

[9]   Erika Hagelberg, B. Sykes, and R. Hedges, "Ancient Bone DNA Amplified," *Nature* 342 (1989): 485; Erika Hagelberg et al., "Ancient Bone DNA: Techniques and Applications," *Philosophical Transactions of the Royal Society of London B* 333 (1991): 339–407; Erika Hagelberg and J. B. Clegg, "Isolation and Characterization of DNA from Archaeological Bone," *Proceedings of the Royal Society of London B* 244 (1991): 45–50; S. Horai et al., "DNA Amplification from Ancient Human Skeletal Remains and Their Sequence Analysis," *Proceedings of the Japanese Academy of Science* 65 (1989): 229–33; G. Hanni et al., "Amplification of Mitochondrial DNA Fragments from Ancient Human Teeth and Bone," *C. R. Academy of Science*, 3rd series, 310 (1990): 356–70; Susanne Hummel and Bernd Herrmann, "Y-Chromosome-Specific DNA Amplified in Ancient Human Bone," *Naturwissenschaften* 78 (1991): 266–67; D. A. Lawlor et al., "Ancient HLA Genes from 7500-year-old Archaeological Remains," *Nature* 349 (1991): 785–88; E. Beraud-Columb, J. M. Tiercy, and G. Querat, "Human Beta-thalassemia Gene Detected in 7000-year-old Fossil Bones," in *Proceedings of the 3rd International Congress on Human Paleontology, Jerusalem, Israel, August 23–28, 1992* (1992), 146 (abstract); K. Thomas et al., "Spatial and Temporal Continuity of Kangaroo Rat Populations Shown by Sequencing," *Journal of Molecular Evolution* 31 (1990): 101–12; Scott R. Woodward et al., "Amplification of Nuclear DNA from Teeth and Soft Tissue," *PCR Methods and Applications* 3/4 (1994): 244–47; and Pääbo, Higuchi, and Wilson, "Ancient DNA and the Polymerase Chain Reaction," 9709–12.

tal remains.[10] Lawlor and others succeeded in analyzing an ancient class I HLA heavy chain gene locus from a 7500-year-old human brain from the Windover pond, Florida.[11] Investigations of genetic disorders in aDNA samples are just beginning. Beraud-Colomb and colleagues[12] analyzed DNA isolated from a suspected thalassemic bone specimen with cranial porotic hyperostosis, dated 7000 years BP, and found a single base deletion in codon 6, corresponding to a known beta-thalassemia mutation (frameshift 6), observed in modern Mediterranean populations. PCR has been successfully applied to the analysis of ancient mtDNA from a variety of soft tissue remains, including a 7000-year old human brain,[13] an extinct marsupial wolf,[14] and, particularly relevant to this study, the preserved museum skins of over thirty kangaroo rats.[15] Numerous reports exist of the successful extraction and amplification of aDNA from museum skins and field-collected specimens.[16] These have included both naturally preserved (mummified) and actively treated skins from a wide variety of organisms, especially birds and mammals. The aDNA recovered from these skins have been used to successfully amplify aDNA and to determine DNA sequences that have been used in evolutionary and phylogenetic studies.[17] Some of these skins have been subjected to the same conditions that we expect to exist in the scroll parchments. The

---

[10]   Hummel and Herrmann, "Y-chromosome-specific," 266–67; Svante Pääbo, "Ancient DNA: Extraction, Characterization, Molecular Cloning and Enzymatic Amplification," *Proceedings of the National Academy of Sciences* 83 (1989): 1939–43.

[11]   Lawlor et al., "Ancient HLA Genes," 785–88.

[12]   Beraud-Colomb, Tiercy, and Querat, "Human Beta-thalassemia Gene," 146.

[13]   Lawlor et al., "Ancient HLA Genes."

[14]   R. H. Thomas et al., "DNA Phylogeny."

[15]   K. Thomas et al., "Spatial and Temporal Continuity of Kangaroo Rat Populations," 101–12.

[16]   R. H. Thomas et al., "DNA Phylogeny"; K. Thomas et al., "Spatial and Temporal Continuity"; M. Culver, personal communication.

[17]   K. Thomas et al., "Spatial and Temporal Continuity."

extraction procedures for such specimens are not substantially different from those used by us in previous studies of aDNA.

Methodology

In spite of these and other reports on successful studies employing aDNA analysis, many difficulties and methodological problems are still encountered. The PCR technology is extremely sensitive and affected by artifacts because of contamination by nonrelevant DNA material. The source of contamination may be other personnel working in the field and laboratory or microorganisms such as bacteria. Another problem is the presence of inhibitors of unknown origin in aDNA extracts which interfere with the PCR reaction.[18] In our laboratories all work is routinely carried out using rooms, equipment, and reagents kept only for aDNA analysis. All personnel wear masks and sterile gloves to minimize contamination, and extensive controls are routinely used in all stages of DNA extraction and amplification. Specimens are thoroughly cleaned before sampling, and only sterile instruments that have been exposed to ultraviolet light to destroy DNA are used. Approaches have been developed to overcome the inhibitor effect, either through dilution of the inhibitor prior to PCR[19] or alternate purification techniques. Contamination by contemporary human DNA will not pose a serious problem to this study because if it does occur it will be easy to differentiate the contaminating human DNA from animal DNA obtained from the parchments using sequence analysis.

aDNA obtained from the parchment fragments may help answer some very interesting questions. These questions include:

---

[18]   Hagelberg and Clegg, "Isolation and Characterization," 45–50; Pääbo, "Ancient DNA: Extraction."
   [19]   Hagelberg and Clegg, "Isolation and Characterization"; Pääbo, "Ancient DNA: Extraction."

• **What species of animals were used for parchment production?**

Currently it is thought that most of the scrolls were written on goat or sheep skins. However, physical variations of texture, color, thickness, and follicle number and distribution in the surviving parchments may indicate a wider range of species used for parchment production. Based on microscopic examination of the distribution of hair follicles remaining in the parchment fragments, Ryder[20] was able to determine four different groups representing the possible species of origin for twenty samples of parchment from the Dead Sea area. He determined that one sample group derived from calf, one from a fine-wooled sheep, one from a medium-wooled sheep and one from a "hairy animal" that could have been either a sheep or a goat. However, the exact species identification is impossible using this technique.

It is likely that scrolls destined to contain religious writings were produced from ritually clean animals. According to Maimonides, "a scroll of the Law or phylacteries written on skins not expressly tanned for those purposed, is unfit for use."[21] Evidence from both biblical sources and from at least one of the Judean desert scrolls (*Temple Scroll*) shows that very strict requirements were placed on purity of animals skins. In particular, the skins that would be brought into the Temple or the Temple city had extra requirements placed on their origin and preparation. According to Yadin, skins that were to be brought into the Temple had not only to be pure but to be "surpassingly holy and pure." In the *Temple Scroll* this requirement is stressed.

> Skin, even if it was made from the hide of a clean animal, unless the animal had been sacrificed in the Temple [should not be brought to the Temple city]. Such

---

[20] W. Ryder, "Remains Derived from Skin," in *Microscopic Studies of Ancient Skins* (Oxford: Oxford University Press, 1965).

[21] Maimonides, as quoted by Yigael Yadin in *The Temple Scroll* (Jerusalem: Israel Exploration Society, 1983), 1:315.

ordinary skins are, indeed, clean for the need of all labour in other cities, but "into the city of my temple they shall not bring [them]."[22]

In addition, Maimonides continues in his description of preparation of leather for phylacteries "that even though you could use sinews from animals that were nevelah or terefah, the leather must be prepared by an Israelite for the express purpose of a phylactery."[23]

It seems possible that some of these parchments may have had less strict requirements for cleanliness and purity applied to them. It would therefore be possible to use skins from species of animals that would be clean, but not necessarily ritually pure and used for sacrifice in the Temple. These "clean," but not "temple-city worthy" animals could include a number of animal species such as gazelle, ibex, dishon, or deer.

By identifying the species of animal used for the production of a specific parchment, it may be possible to place a biologically based hierarchy of importance on the different manuscripts. Some would have been intended for use in the temple or synagogue and other important sites within the temple city or community, and others may have had lesser religious significance. Species identification by DNA analysis is a straightforward procedure and would be helpful for evaluation of the scroll parchments.

• **How many different manuscripts are represented in the collection of fragments at the Rockefeller and Israel museums?**

Unfortunately, most of the recovered parchment material is of a very fragmentary nature, making it difficult to establish physically contiguous pieces of manuscripts. It is estimated that the approximately 10,000 fragments can be grouped into per-

---

22 Yadin, *The Temple Scroll*, 1:309.
23 Maimonides, as quoted in ibid., 1:315.

haps 800 different manuscripts. It would be of tremendous value to be able to reconstruct the physical relationships of the different fragments of parchment. Obtaining DNA signatures unique to each manuscript will make it possible to sort out the physical relationships of scroll fragments. Such information should prove particularly useful in sorting out the huge number of small fragments that cannot be confidently grouped on the basis of fragment shape, style of handwriting, or text and could provide unique insights into the subsequent interpretation of the scrolls.

• **Which fragments can be grouped together as originating from the same manuscript because they are from identical or closely related parchments?**

Because individual animals can be identified by a unique genetic signature, it is theoretically possible to identify the unique origin of each of the parchment fragments based on their genetic information. Using the techniques of aDNA analysis, fragments belonging to the same or closely related skins can be grouped together. This could assist both in the reconstruction of manuscripts and in the verification of assemblies already made.

• **Did more than one scribe work on a single document or did different scribes use parchment originating from the same source for different manuscripts?**

There are examples in which two or more scribes worked on the same manuscript, as was the case with the *Temple, Thanksgiving*, and several other scrolls. If more than one scribe participated in the production of a single scroll, which was then subsequently damaged and today is represented by many fragments, the critical analysis based only on paleography could falsely identify separate origins of the text.

In the case of the *Temple Scroll*, it would be valuable to determine whether the parchment of the first sheet, which was used by scribe A, is biologically related to the rest of the manuscript. If it is, it could reflect the degree of genetic distinctness of the herds over a time span, supposing of course that the material written by scribe A is a repair of the manuscript effected by the same group as the original producers of the manuscript.

Because of their size, some of the scrolls (i.e. the Isaiah, *Manual of Discipline*, and *Temple* scrolls) are composed of parchments produced from a number of different animals. The *Temple Scroll* is written on nineteen separate sheets of parchment, each of which are between 37 to 61 centimeters in length.[24] It is probable that no more than two or four sheets were derived from the same animal. Analysis of fragments from each section of these scrolls will allow us to determine the degree of relatedness of the parchments in a single scroll and whether they are derived from identical or closely related animals. This analysis could also be applied to repair patches that would give us information concerning where a scroll was when it was patched. Is the parchment for the patch from the same herd as the original manuscript? Does the patch represent a herd from a different region, reflecting mobility of either the original scroll or the herd. Perhaps parchment was a trade item that was brought from one or a number of different sources. The resulting data, revealing the level of relatedness of the parchment from a single scroll, will establish benchmarks valuable for the subsequent interpretation of the genetic data obtained by analysis of the aDNA from the fragments.

• Does the collection represent a unitary library from a single locality or is it a collection representing contributions from a wide region?

By comparing DNA fingerprints recovered from the parchments and those obtained from archaeological remains of animals found in ancient sites throughout Israel, the origins or source of the parchment will be determined. In the ancient

---

[24]   Yadin, *The Temple Scroll*, 1:9–10.

populations of domestic animals in Israel it is likely that certain alleles became fixed by inbreeding in local herds. This is especially true if a group such as that at Qumran was isolated and closed.[25] Biblical examples of the importance of separating flock and herds are reflected in Genesis 13:5–9 when Abram and Lot separate their herds to different locales and again in Genesis 30:40 when Jacob separates his herds from his father-in-law Laban.

It was apparently critical that animals for the production of skins to be used in Jerusalem or the "temple city" were derived from flocks and animals "that were known to their ancestors."[26] This would suggest that flocks and herds were carefully observed and may have been guarded against "contaminating" crossbreeding. Such patterns of husbandry would effectively produce closed breeding groups and have predictable genetic consequences. Fixed allele patterns would establish specific markers in the population that could be used to identify and differentiate local herds. Analysis of aDNA extracted from goat bones excavated at Qumran and other archaeological sites within present-day Israel could reveal any fixed allele patterns and will be compared to the alleles found in the parchments. Such analysis will allow us to determine if the sampled parchments were produced locally at Qumran or, alternatively, collected from different locations. A test of the sensitivity of this procedure could be performed comparing genetic fingerprints from scrolls such as *1QS* (the *Manual of Discipline* or *Rule of the Community*), which were likely composed at Qumran, and others such as *1QIsaᵃ* (the Isaiah scroll) that were possibly brought to Qumran from another location in Palestine.[27] Another potential source to

---

[25]   James H. Charlesworth, "Foreword," in *Jesus and the Dead Sea Scrolls* (New York: Doubleday, 1992), xxxiii; Emmanuel Tov, "Textual Witness of the Bible," in *Textual Criticism of the Hebrew Bible.* (Minneapolis: Fortress, 1992), 102.

[26]   Josephus, *Antiquities of the Jews* XII, 8, 4.

[27]   Norman Golb, "The Problem of Origin and Identification of the Dead Sea Scrolls," *Proceedings of the American Philosophical Society* 124

determine the origin of manuscripts would be to compare DNA sequence with "autograph" documents, several of which may now have been identified in the Qumran collections.[28] These autographs may be considered to have been authored by the people at Qumran and would provide a fingerprint of parchment used by these individuals.

The molecular identification of parchment fragments involves a number of complex steps. However, none of the steps is without precedent. We first demonstrated the ability to isolate and amplify aDNA from parchment on "modern parchment," animal skins that have been treated in a similar way to that which we believe to have been practiced anciently. The modern or ancient skin fragments were pulverized in liquid nitrogen, dissolved and lysed in a highly chaotropic solution and the DNA recovered by collection on silica beads. We have extracted DNA from museum skins of rabbits and commercially prepared deer and sheep skins. This DNA has been successfully amplified using a primer set for a 135-base pair fragment of cytochrome b (see fig. 1, p. 229). These fragments were sequenced and shown to be specific for rabbit, deer and sheep respectively. These procedures were then used to obtain aDNA from the ancient parchment.

After we demonstrated that it was actually possible to obtain DNA from treated skins, the next step was to identify in modern goats—both domestic and wild—and other potential parchment sources the appropriate DNA sequence changes, or polymorphisms, capable of either individual, herd, or species differentiation. A specific region of DNA that has been used extensively to differentiate and establish the level of relatedness between species of the same genus is the mitochondrial cytochrome b gene. In addition, the D-loop region of mitochondria DNA has been used to identify differences within a species but unique to a

---

(1980): 1–24; Norman Golb, "Who Hid the Dead Sea Scrolls?" *Biblical Archaeology* 48 (June 1985): 68–82.

[28]   Golb, "The Problem of Origin," and Golb, "Who Hid the Dead Sea Scrolls?"

closely related herd or group. To identify individual specific polymorphisms, regions of nuclear DNA associated with microsatellite loci will be amplified with PCR, sequenced and used to delineate highly polymorphic markers. DNA was isolated from modern domestic goats, wild goats, sheep, ibex, and other animals possibly used for parchment production, and amplified using the polymerase chain reaction (PCR) with separate primer sets specific for the entire cytochrome B gene (approximately 1200 base pairs) and the D-loop region (650 base pairs). Some of these amplified DNA fragments have been sequenced and compared to identify polymorphisms that are both species and herd specific. From our preliminary results it is clear that unique DNA regions will be identified that will give good differentiation at the species and herd level.

Because of the degraded and fragmentary nature of aDNA, primers spanning small regions of nuclear and mitochondrial DNA must be used for aDNA PCR. Therefore as polymorphic regions were identified in modern goat, sheep, and wild animal populations, primers flanking these polymorphic regions were designed to amplify small (approximately 150 to 250 base pairs in length) fragments of aDNA recovered from parchment pieces.

Results

We have begun to extract aDNA from small portions of parchment fragments of the Dead Sea Scrolls, amplify biologically active DNA using the polymerase chain reaction (PCR), obtain DNA sequences, and identify unique genetic signatures of the fragments. This has shown that the process is feasible and can be used to reestablish the physical relationships of scroll fragments that may assist in clarification of translation and interpretation of the scrolls.

We have extracted DNA from eleven small pieces (approximately 0.5 cm^2) of parchment from the area and time period corresponding to the Dead Sea Scroll parchments. DNA from these fragments has been successfully amplified and sequenced using primers corresponding to an area of the same region of the cytochrome B gene in the mitochondria as above. This sequence is used for differentiation at the species level. The sequence from the parchment is most closely related to, but not identical with, the sequence corresponding to both wild and domestic goats. It is very different from the human sequence, which demonstrates that the parchment material was not contaminated by human contemporary DNA either in the handling of the parchment during collection or during the laboratory manipulations (see fig. 1). The number of differences between the aDNA and the contemporary goat DNA is greater than expected because of the accumulated normal evolutionary mutations over the 2000-year interval. It is likely that the aDNA is not from the same species as the contemporary goat samples. However, fewer differences occur between the ancient sample and the modern goat than between the ancient sample and either sheep or cow. This suggests a closer relationship to a goatlike animal than to a cow or sheep. We then compared it with sequences that we have determined for the modern ibex and gazelle. Based on these comparisons it is possible that the first two fragments derived from either a gazelle or ibexlike animal.

We have also examined six fragments from five different sheets of the *Temple Scroll*. These have all been shown to be derived from goat (see fig. 2). Also, no difference exists at this gene locus between ancient and modern goats. We are currently in the process of identifying individual DNA polymorphisms in those fragments to determine the degree of relatedness of the animals used to produce the parchment in the scroll.

We have also been able to isolate and amplify DNA from archaeological bones of ibex and goats found at Masada. In most of the instances, horn cores that have been identified by morphology to the species level have been used as the source of DNA. This demonstrates our ability to recover the necessary genetic information from ancient animal remains that will enable us to make comparisons between the scroll fragments and the animals from which they were derived. This level of sequence

DSSF-1	C	CTA	GCA	ATT	GTT	CCC	TTA	CTC	CAC	ACC	TCT	AAA	CAA	CAA	AGC	ATA	ATA	TTT	CGT	CCT
DSSF-2	.	:::	:::	:::	:::	:::	:::	:::	:::	:::	:::	:::	:::	:::	:::	:::	:::	:::	:::	:::
C. hircus	.	T..	.T.	C..	.A.	.C			.A					.G.				.C	.C	.A
G. gazella	.	.T.			A..									.C	G..				.C	..
C. ibex									.A	.?	??		??				.?	.C	.C	.A
C. ibex	.		T..			C.C		.?	.A	.C		.G	G..				.C	.C	.C	.A
O. aries	.	T..	C.A	A.A	C.C		.A	.T	.A	.A	.G	.GG				.C	.C	.C	.A	.A
B. tarus	T	.T	.T	C.A	C..	.A			.C	.C			.G.				.C	.A	.A	.A
H. sapiens	.		.A	A.C	A.C	A.C		.T	.TA	.C			.G.				.C	.C	.C	.A

DSSF-1	ATC	AGC	CAA	TGC	ATA	TTT	TGA	ATA	CTG	GTA	GCA	GAT	CTA	TTA	ACA	CTA	ACA	TGA	ATT
DSSF-2	.?	.?							.?	?..									
C. hircus	:::	:::	:::	:::	:::	.C	:::	.C	:::	:::	:::	:::	:::	.C	:::	:::	:::	:::	:::
G. gazella	C.T	.T			C..		T..	.A	AC.	.T			C.C			.C			
C. ibex	?.A	.A			.?	?.	?.	.C	.C	.C		.C	C..			.C			
C. ibex		.C		.C	.C		.C	.C	.C		.C	C..			.C			
O. aries		T..	.T		.C	.C	.C	.A	.A	.C	.C		.C			.C			
B. tarus	C..		C..	.C	.A	.C	GCC	.A		.C	.C	G	C.G			.C			
H. sapiens	C.A		CA	C.T	A.	C.C	C.C	.A	CC	.A	.CC		C.C	.TT		.C		.C	

Figure 1. Comparisons of Dead Sea Scrolls Fragments DSSF-1 and DSSF-2. The dots on succeeding lines mean that the sequence is identical to the top line.

First alignment block

C. hircus	C	TTA	GTA	CTT	GTA	CCC	TTC	CTC	CAC	ACA	TCT	AAA	CAA	CGA	AGC	ATA	ATA	TTC	CGC	CCA
11QT 1	.	:	:	:	:	:	:	:	:	:	:	:	:	:	:	:	:	:	:	:
11QT 3	.	:	:	:	:	:	:	:	:	:	:	:	:	:	:	:	:	:	:	:
11QT 5	.	:	:	:	:	:	:	:	:	:	:	:	:	:	:	:	:	:	:	:
11QT 5a	.	:	:	:	:	:	:	:	:	:	:	:	:	:	:	:	:	:	:	:
11QT 7	.	:	:	:	:	:	:	:	:	:	:	:	:	:	:	:	:	:	:	:
11QT 9	.	:	:	:	:	:	:	:	:	:	:	:	:	:	:	:	:	:	:	:
DSSF-12a	.	:	:	:	:	:	:	:	:	:	:	:	:	:	:	:	:	:	:	:

Second alignment block

C. hircus	ATC	AGC	CAA	TGC	ATA	TTC	TGA	ATC	CTG	GTA	GCA	GAT	CTA	TTA	ACA	CTC	ACA	TGA	ATT
11QT 1	:	:	:	:	:	:	:	:	:	:	:	:	:	:	:	:	:	:	:
11QT 3	:	:	:	:	:	:	:	:	:	:	:	:	:	:	:	:	:	:	:
11QT 5	:	:	:	:	:	:	:	:	:	:	:	:	:	:	:	:	:	:	:
11QT 5a	:	:	:	:	:	:	:	:	:	:	:	:	:	:	:	:	:	:	:
11QT 7	:	:	:	:	:	:	:	:	:	:	:	:	:	:	:	:	:	:	:
11QT 9	:	:	:	:	:	:	:	:	:	:	:	:	:	:	:	:	:	:	:
DSSF-12a	:	:	:	:	:	:	:	:	:	:	:	:	:	:	:	:	:	:	:

Figure 2. Sequence Comparisons of *Temple Scroll* Fragments. All fragments demonstrated an identical DNA sequence to Capra hircus. This means that the *Temple Scroll* and the random fragment DSSF-12a were derived from goat skin as opposed to sheep or other animal skin.

polymorphism will allow geographical localization of the parchment sources. It is interesting to note that the ibex sequence obtained from archaeological remains at Masada differs slightly from the sequence of the modern ibex. This may represent either a population polymorphism or a possible evolutionary event in the species *Capra ibex*.

In conclusion, we have demonstrated the ability to recover aDNA from parchment on which the Scrolls were written. We have also shown that it is possible to recover authentic sequence from this material and use it to make comparisons with other sequences. Our early results indicate that, based on the mitochondrial cytochrome B gene, the skins from which the first two ancient fragments were derived are not goat skins, either contemporary domestic goat or wild goat, but likely a wild species of gazelle or ibex. We have determined that seven other random fragments are derived from goat; six of these fragments belong to the *Temple Scroll*. These analyses differ from the classifications made by Ryder,[29] using microscopic analyses of similar parchment fragments from the same area. We have not yet identified any parchment from a species of sheep.

This project is the beginning of a fruitful collaboration that will continue over the next few years. It is hoped the analysis of DNA from parchment fragments will add a new level of critical analysis to scroll scholarship.

---

[29]   Ryder, "Remains Derived from Skin."

Appendix: Methods and Materials

Identification of polymorphisms

DNA will be extracted from the tissue or blood of eighteen modern goats representing at least three different herds using established protocols.[30] Goats will be picked at random from native herds. PCR amplifications will be as outlined below for aDNA. PCR fragments will be directly sequenced as follows:[31] Double-stranded PCR product will be separated from excess primers by agarose gel electrophoresis. Asymmetric amplification will be performed and separated from excess primers by ethanol precipitation or by filter centrifugation. Twenty microliters (ul) of the PCR product will be combined with 70 pmol of sequencing primer, heated to 80°C, allowed to cool to room temperature and placed on ice. Alternatively, double-stranded DNA will be sequenced directly after isolation from low-melting agarose gels. Sequencing reactions are as outlined for Sequenase (United States Biochemical) with the labeling reaction performed on ice with the labeling mix diluted to 1:16. Regions of polymorphic DNA will be determined by comparison of DNA sequence. The mitochondrial cytochrome b and D-loop sequences will be used to identify genus and herd-specific polymorphisms, respectively, and a nuclear locus flanking microsatellites[32] will identify highly polymorphic regions suitable for unique identification of each individual. PCR primers corresponding to short (150–250 base pair) fragments contain-

---

[30]   Lin Zhang et al., "Whole Genome Amplification from a Single Cell: Implications for Genetic Analysis," *Proceedings of the National Academy of Sciences* 89 (1992): 5847–51.

[31]   M. Orita et al., "Rapid and Sensitive Detection of Point Mutations and DNA Polymorphisms Using the Polymerase Chain Reaction," *Genomics* 5 (1989): 874–79.

[32]   E. Sullivan, personal communication.

ing diagnostic polymorphisms will be designed to amplify the aDNA. It is possible that a combination of two or more loci may be needed to identify individuals unambiguously.

As described above it is likely that certain alleles have become fixed in local ancient populations of goats. These alleles will be used as markers for each population and will serve as a biological identification marker for each piece of parchment.

Recovery of aDNA

Three manual methods of DNA extraction are currently used in our laboratory. The first is a standard lysis and deproteination procedure.[33] The tissue for extraction is either placed in an acid-washed mortar and ground to a fine powder with a pestle in the presence of liquid nitrogen, or the tissue is powdered using a small drill and bit. This powder is placed in lysis buffer (10 mM Tris HCl/10 mM EDTA) with SDS and Proteinase K at final concentrations of 0.5% and 0.2 mg/ml respectively, and incubated at 56°C overnight. The sample is then extracted with phenol/chloroform/isoamyl alcohol (25:24:1) three times and precipitated by adding 1/10 volume of 3M NaOAc and 1.5 volumes of isopropanol. The extracted DNA is suspended in TE.

The second method is very simple and has resulted in a high percentage of successful amplifications of target DNA from ancient samples. In this procedure a very small piece of tissue (0.5 mm square) or powdered material is placed in an eppendorf tube with 500 ul of a 0.5% Chelex solution (w/v in H_2O). This sample is vortexed for 1 minute, incubated at 56°C for 15 minutes to overnight, vortexed for 1 minute, brought to 95°C for ten minutes, vortexed and then centrifuged at 12,000 X g for three minutes. The supernatant is removed and stored at -20°C. This is then used in the PCR reaction. Boiling in Chelex is a simple and reliable primary method of DNA extraction for use in the PCR reaction. The probability of contamination from outside sources of DNA is decreased by the limited handling and a

---

[33]   K. Thomas et al., "Spatial and Temporal Continuity."

reduction in the number of different reagents that come in contact with the ancient sample. The ability to recover biologically active DNA from aDNA has been enhanced over other procedures by using the Chelex extraction method. However, the total amount of DNA extracted is small. This method will be used to extract DNA for single amplification or as the source of templates for the primer-extension preamplification method,[34] but other extraction procedures will also be used for larger quantity extractions.

A third method that has also been used successfully in our laboratory for extracting aDNA is the use of a highly chaotropic agent, guanidine thiocyanate. This can be used for both soft tissues as well as bone and teeth. The sample is pulverized as above before chemical extraction. Powder from bone and teeth can be used in the same manner. To facilitate this, a small drill is used to remove surface material from the tooth or bone. This powder is discarded. The drill is reintroduced to the original hole using a smaller diameter bit and between 0.05 g and 0.5 g of powdered bone material is collected. This is suspended in up to 2 ml of 4M guanidine thiocyanate, 0.5% sarkosyl, 25 mM EDTA, 100 mM NaCl, 0.1M 2-beta-mercaptoethanol, adjusted to pH 7.0 with 4M NaOH, and incubated at 56°C overnight with agitation. This is centrifuged at 2000 X g to sediment the particulate matter. The supernatant is collected and an equal volume of 5M NH_4OAc added. Two volumes of absolute ethanol are added and mixed, and placed at -20°C for 1 hour. DNA is pelleted by centrifugation at 2400 X g for 30 minutes and the pellet suspended in 1 ml of TE. Alternatively the supernatant is brought to a 2M Na concentration and the DNA is adsorbed on

---

[34] D. Irwin, Thomas D. Kocher, and Allan C. Wilson, "Evolution of the Cytochrome B Gene of Mammals," *Journal of Molecular Evolution* 32 (1991): 128–44.

silica beads, washed with an ethanol and salt wash, and eluted in distilled H_2O or TE.[35]

Amplification of aDNA

Amplification of single gene loci is performed in a volume of 25 ul in a Perkin Elmer-Cetus 480 temperature cycler. The basic temperature profile consists of a denaturation step at 94°C for 2 minutes, an annealing step at 42° to 60°C for 15 seconds to 1 minute, depending on the specific primer-set conditions, and an elongation step at 72°C for 30 seconds. The reaction mixture contains 67 mM Tris pH 8.8, 2 mM $MgCl_2$, 16.7 mM $(NH_4)_2SO_4$, 10 mM 2-beta-mercaptoethanol, 0.2 mM dNTP's, 1 uM each primer and DNA. Control reactions are set up as follows. Negative controls: In place of the aDNA, an equivalent volume of (1) a blank extraction solution supernatant (subjected to the same protocol as the aDNA extractions), (2) extraction supernatant in which the tools used to powder the samples had been rinsed between samples (to insure there was not any carryover from sample to sample), and (3) water only was used. Positive controls included (1) contemporary DNA in water and (2) contemporary DNA in the presence of a blank extraction supernatant. Separate micro pipettors will be used in the DNA extractions, preparation of the PCR reactions, and PCR product evaluations. The PCR setup, amplification, and evaluation are each done in a separate room. Evaluation of the PCR product will be performed on 2.5% NuSieve agarose gels in tris-acetate buffer containing ethidium bromide. Positive bands for secondary amplifications will be cored with a Pasteur pipette, placed in a 0.5 ml eppendorf tube, diluted to 100 ul in double distilled sterile water and heated to 50°C for 10 min.

---

[35] M. Hoss and Svante Pääbo, "DNA Extraction from Pleistocene Bones by a Silica-Based Purification Method," *Nucleic Acids Research* 21 (1993): 3913–14.

Primers for amplification

Three sets of PCR primers will be use in the initial investigation of the modern goat DNA. These correspond to the cytochrome b gene, W116, and W117.[36] These primers amplify a 172 bp fragment of the mitochondrial genome. Primers W152 5' AAT TAA GCT AAA TCC TTA CT 3' and W153 5' ATT GAA TTG CAA ATT CAA AG 3' flank the L-chain replication origin in goat specific mitochondrial DNA. Primers to be used to amplify nuclear genome regions corresponding to microsatellite loci will be determined during the course of this study based on polymorphisms in modern native goat populations. The first nuclear locus to be amplified corresponds to a $(CA)_{15}$ repeat flanked by the primers W154 5' CAA AGC ATA GTT CAT TCA CA 3' and W155 5' GGA GTC ACA AAG AGT TGA AC 3'; this primer set produces a fragment approximately 151 bp in length. Because aDNA is of a very fragmentary nature the large PCR fragments expected from modern DNA cannot be obtained; therefore, primers spanning 150 to 250 bp corresponding to polymorphic regions of the sequences have been and will be designed.

Analysis

Polymorphic regions of the aDNA corresponding to parchment fragments will be determined by a combination of single-stranded conformation polymorphism (SSCP) analysis[37] and direct sequencing.[38] Sequences will be read by hand and entered into the data base manually. Sequence alignment will be assisted by computer analysis. It is expected that the cytochrome b gene polymorphisms will differentiate individuals at the genus level.

---

[36] Scott R. Woodward, Nathan J. Weyand, and Mark Bunnell, "DNA Sequence from Cretaceous Period Bone Fragments," *Science* 266 (1994): 1229–32.

[37] Orita et al., "Rapid and Sensitive Detection of Point Mutations."

[38] Horai et al., "DNA Amplification from Ancient Human Skeletal Remains."

This will allow us to identify differences between animals from divergent geographical locations. The L-chain polymorphisms will identify between-herd or local differences. The nuclear locus will identify sequence polymorphisms unique at the individual level and will be used for the identification and assignment of fragments to the same original parchment. Depending on the level of heterozygosity exhibited in the different herds as shown by the aDNA from bone at Qumran and other archaeological sites, it will be possible to determine the level of heterozygosity expected in scrolls produced from the same herd. Analysis will consider both within-scroll variation (determined by the analysis of large scrolls such as the Isaiah and *Temple* scrolls) and between-scroll variation (determined by analysis of material from scrolls such as *1QS* and *1QIsa^a*) to establish parameters for determining the location of the production of the parchment.

The most difficult problem associated with this work is the isolation of biologically active (PCR amplifiable) aDNA. Two main causes can be responsible for these difficulties: (1) The DNA remaining in the parchments is of such poor quality that established techniques will not be able to recover amplifiable fragments of aDNA, and (2) inhibitors in the aDNA copurify with the DNA such that amplification is prohibited. In the case of excessively degraded DNA it may be possible to repair some of the damage by a preamplification primer extension (PEP) reaction.[39] In this procedure the degraded DNA is preincubated in the presence of random small primers and polymerase. Any small piece of aDNA present in the sample is randomly amplified establishing a large pool of repaired starting material recognized by the specific primers used in the experimental protocol. If the DNA is universally poorly preserved, it may not be possible to recover any DNA. This likelihood is small, based on both our experience and the published results of others. Inhibitors of

---

[39]   Irwin, Kocher, and Wilson, "Evolution of the Cytochrome B Gene of Mammals."

amplification have been successfully overcome by alternate purification methods, dilution, and the addition of other reagents in
the PCR reaction such as bovine serum albumin.[40] A major
problem associated with all types of aDNA work is contamination with extraneous modern DNA. This should not be a serious
problem in this study because even though the scrolls have been
handled extensively, the most likely contamination would be
from human DNA. Human and goat DNA are easily differenti-
ated at the DNA loci that will be used in this study and would
not confound the results. Another potential problem may be that
the level of heterozygosity in the ancient animals used to produce the parchments would be so low because of local inbreeding within herds that polymorphisms for the individual fingerprinting would be difficult to identify. This would require the
amplification and sequencing of more loci. This is not a technical problem, but it would probably require the analysis of more
genetic loci.

---

[40] Woodward et al., "Amplification of Nuclear DNA," 244–47;
Pääbo, Higuchi, and Wilson, "Ancient DNA and the Polymerase Chain
Reaction," 9709–12.

The Dead Sea Scrolls CD-ROM Database Project

DONALD W. PARRY

Brigham Young University

STEVEN W. BOORAS

Foundation for Ancient Research and Mormon Studies

For the first time, scholars in history, religious studies, Near Eastern languages, archaeology, and biblical studies, among others, will be able to access the Dead Sea Scrolls (DSS) and related literatures quickly and effectively via the computer for whatever additional light these texts might shed on their disciplines. The goal of this paper is to introduce the reader to the DSS CD-ROM Database Project (Database), which is being developed jointly by the Foundation for Ancient Research and Mormon Studies (FARMS) and Brigham Young University.[1]

---

[1]   We acknowledge the work, dedication, and expertise of several individuals who have made the dream regarding the DSS Database become a reality. We appreciate the collaborative efforts and ongoing encouragement of both Emanuel Tov, Editor-in-Chief of the Dead Sea Scrolls publication project and professor at Hebrew University, Jerusalem, and Weston W. Fields, executive director of the DSS Foundation. We are grateful to Stephen J. Pfann, Center for the Study of Early Christianity, for the DSS transcription files and to James A. Sanders, president of the Ancient Biblical Manuscript Center, Claremont, CA, for the scroll/fragment photographs. We also recognize FARMS and BYU, both of which have produced many resources in the form of personnel, services, and consultative assistance. In particular, we thank Noel B. Reynolds, professor of political science, BYU, president of FARMS, and producer of the DSS CD-ROM Database Project;

The objective of the DSS CD-ROM Database Project is to produce a comprehensive, fully indexed, and cross-linked computerized database of all texts, images of texts, and reference materials of importance for scholarly work on the Dead Sea Scrolls and related literatures. The Database will make available to a wide range of students, scholars, and informed lay persons a fully integrated and computerized collection of transcriptions, translations, and digitized images (or photographic images) of the DSS, as well as other important texts of the same general period and geographic area. The combination of modern computer power with sophisticated text-manipulating software offers the prospect of combining all these materials into a single database that can be analyzed simultaneously and instantaneously by scholars and researchers at a relatively low cost.

Comprehensive indices of all textual terms will prove invaluable for translations and linguistic studies. The ability to check for all occurrences of words and phrases in associated texts will greatly enhance commentaries. The primary scholarship that has been performed on the scrolls to this point has often been done without full knowledge of the content of related texts. The next round of scholarly work on these materials will have the advantage of access to fully automated comprehensive reference materials, thereby making integrated studies possible.

The project will itself *not* offer interpretations or scholarly analyses of the scrolls. It aims only to provide comprehensive reference materials in the most accessible format possible. Nor does the Database pretend to offer authoritative or new readings of texts. It will provide the most accurate possible digitizations of readings that have already been offered by DSS scholars.

Monte F. Shelley, director of Instructional Applications Services, BYU, and his colleagues James S. Rosenvall, manager of WordCruncher Development Team; William A. Barrett, associate chair of Computer Science Department; and Daniel R. Bartholomew and Jason W. Dzubak, senior programmers. We also wish to thank Dr. E. Jan Wilson, Hebraist; Dana Pike, assistant professor of ancient scripture, BYU; and Terry Szink, Ph.D. candidate in Near Eastern Languages and Cultures, UCLA, for their professional assistance.

Computer Power

The use of computers makes possible the meaningful publication of huge databases of texts and graphics. The electronic accessibility of the DSS materials will be a major boon to both scholars and informed students. Users of the Database will want to access the published material from a variety of perspectives and for different reasons. Accessibility is one primary objective to be achieved with this software. The Database will provide the ability to:

- access large quantities of material, both textual and graphic;
- search textual material for words and phrases;
- display graphic images of the scrolls and fragments;
- conduct a word-print analysis to assist in the determination of authorship;
- store and retrieve earlier searches for modification and reexecution;
- present lists of units within which a search has found matches;
- copy blocks of material to user files or directly to a printer;
- add researcher notes to the Database;
- execute external programs during the use of the Database software;
- create a single concordance (digitized or hard copy) of any single text or part of a text;
- find the number of times a given word is attested in a document or number of documents and study its usage in a number of contextual settings to determine meaning;
- ask numerous questions of the Database and research items in a way not possible a generation ago;
- provide collocation tables, lexical searches, and morphological notations.

The DSS CD-ROM Database Library

The DSS CD-ROM Database library may include the following DSS materials (as permissions can be secured): (1) photographic images (binary facsimiles) of the DSS; (2) transcriptions of the DSS; (3) translations of the DSS; and (4) secondary literature directly related to the DSS, including commentaries, journal articles, bibliographies, monographs, and other secondary works.

In addition, the Database may eventually contain a number of other primary sources from the Second Temple and post-destruction era, which may cast a reflection upon the DSS, including: (5) various versions of the Bible (the Masoretic Text, the Septuagint, the Greek New Testament, the Vulgate, and a number of English Bibles); (6) apocryphal and pseudepigraphic materials (i.e., the Old Testament pseudepigrapha, the New Testament pseudepigrapha, and the apocrypha); (7) rabbinic materials (i.e., the Mishnah, the Babylonian and Jerusalem Talmuds, and the Tosephta); (8) the writings of hellenized Jewry (i.e., Josephus and Philo of Alexandria); and (9) a number of lexical materials and aids.

Graphics Presentation of the Facsimile or Photograph

The Database allows the user to open a number of windows (limited by the amount of available computer memory) that feature digitized images of photographs of the scrolls (see fig. 1).

The Database permits the user to create graphical hotspots which link the photograph to the transcriptional text, a translation, a commentary, or other graphics. This is accomplished by marking any section of the graphic (in the form of a square or rectangle) with the cursor; then the marked section (the hotspot) will take the user to the transcriptional text. The user may also view alternate images (such as duplicate images taken under different conditions, with different methods and at different times)

Figure 1. Digitized image of *1QSa (Rule of the Community)*

and images linked to other images, allowing quick scrolling through continuous columns of a manuscript (see fig. 2). The user may also mark part of the facsimile with the cursor and transport it elsewhere, perhaps into a graphical software or onto the user's hard drive for storage.

Zooming the Graphics

Graphics can be zoomed in two different ways: (1) by dragging a rectangle over a section of the photograph, after which the section will repaint to a larger size; or (2) by moving the cursor to the "zoom size edit box" to automatically adjust the size of the facsimile. If the scanning is conducted in the beginning with proper equipment, the zooming assures the retention of high resolution. The horizontal and vertical scroll bars permit the graphic image to be scrolled up or down, right or left.

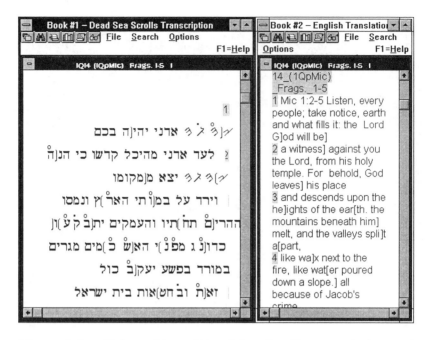

Figure 2. Parallel scrolling of Dead Sea Scrolls transcription and English translation.

Presentation of the Transcription—Search Capabilities

The Database permits the user to perform both single and multiple word searches by the use of a WordWheel that lists every word with the number of occurrences of each word and a total count in a given text. The WordWheel presents the words in alphabetical order in the text language (Hebrew, English, Greek, etc.), and text windows are created by clicking on a word with the mouse. The search apparatus permits searching by using wildcards (* = multiple characters or ? = a single character), wherein the user types in three or four characters of a word (which may appear at the beginning, middle, or end of the word) and then the search engine seeks all attestations of the characters in the document.

The results of the search (called hits) are shown immediately and can be viewed in the Reference List display or within a number of windows, one reference per window (see fig. 3). The total number of hits are listed almost instantaneously, and the results are shown in windows. The windows can be adjusted (i.e., enlarged or reduced) to show several lines of text or can be limited to show one or two lines of text. The windows may be scrolled down so the user can see all of the hits one after another. The user may browse the results of the window, call up the entire text, or show the references. The user may also click on a particular hit and call up the entire text, showing the text displayed on the screen.

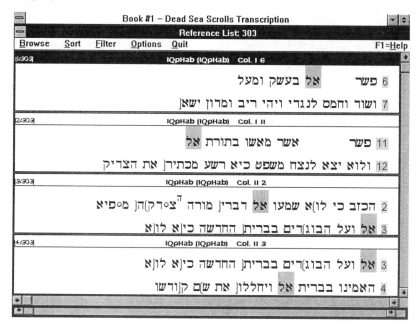

Figure 3. Four of 303 occurrences of the word אל.

The user may print the results or store them onto the disk for recall at a later time. Multilingual files may also be retrieved simultaneously as well as external files, including thesauruses, facsimiles of the DSS, and other materials.

Word Searches

Searching capabilities permit collocation analysis—the user may search words that are either immediately adjacent to each other or within several words of one another. For instance, if the searcher wishes to discover how many times the word *sons* appears within ten words before or after the word *light*, the command would take a just a moment and the results would appear on the screen instantaneously (see figs. 4 and 5).

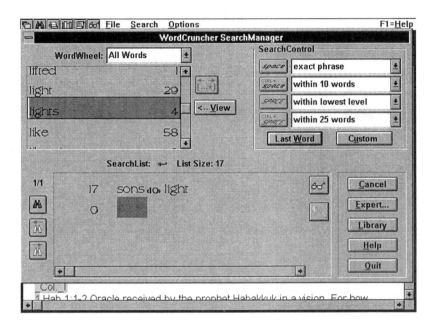

Figure 4. Searching for the words *sons* and *light* within ten words of each other.

One significant feature of the Database is its capability to search for Hebrew words according to their root forms. This feature, for example, permits the user to search for *lamed=he* verbs, *peh=nun* verbs, *peh=yod* verbs, *hitpael* verbs with sibilants that have experienced metathesis, or hollow verbs

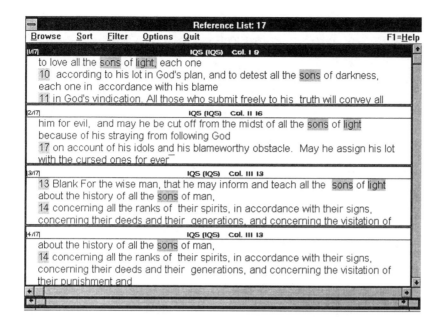

Figure 5. Four of 17 occurrences of the words *sons* and *light* in close proximity.

where one or more of the root letters is missing (see fig. 6). The user can also search for verb roots even with prefixes or suffixes, such as prepositions, the *waw* conjunction, pronoun suffixes, or other similar affixes.

Editing Capabilities

The program permits various text-editing functions, including cross-referencing to either internal or external locations—such as other software packages, video or audio glyphs—editing of graphics, creating notes by the user, or the copying of a text and its insertion into a word-processing file. Such text editing has no impact upon the primary texts or index. Further, the user may alter the appearance of the text by using italics, underlining, bold, strikeout, or other formatting features.

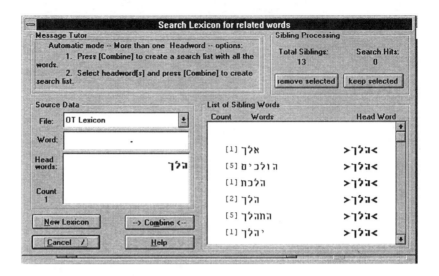

Figure 6. Searching for Hebrew words according to their root forms.

Display of windows

The user may have a large number of windows open at the same time (our computer technicians have opened up to twenty-nine windows before they ran out of room on the monitor) and each window may be resized larger or smaller or moved on the screen independently of other windows (see fig. 7). Windows may be placed one on top of the other.

For instance, the user may open multiple windows related to a single document, including a facsimile of a scroll, a Hebrew transcription, three English translations, a French translation, the Hebrew Bible, the pseudepigrapha, a bibliography, and several scholarly journal articles. The user may also make notes and comments in a separate window.

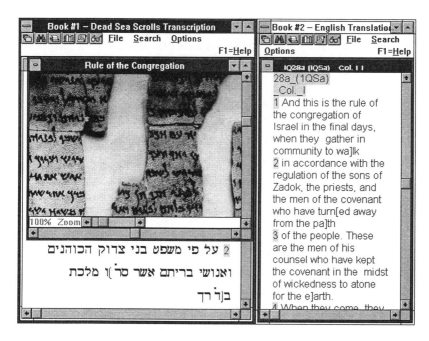

Figure 7. Multiple windows open simultaneously.

Links

The Database will eventually include an entire library comprised of several bookshelves of ancient primary materials that will be linked to each other. The bookshelves may appear either in an icon format or in a table of contents format. Searches may be made within a single document (e.g., *4QSam^a*) or among the entire library of materials located on the bookshelf (e.g., the entire Dead Sea Scroll corpus, the Hebrew Bible, etc.). The Database contains a linkage tool that links the materials together. The linkage system also links materials such as internal references, external references, or graphical objects.

Synchronized files

The Database supports the synchronization of two or more files simultaneously if they possess marked codes. Multiple books, documents, or texts can be linked together so that information in the same sections of each text are shown simultaneously in different text windows. As the user scrolls down one text, the computer automatically repositions the other text(s) to the same section as the text being scrolled.

The synchronous files may include several different languages, including a read left-to-right language such as English or a read right-to-left language such as Hebrew. Hence, the software accommodates Hebrew language idiosyncrasies. For example, as the user searches or scrolls down the Hebrew transcription of certain DSS texts, the same navigation and tracking occurs in the English language, permitting the user to ask questions of the texts and compare the translation. Synchronized files may also consist of a Hebrew facsimile (photograph), transcription, translation, commentary, and parallel texts, all linked together to permit the user to access a large amount of material.

The DSS CD-ROM Database Project is bringing scholarship and state-of-the-art technology closer together. The Database is dynamic, meaning that its creators will continue to update, add, or change the Database as new and improved technology and textual materials—both primary and secondary—become available.

Indexes

Index of Passages

Bible

Dead Sea Scrolls

Jewish Authors and Works

Early Christian Authors and Works

Index of Subjects

copy of, preserved in paleo-
Hebrew script, 170
passages in Qumran sectarian
literature that quote or might
relate to, 189–91
significance of, for covenant
community at Qumran, 166
texts of
in Caves 1 and 2, 169–72
in Cave 4, 172–73

—O—

oral tradition, beginnings of
scripture, 90
orthography, differences in
editions, 93

—P—

parchment, species sources of,
221–22
Pentateuch, interwoven from
several sources, 90
people of God, 28–29
polymerase chain reaction (PCR)
technology, sensitive to
contamination by nonrelevant
DNA material, 220
poverty, term used in sectarian
texts from Qumran, 198
predestination, Qumran view of,
160
priesthood, restoration of, 19
priestly blessing, 180–82
Prince of Light, 27
Melchizedek identified with, 24
Prince of the whole congregation,
34, 36
prophet
as a messianic figure, 31–32
in *4Q521*, 39
as a precursor to the heavenly
messiah, 30
as forerunner of the messiahs,
38

as Interpreter of the Law, 32–33
eschatological, 30
messianic character of, 18
Prophet like Moses, 31–32, 38
future coming of, 19
prophetic collections, history of,
90
Proverbs, as a collection, 90
Psalter, as a collection, 90
Ptolemies, defeat of, 9–10

—Q—

Qumran documents
principal corpus of, 175–76
use of biblical materials in,
188, 192
use of passages from Numbers
in, 192
Qumran scribal practice
misleading term, 94
orthography and morphology
in, 93

—R—

raz nihyeh
as inspired instruction, 135
background of, 134 n. 18
definition of, 134
repair patches of scrolls, analysis
of, 224
resurrection
doctrine of, 4
of the righteous, 143

—S—

salvation as a present reality, in
Sapiential Work A, 144
Samaritan Pentateuch
compared to traditional biblical
text, 80
use of scribal markings in, 45
Sapiential Work A
apocalyptic motifs in, 136

Index of Modern Authors

STUDIES ON THE TEXTS
OF THE DESERT OF JUDAH

1. WERNBERG MØLLER, P. *The Manual of Discipline.* Translated and Annotated, with an Introduction. 1957. ISBN 90 04 02195 7
2. PLOEG, J. VAN DER. *Le rouleau de la guerre.* Traduit et annoté, avec une introduction. 1959. ISBN 90 04 02196 5
3. MANSOOR, M. *The Thanksgiving Hymns.* Translated and Annotated with an Introduction. 1961. ISBN 90 04 02197 3
5. KOFFMAHN, E. *Die Doppelurkunden aus der Wüste Juda.* Recht und Praxis der jüdischen Papyri des 1. und 2. Jahrhunderts n. Chr. samt Übertragung der Texte und Deutscher Übersetzung. 1968. ISBN 90 04 03148 0
6. KUTSCHER, E.Y. *The Language and linguistic Background of the Isaiah Scroll (1 QIsaᵃ).* Transl. from the first (1959) Hebrew ed. With an obituary by H.B. ROSÉN. 1974. ISBN 90 04 04019 6
6a. KUTSCHER, E.Y. *The Language and Linguistic Background of the Isaiah Scroll (1 QIsaᵃ).* Indices and Corrections by E. QIMRON. Introduction by S. MORAG. 1979. ISBN 90 04 05974 1
7. JONGELING, B. *A Classified Bibliography of the Finds in the Desert of Judah, 1958-1969.* 1971. ISBN 90 04 02200 7
8. MERRILL, E.H. *Qumran and Predestination.* A Theological Study of the Thanksgiving Hymns. 1975. ISBN 90 04 042652
9. GARCÍA MARTÍNEZ, F. *Qumran and Apocalyptic.* Studies on the Aramaic Texts from Qumran. 1992. ISBN 90 04 09586 1
10. DIMANT, D. & U. RAPPAPORT (eds.). *The Dead Sea Scrolls.* Forty Years of research. 1992. ISBN 90 04 09679 5
11. TREBOLLE BARRERA, J. & L. VEGAS MONTANER (eds.). *The Madrid Qumran Congress.* Proceedings of the International Congress on the Dead Sea Scrolls, Madrid 18-21 March 1991. 2 vols. 1993. ISBN 90 04 09771 6 *set*
12. NITZAN, B. *Qumran Prayer and Religious Poetry* 1994. ISBN 90 04 09658 2
13. STEUDEL, A. *Der Midrasch zur Eschatologie aus der Qumrangemeinde (4QMidrEschatᵃ·ᵇ).* Materielle Rekonstruktion, Textbestand, Gattung und traditionsgeschichtliche Einordnung des durch 4Q174 („Florilegium") und 4Q177 („Catena A") repräsentierten Werkes aus den Qumranfunden. 1994. ISBN 90 04 09763 5
14. SWANSON, D.D. *The Temple Scroll and the Bible.* The Methodology of 11QT. ISBN 90 04 09849 6
15. BROOKE, G.J. (ed.). *New Qumran Texts and Studies.* Proceedings of the First Meeting of the International Organization for Qumran Studies, Paris 1992. With F. García Martínez. 1994. ISBN 90 04 10093 8
16. DIMANT, D. & L.H. SCHIFFMAN. *Time to Prepare the Way in the Wilderness.* Papers on the Qumran Scrolls by Fellows of the Institute for Advanced Studies of the Hebrew University, Jerusalem, 1989-1990. 1995. ISBN 90 04 10225 6
17. FLINT, P.W. *The Dead Sea Psalms Scrolls and the Book of Psalms.* 1995. ISBN 90 04 10341 4

18. LANGE, A. *Weisheit und Prädestination.* Weisheitliche Urordnung und Prädestination in den Textfunden von Qumran. 1995. ISBN 90 04 10432 1
19. GARCÍA MARTÍNEZ, F. & D.W. PARRY. *A Bibliography of the Finds in the Desert of Judah 1970-95.* Arranged by Author with Citation and Subject Indexes. 1996. ISBN 90 04 10588 3
20. PARRY, D.W. & S.D. RICKS (eds.). *Current Research and Technological Developments on the Dead Sea Scrolls.* Conference on the Texts from the Judean Desert, Jerusalem, 30 April 1995. 1996. ISBN 90 04 10662 6